Y0-EAG-400

The Leaders and the Led

Marigum's Genealogy

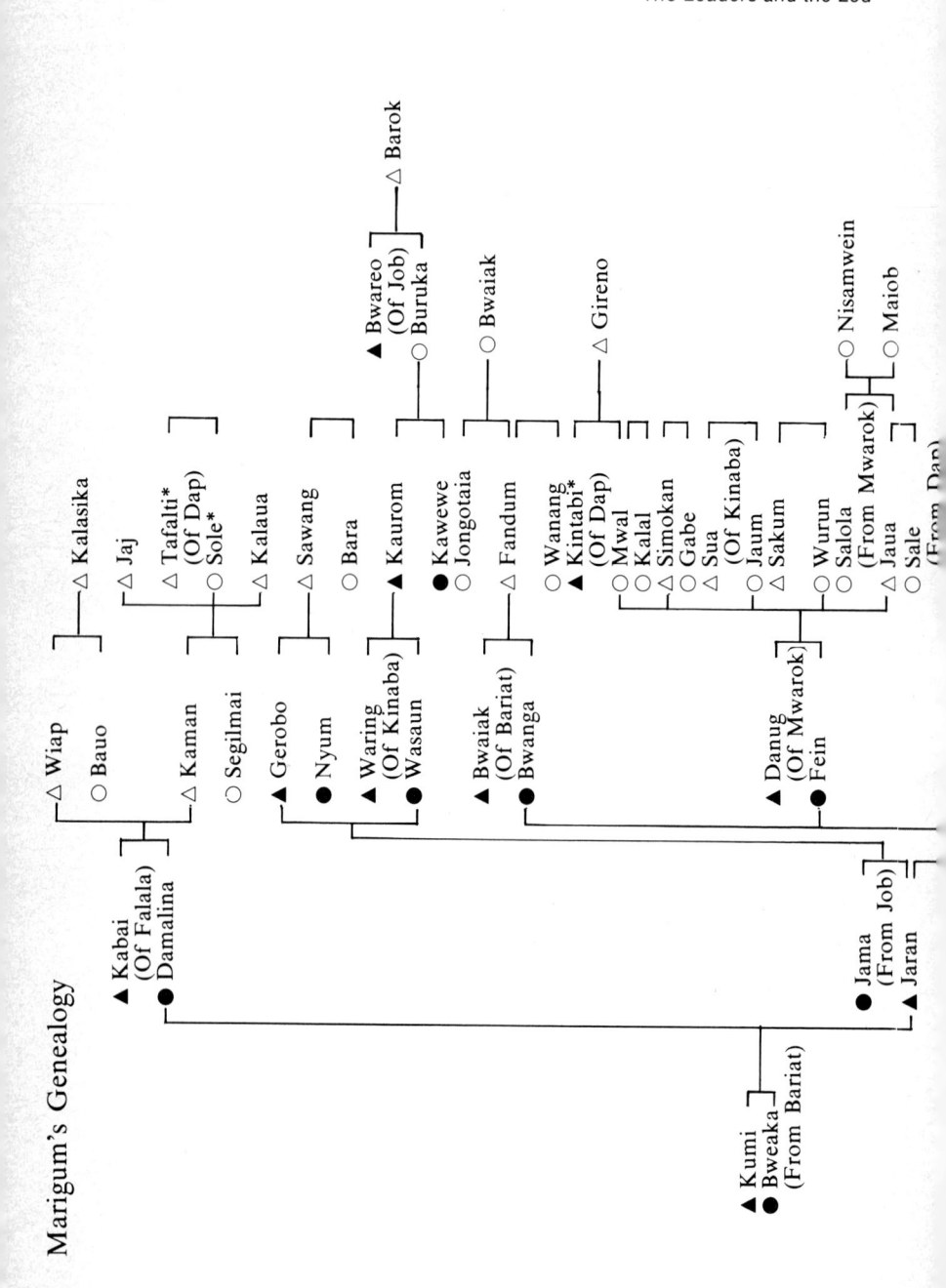

Marigum's Genealogy

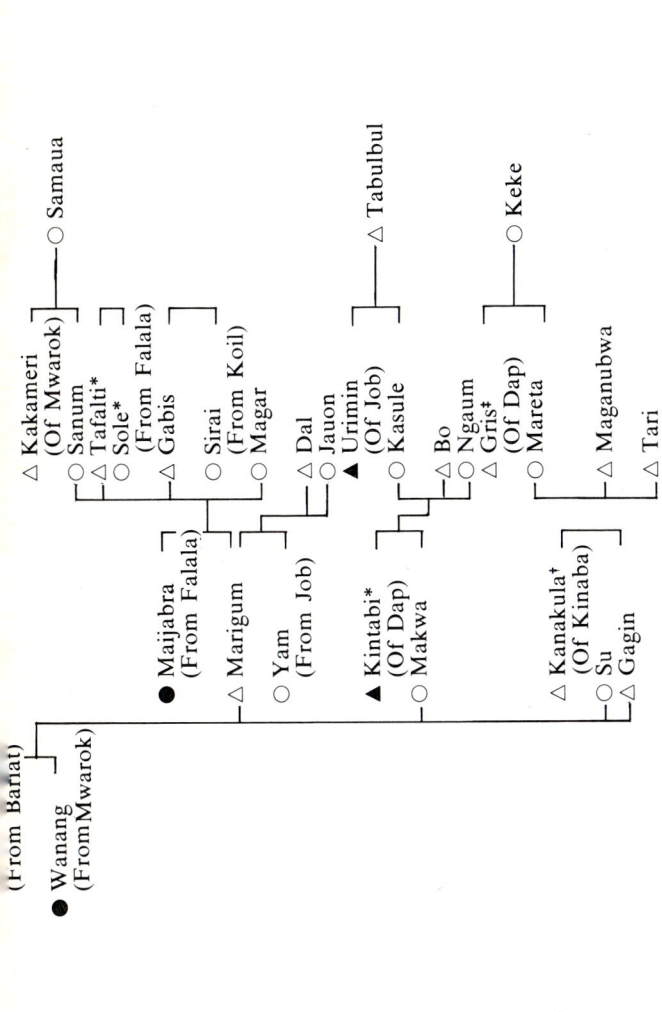

(From Barlat)
● Wanang (FromMwarok)
△ Kakameri (Of Mwarok) — ○ Samaua
 ○ Sanum
 △ Tafalti*
 △ Sole* (From Falala)
● Maijabra (From Falala) — △ Gabis
△ Marigum — ○ Sirai (From Koil)
 ○ Magar
○ Yam (From Job) — △ Dal
 ○ Jauon
▲ Kintabi* (Of Dap) — ▲ Urimin (Of Job)
 ○ Kasule
▲ Makwa — △ Bo
 ○ Ngaum
 △ Gris‡ (Of Dap) — △ Tabulbul
 ○ Mareta — ○ Keke
△ Kanakula† (Of Kinaba) — △ Maganubwa
 ○ Su
 △ Gagin — △ Tari

Many persons, living and dead, have for reasons of space been omitted (e.g. two of Marigum's wives are not shown).
▲ Male Deceased   △ Male Living
● Female Deceased ○ Female Living
A linkage after names indicates marriage.
* Persons who appear twice
† Elsewhere, for reasons explained, I have changed Kanakula's name to Tago.
‡ Elsewhere, for reasons explained, I have changed Gris's name to Gireno.

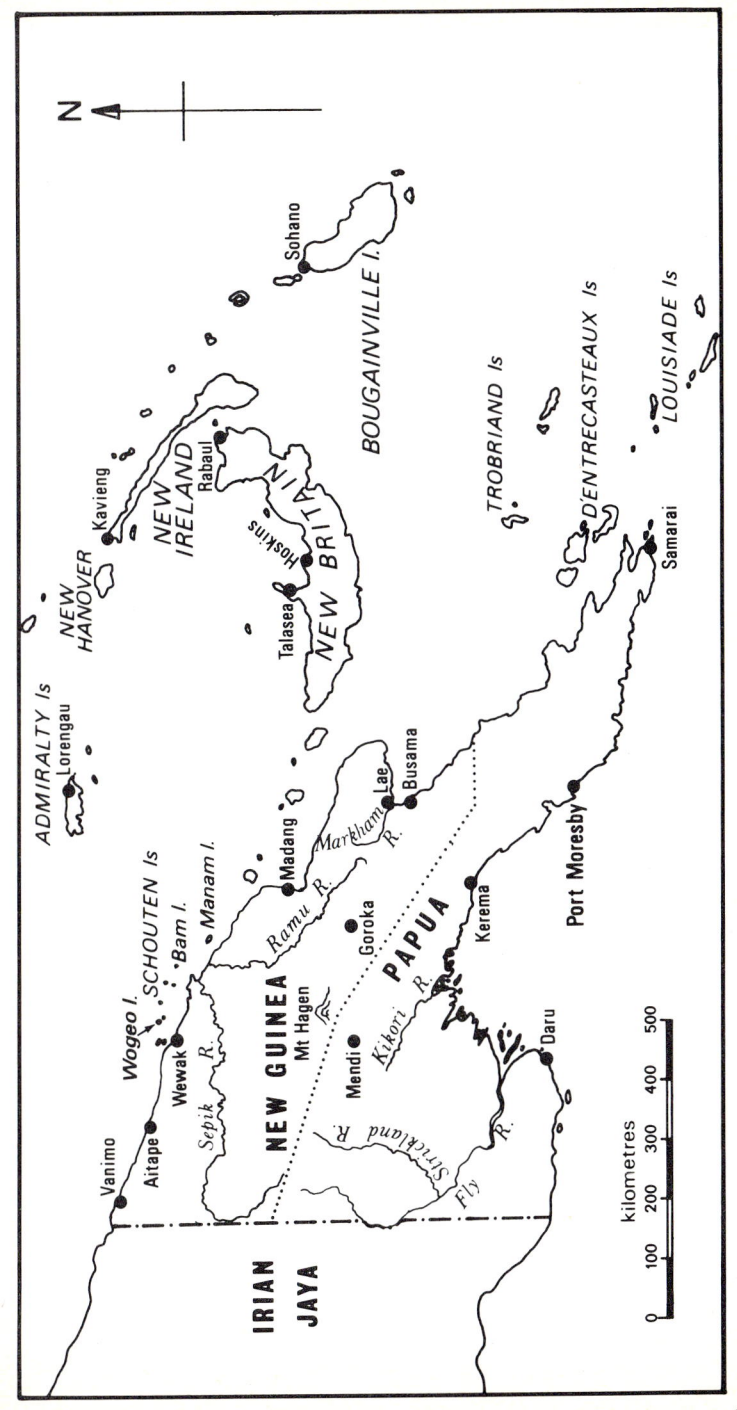

Papua New Guinea

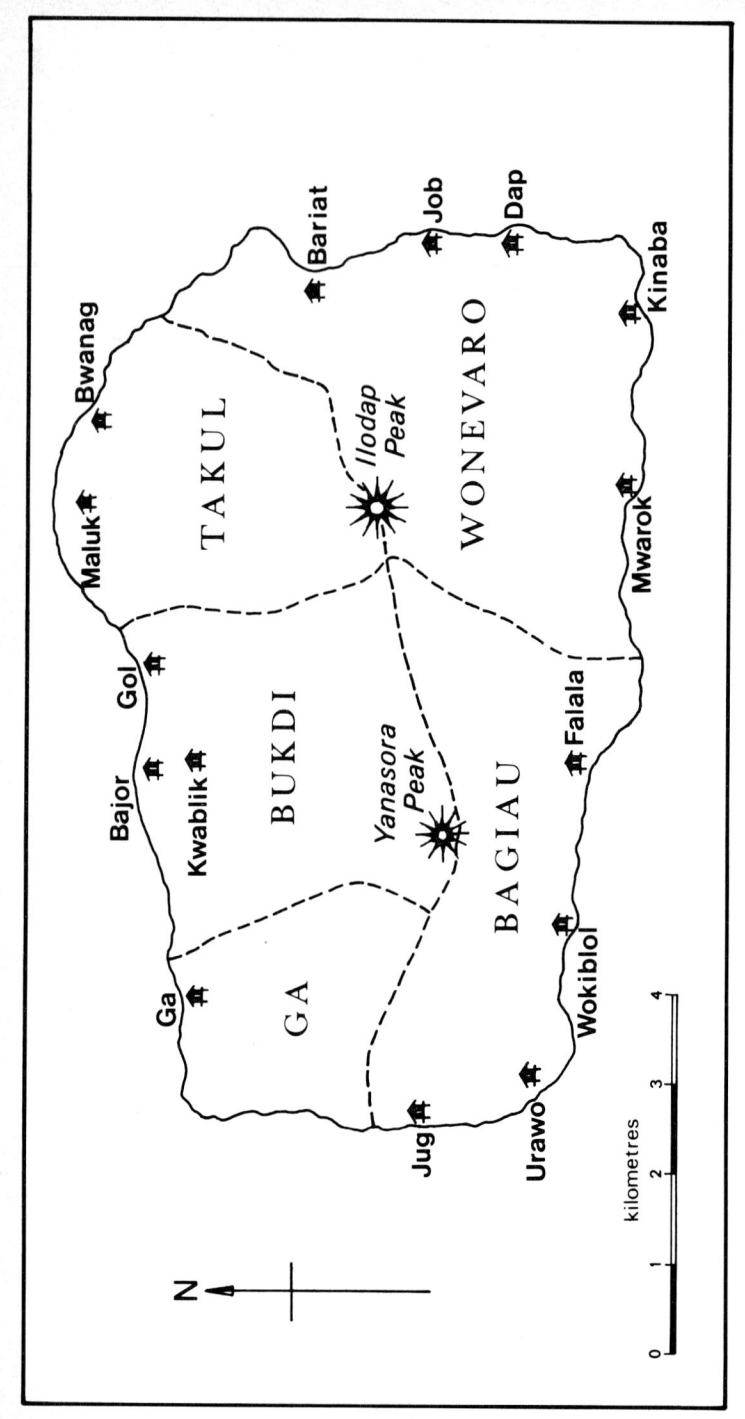

Wogeo Island

1 Introduction

My acquaintance with the Wogeo islanders began early in January 1934, when an anthropologist in the service of the New Guinea government, E. W. P. Chinnery, informed me that they would be worthy of investigation, though I have now forgotten why.[1] Probably his reason had little to do with my own interest, but I accepted the advice.

The present-day port of Wewak, on the New Guinea mainland 80 kilometres away, did not then exist. A single junior officer with a small squad of police manned a patrol post located on the site, at that time referred to as Wiwiak. Not till several months had gone by was the main administrative station of the Sepik District moved down from Aitape some 150 kilometres to the west, a spot convenient when first selected but now too isolated; moreover, it provided but poor anchorage for ships of any size. When I left in the following December a full-scale settlement was being established — the government headquarters, a hospital, a gaol, a warehouse for cargo, and a couple of stores.

I landed from the Sydney steamer at Boram plantation three kilometres away and perforce threw myself on the hospitality, well known throughout the region, of Tom and Mollie Ifould, the proprietors. Communications with Wogeo were irregular and unreliable, and I was obliged to charter their schooner as transport. I also arranged for the replenishment of my supplies after six months had elapsed and for my departure six months later again. During the year I had only four or five callers — the District Officer taking the census (the figure was 929 including absentees, made up of 316 male adults, 177 male children and adolescents, 297 female adults, and 139 female children and adolescents), a couple of recruiters enlisting or returning labourers, and missionaries seeking to found a station. Those were the days of steam anthropology. Not only were tape recorders and colour photography unknown, but transistor radios were still in the future, and the film of the day was so slow that usually I was obliged to operate my camera

3

on a tripod. At one period I was for four months without any news of the outside world.

Wogeo has two main anchorages, at Dap village protected from the monsoon and at Mwarok village with shelter from the southeast trade winds. This was the monsoon season, so it was at Dap that I first landed. The settlement was large by local standards, with over sixty inhabitants, and I decided that here would be a suitable base. But first I needed a place in which to live. I arranged for the construction of a dwelling and then departed for Mwarok to wait in the government rest hut till its completion.

The house was ready after about three weeks, and I moved in at once. The choice proved fortunate. One of the two headmen, Marigum, was highly respected everywhere, and I was within easy walking distance of nearly half the population, around 400 people. Marigum treated me amiably from the start and within a couple of months had adopted me as a younger brother. He suggested that his favourite son, a youth of seventeen or eighteen named Dal, should enter my employment as a personal servant (my cook, a youth of similar age called Gris, was from Mwarok), and his half-sister's son Jaua and the man Waru, whom he regarded as a brother though neither knew exactly how they were related, became two of my closest associates. A third, Wiawia, was the brother of the other Dap headman, a person of lesser importance in island affairs.

Marigum had ties with Kawang, a headman of equal prestige from Gol on the far side of the island. Kawang's younger brother Sangani and I soon became friends, and shortly after my adoption by Marigum he declared me to be a member of that family also. The relationship meant that I was sure of food and shelter when I made the journey across to attend ceremonies, seek information, or confirm material gathered in other places. A deserted house in the centre of the village was refurbished for my use, and I often lived in it for a week or two at a time.

The German government had annexed northeastern New Guinea under the name of Kaiser Wilhelm's Land together with the outlying islands further east in 1884, and Wogeo men had been employed as wage labourers on the coconut plantations owned by Europeans in the more developed areas since about 1909 or 1910. After the outbreak of war in 1914 an Australian Force captured the country from the Germans, and eight years later the new administration set up by Australia under mandate from the League of Nations declared the Wogeo people to be now fully under control. Yet, apart from the substitution of steel axes and

1 Introduction

knives for those made of stone, they were living in almost the same conditions as during the previous century. In anthropological terms their society was typically primitive — isolated, self sufficient, and technologically simple. Officials made a short patrol once annually at most, and the result was that outbursts of violence had by no means ceased. An avenging party during 1933 slew a man judged to be a sorcerer; my presence saved the life of another in 1934, though I had neither commented on his actions nor made any move to protect him; a third was stabbed to death in 1935; a fourth, my nephew Jaua, in 1948; and in 1949 a group from the Dap neighbourhood beat and kicked an alleged sorcerer from a village near Gol with such fury that he expired; they then went on to strangle his supposed companion in crime. These last two murders alone were reported, and the persons responsible for the rest remained unpunished — indeed, some of them gained honour as killers.

Again, missions had not yet begun preaching Christianity, and the pagan religion flourished unhindered and was subject neither to outside criticism nor to condemnation. A New Guinean[2] catechist of the Roman Catholic Society of the Divine Word had landed with his family a day or two before my own arrival, but by the end of the year he had still not persuaded the people to build a school for the children, much less a church. In other words, his presence had so far exerted no influence.

Finally, there was no commercial agriculture, nor did traders call to pick up copra (1934 was the height of the Great Depression, and prices for all tropical products had never been so low). The only way to earn money was to continue taking indentured employment on the plantations, where the monthly wage for an unskilled worker was fifty cents, plus rations and housing.[3] Such Western goods as the villagers owned — confined almost entirely to simple tools, strips of calico worn as clothing by the younger men, and cosmetics — had been brought back by the returning labourers on the expiry of their contracts.

All the men between about twenty years old and early middle age spoke pidgin English, the New Guinea lingua franca, and through this medium I made my attempts to learn the vernacular. (Old people, lacking teeth, are too indistinct to act as teachers.) Fortunately it was of Austronesian type and therefore not excessively complicated, though Papuan influences were present here and there — the numerical system, for instance, lacked the common unit of five or ten. I was already familiar with certain of the Austronesian languages after a couple of years' experience in the

Solomon Islands and at the end of four or five months was sufficiently fluent to be able to follow a good deal of most conversations. Yet my grammar till the end was lamentable. The people were continually correcting me — as a rule after they had enjoyed a laugh at my expense.

Connections with the administration during and after World War II gave me an opportunity for another visit lasting for a few weeks in 1948. The country, still in the care of Australia, had by that time become a Trust Territory of the United Nations. I was primarily interested in investigating the effects of the conflict, if any. Despite a little harmless bombing — by which side is unknown — and a short Japanese occupation, these proved to be mainly indirect. The worst disaster occurred when a detonating device, probably a mine, drifted to a beach near Dap. A crowd of children dragged it ashore and, ignorant of the danger, began throwing stones. In the subsequent explosion several were blown to pieces and two or three injured. The main result otherwise was a fall in population, which now stood at 839. Wewak had been in the hands of the Japanese from December 1942 till their surrender nearly three years later, but the Allied naval victory in the Battle of the Bismarck Sea meant that after March 1943 enemy shipping could rarely reach any point on the coast, and the various garrisons were obliged to maintain themselves as best they might with no reinforcements and scarcely any replacement of stores. Every adult able-bodied male from the surrounding areas, including Wogeo, was conscripted for cultivating food gardens. Despite constant Allied bombing not one was killed, probably on account of the concentration on purely military targets. The Australian Army returned the conscripts after the capitulation but later had second thoughts, so great was the chaos. Thanks to Major G. C. O'Donnell M.C., who was Assistant District Officer in the administrative unit, the Wogeo, however, were allowed to stay at home with their families.

The only mission then operating in the Sepik District, the Society of the Divine Word, had suffered the loss of every European priest, every lay brother, and every nun. The Japanese despatched some at once, convinced that they were spies, and Bishop Loeks, together with thirty-three other men, twenty-five women and three children (the vast majority of German nationality), were compelled to board the destroyer *Akikaze* and while the ship was at sea shot one by one; the bodies went overboard. This happened on 17 March 1943.[4] In the circumstances, it was surprising that work could start

1 Introduction

up again so soon. The first mission call at Wogeo was in October 1947.

Evidence of success in conversion between 1935 and 1942 was manifest everywhere. The majority of the islanders over the age of thirty were still pagan, but everyone younger professed to be a Christian. Many of these had been to school and were able to read and write in pidgin. The initiation ceremonies, with their accompanying flutes, had already been abandoned, but the masked dances of the *tangbwal* monsters occasionally took place still.

Marigum was blind by 1948 and his daughter Jauon, a toddler in 1934, led him everywhere. Yet he retained his compelling presence and gave me a warm welcome. His son Dal, my former servant, had already married a first wife, who had given birth to a son, then learning to walk. Presumably this child was born late in 1946 or early 1947. I have no recollection of doing so, but learned in 1974 that I had often carried him about the village. His local name was Gagin, after Marigum's youngest brother, but at the age of three he was baptized Bernard. Twenty-six years later, now a mature young man, he arranged for me to go back for a third visit. Eastern New Guinea and the islands as far as the northern Solomons were by then self-governing and on the brink of independence, which came within nine months, on 16 September 1975.[5]

In 1968 I had received a letter signed Bernard Dalle Gagin from a pupil at the Mission High School on Kairiru Island near Wewak. He said, rightly, I would not know who he was (clearly he also had no recollection of our earlier meeting) but that he was the son of Dal and grandson of Marigum, both now dead, whom I certainly would remember. His history master had shown him an article of mine dealing with Wogeo in the journal *Oceania*, and after reading it he decided on a personal approach. He also reminded me that as I was Marigum's adopted brother, it followed that in the local kinship terminology I had the status of a grandfather. We thus inherited many mutual responsibilities, all of which on his side have been amply fulfilled.

We began a correspondence, and in 1970 and 1971, when I was in New Guinea as an external consultant to the recently established University of Papua New Guinea, I spent weekends as Bernard's guest at the Teachers' College in Goroka, whither he had proceeded after completing his schooling. New Guinea personal names are not yet standardized and often people decide to be somebody different (a great embarrassment to institutions awarding degrees and diplomas). Bernard had now elected to take 'Dalle', his spelling of my 'Dal', as a surname and to shift Gagin to the middle. He was by then therefore Bernard Gagin Dalle.

At the Teachers' College I met a second grandson, Tom Fandim, the son of the daughter of my brother Sangani of Gol. Both Bernard and Tom gave me valuable information now incorporated into this book, and Bernard also criticized sections of the typescript. He disapproved chiefly of some of my spellings, and I am sure he was right. With so much material already published, however, I would have caused confusion by making alterations. I apologized but felt I had to persist in my errors. The main faults were to mix up *l* and *r* (*ruma* not *luma*, house, and Takur not Takul) and *p* and *b* (Dab not Dap) and sometimes to hear what should really be *o* as *wa* (Morok not Mwarok). Marigum also should be Maurigum. Yet I must say in my defence that those whose mother tongue is the Wogeo language still disagree over some things. I have seen the district I call Wonevaro variously spelled Wanevaro, Wanewaro, and Onevaro. The *s* of 1934 was forty years later also on the way to becoming *h*; Bagasal, for example, now sounded like Bagahal.

In 1973 Bernard, appointed a science master at a high school in the Central Highlands after his graduation, began insisting that I must be his guest for the Christmas holidays either that year or the next. I was at length persuaded, partly because I wanted to see the place again, partly to set the record straight about the events following on Marigum's death in 1949. Father Meyer, the then missionary, had sent me an account, but I wished to fill in a number of gaps. I shall tell the story in its proper place in the following pages. This time the governing authorities of Macquarie University defrayed my travelling expenses, and I am most grateful to them as well as to Bernard.

I set out from Sydney by air in December 1974 and reached Wewak eight hours later, a journey that forty-one years before had taken three weeks by ship. Bernard met me at the airport, and we embarked next day for Wogeo in a boat he had chartered. I remained on the island for a month.

Wewak, which I had not seen since 1948, was now the fifth largest town in Papua New Guinea — after Port Moresby (the capital), Lae, Rabaul, and Madang. It was the governing headquarters of the East Sepik District (the old Sepik District had been divided in two), the seat of a bishop, and the chief commercial centre on the eastern side of the Indonesian border of Irian Jaya. There was a long wharf for shipping, warehouses, a large hospital, half a dozen schools, two streets of shops, three hotels, and extensive markets for the sale of local produce.

On arrival in Wogeo the first thing I noticed was the complete absence of the traditional clothing. The men all wore a shirt and shorts or trousers and the women cotton blouses and skirts. Many people also preferred sandals or shoes to bare feet.

I was introduced to my great-grandson, the son of Bernard's only married sister. He had been christened Tom, but his place name was Hogbin (why this and not Ian is unexplained). People also pointed out that the site of my house of 1934, where the clinic now stood, retained the name Ambola, actually a corruption. The earlier generation had requested me to say what I wanted the place to be, and I chose Ambuala, where I had lived in Malaita, Solomon Islands, during the previous year.

Everyone knew me by reputation and took it for granted that I would fit in as one of themselves. They related many of my doings learned in childhood, some true, some apocryphal.

All those older than I were dead, as well as most of my contemporaries. Unfortunately, the survivors looked to be at least eighty. Kalaua, who appears in the following pages, was in fact sixty-six, but seemed much more, and his wife Magar, who in 1934 had been seventeen, could have passed for the same age. Most of them had lost their teeth, some were almost blind, and none was capable of an active day's work.

Many other changes were apparent. To begin with, almost no pagans were left. The majority had been baptized as Roman Catholics, though there was a New Guinean Seventh-Day Adventist pastor with a very small flock.[6] Wogeo was part of an extensive island parish with its own priest, Father Hugo Schulz, who spent much of the time travelling in his ship M.V. *Gabriel* to look after the several congregations. In Wogeo there were two churches, one in the south and the other in the north, both dedicated to St Thérèse of Lisieux, patroness of missionaries. Father Schulz happened to spend Christmas 1974 with us. On the evening of 24 December we had a film show — two American comedies, a New Guinea documentary with a pidgin commentary about the work of the Teaching and Nursing Sisters, and a version of the birth of Jesus made in Spain with American actors (some members of the audience were highly critical of Mary, pointing out that she was neither pregnant at the start nor a young mother with full breasts at the end). This was followed by midnight mass, at which nearly 200 were present. The service, as always, was in pidgin English. (Two translations of the New Testament into pidgin have been printed, one Roman Catholic, the other Protestant, and several Old-Testament stories have also been made over.)

The mission ran a couple of primary schools, with New Guinean teachers, and literacy in pidgin was universal. The people could thus conduct a correspondence with relatives in employment on the mainland and also make themselves understood everywhere when travelling. Many had radios and listened regularly to the news broadcasts in pidgin and other programmes transmitted over the national networks from Port Moresby and Wewak. Pop music was most favoured and ran on and on like a dripping tap.

The best students, perhaps four annually, passed on to the secondary schools in or near Wewak, where teaching was in English. On finishing this course they might enter one of the better paid jobs where literacy in English was essential or else accept a scholarship to attend a tertiary establishment — a technical or teachers' training college or the University of Papua New Guinea. Already three others besides Bernard had entered the professions. These men, although domiciled in one or other of the towns, liked to spend holidays back in Wogeo.

There was progress also in commerce. Wages were, of course, very much higher and constantly increasing. Then on the island itself the coconut groves had been greatly extended, and householders regularly cut and smoked copra. I also saw a few stands of young coffee trees. One group owned a boat, M.V. *Paulus*, which had a regular run between Wewak and Wogeo.[7] It carried copra and coffee to the trading firms and such goods as pigs, chickens, tobacco, areca nuts, betel pepper, almonds, fruit, and vegetables for sale in the Wewak markets. Another group, the Wogeo Island Co-operative Development Society, had two stores stocking rice, canned meat and fish, clothing, tools, pots and pans, kerosene, nails, razor blades, dried and condensed milk, toilet articles, cigarettes and other items now deemed necessary for normal living.

Co-operation remained important for many undertakings. Thus fifteen men, not necessarily always the same ones, were occupied daily for a period of four weeks to complete a house for Bernard, and on one occasion twenty-one men took about five hours to capture a domestic pig that had taken to the bush. Kinship ties were the basis of requests for help, but the emphasis was more diffuse than it once would have been. This change had come about in a sense by accident. The men's clubhouses had gone, fallen into disrepair and not renewed, and with them the two well-defined clusters of dwellings at each end. The villages, though still said to have three parts — the sides and middle — were no longer compact but scattered over a wide area. The fundamental small groups consisting of the residents of a cluster, the unit that in some of my earlier publications I wrongly referred to as a patrilineage or clan, had therefore disappeared. The kindred, always significant but hitherto in the background, was now the main unit, though relatives who were also neighbours tended to be found together more often than those living further away. Residence was usually patrivirilocal, and brothers' sons shared daily tasks whereas sisters' sons and the sons of a brother and a sister might collaborate once or twice a month.

The change in village plan had been followed by innovations in architecture. The distinctive style of the past, a main room with apses at opposite ends, had been succeeded by what might be described as 'New Guinea universal', a simple rectangle sometimes divided in halves. The timbers were nailed in place instead of being lashed with cord, and a few houses had a corrugated-iron roof — one or two even had glass windows.

The hereditary headmen were also no more. Their place was taken by an elected councillor, one for the entire island, who settled minor disputes, brought serious offenders before the courts, kept a record of births and deaths, saw the roads were in good repair, and acted as a channel for the transmission of official instructions.

The religious system had collapsed, and my book *The Island of Menstruating Men: Religion in Wogeo* (Scranton, 1970) might as well have been written about a people living in the Middle Ages. No young man had been initiated and no older one hacked his penis in ritual purification till the blood flowed, and the sacred flutes and masks had rotted away or been burned.

I am not implying a policy of deliberate destruction by the mission, though it may have actively discouraged a few practices. The explanation is to be sought rather in the iconoclastic zeal of the original converts. In Wogeo, as so often in Melanesia, these seem to have found their previous approach to the world of the supernatural a subject for abiding shame, and as a result they did all they could to ensure that their successors should learn little or nothing about it. Bernard told me that his uncles absolutely refused to answer any questions concerning what went on before the missionaries came. Also important in the breakdown were the new conditions brought about by increasing contact with Western goods and ideas. The old rites belonged to a society that faced other problems and had other needs.

The only surviving relics of earlier beliefs were vague notions about pollution in respect to females and the dead. Thus a menstruating woman, though she did not don special clothing to warn others of her condition, refrained from cooking for her husband and family, and one who had just given birth stayed in seclusion for a month in a small hut at the edge of the village. Men and women also sat on different sides of the church during mass and took communion separately (these are common habits throughout Melanesia). Again, at the end of the period of mourning those who had handled the corpse submitted to a ceremonial washing with water in which ginger and Cordyline leaves were soaking — ginger for heat, Cordyline because once it was sacred not only in Wogeo but all over the Pacific. Villagers who had not taken part in the funeral then nicked these folk on the chest, back, shoulders, and calves with a razor blade 'to let out the chill of death'.

Everyone also accepted the efficacy of magic (their word), though not a single spell had survived. Over and over again people lamented their ignorance nowadays of any rites for eradicating the taro blight (see below) or making pigs as fat as they used to be (in fact, because of better breeding, they are much fatter). They admitted that lingering illness could cause death (my blood-brother Kalabai was said to have succumbed to cancer of the throat), but if a man died suddenly, then the consensus was, as before, that sorcery must have been directed against him. 'With each year that passes we have proof that sorcerers still exist — Christianity hasn't made them give up,' one man remarked. 'Nowadays we're helpless against them because we no longer know how to carry out the inquest that could identify them. If you could teach us what to do — surely Marigum must have given you the training — we'd shut them all up in gaol and so be free from harm. Then the population would increase again.' I could only assure him, truthfully as we shall see, that this was the one series of spells that Marigum had withheld.

Undoubtedly the subject of sorcery came up in conversation more often than it had done earlier, a fact that suggests greater fear. I suspect a guilty conscience as perhaps a significant reason. People with money tended to spend it on themselves instead of fulfilling obligations to needy kinsmen and were afterwards not only ashamed of themselves but also alive to the fact that those they had neglected might cherish vindictive feelings.

The last of the great food festivals had taken place more than two decades before. Though the aims were secular, success depended on the performance of too many magical ceremonies at the various stages for the celebrations in the orthodox form

1 Introduction

to retain popular approval. The nearest replacement was the *pati*, a term derived from the English 'party'. A man always held a *pati* to reward the workers who had assisted him in constructing a house, but he did not need such an obvious excuse. He might want to say how pleased he was to return from abroad, end the period of mourning for a dead relative, rejoice at a wedding in the family, or indicate that he was no longer angry with someone who had done him an injury. Whatever the explicit motive, the latent objective, as in the distant past, was to acquire added status by providing great quantities of food and drink, much of it purchased from the stores, and entertaining many guests. The surplus of the new wealth, money, instead of being used to expand business or purchase capital goods whereby ultimately the total sum might go on increasing was thus directed towards improved social standing, the same end as in former times. In a few places in Papua New Guinea the signs of an emerging capitalist society are already apparent, but the experience of the Wogeo islanders was in 1974-5 as yet too limited for such a development. In this particular respect, if in few others, they followed the same kind of pattern as their ancestors. So far not one person had invested a cent in any of the government loans or the public companies.[8]

Bernard's *pati* a fortnight after our arrival was admitted to be bigger than is customary. He wished to pay off the men who had built the new house and also to celebrate his homecoming. It must be borne in mind, however, that he is one of the most highly paid members of the community; moreover, as the legitimate successor, if at one remove, of a famous headman, he has a name to keep up. Before I reached Wewak he had bought for the purpose two bags of rice ($19) — I supplied a third — a case of meat ($8), eight cases of beer, i.e. twelve dozen 400 ml bottles ($48), three bottles of Bacardi rum ($24), and coffee, tea, sugar, tobacco, cigarettes, matches, and such ($30). His total expenditure was thus nearly $130. In addition he supplied three pigs, two of which would have fetched $100 each if sold in the Wewak markets and the third $50, and his relatives contributed between them fish worth $25, over half a tonne of bananas (eighteen bunches, some so large that two men were needed to carry them), hundreds of coconuts, and quantities of sweet potatoes, papayas, breadfruit, areca nuts, betel pepper, and locally grown tobacco, together with newspapers from which cigarettes could be made. The preparations occupied a hundred adult residents of Dap and the surrounding villages for three days. They and their children all attended with a few of Bernard's relatives from elsewhere. The food was set out on platforms, as would have happened formerly, and the older men served the meal at about 8 p.m. In its consumption the sexes were segregated. Then the men betook themselves to drinking around a huge table specially constructed for the purpose. They ended with neat Bacardi at 8 a.m. and, obviously with health unimpaired, began dancing immediately. They continued for the whole morning, backed up by loud thumpings on a wooden slit-gong. The women, indefatigable on over-sweet coffee and tea, had been dancing all night but finished at 9 a.m. They wore imported fibre skirts over their dresses and looked extremely odd.

From then on till our departure almost every fine night there was some woman eager to beat the slit-gong and a small crowd of girls prepared to sing and dance. Incredibly, those who were tired were able to sleep, but not I. There are times when the field anthropologist has to tolerate more handicaps than those suffered by a roadworker with a pneumatic drill at his elbow — the roadworker at least can have peace after knock-off time. Unfortunately the old figure dances and ballets are quite forgotten. We had endless repetitions of the one rhythm, the one tune, the one set of movements, presumably exciting to perform — no other explanation is feasible — but deadly monotonous to watch.[9]

As entertainment had changed for the worse, so also the cuisine. Householders still grated coconut meat, but not one of them ever squeezed out the cream, an essential ingredient of all the best dishes. The frying pan, hitherto unknown, was a popular utensil, and in it people cooked fish, pork, and vegetables in beef dripping purchased in cans from the stores.

One other change must be mentioned, though it had nothing to do with what anyone desired. In 1934 taro had been the staple food, as it was probably in two thirds of the Pacific islands. Soon after that date a type of worm began to attack the crop, and the harvests were much reduced. No insecticide to eradicate the pest has been discovered, and in some islands taro cultivation is now abandoned. The Wogeo turned to bananas and sweet potatoes. The former in 1974–5 provided at least 70 per cent of the diet. Papayas also figured much more prominently, and the pigs were fed on these and coconuts almost exclusively. If some expert was to introduce a method of curing, the Wogeo animals might perhaps become as famous as those of Parma, which, nourished solely on parsnips, provide the world with the exquisite Parmesan prosciutto. 'Papaya-bred ham' would provide a draw card in luxury food shops.

That life was safer than it had been there could be no doubt.

1 Introduction

The fear of being speared or having one's head bashed in no longer crossed anyone's mind. At the same time, the population figure, a total, with absentees, of 798 on 31 December 1974, a reduction of 131 in forty years, or 7 per cent, suggests that health had scarcely improved. (I am not arguing that a fall in population is necessarily bad in itself: Papua New Guinea as a whole is increasing at the rate of 3 per cent annually, and demographers and economists are already expressing alarm at the prospects of double the number in thirty years.) There were two clinics, one on each side of the island, but the orderlies might have had more training, and the nearest hospital at Wewak was not always within reach at short notice. Again, the Malaria Control Unit made occasional visits to spray the inside of the houses with DDT, yet mosquitoes were still present in battalions. I took all the usual precautions but contracted malaria in a stay of only a month. Visits by the child-care nurse were also infrequent.

More comforts were also available. The length of the day could be extended by the use of lamps; literacy, if only in pidgin, conferred many advantages; steel tools of all kinds, from axes and knives to carpenter's levels and drills, made work easier; clothing imported from Hong Kong and Taiwan was cheap; cooking pots could be obtained without the dangers of an overseas canoe voyage; rice, meat, and milk were a valuable addition to the local foods; and galvanized-iron tanks provided better drinking water than pools fouled by pigs (at lower levels there is only one running stream on the entire island).

Yet, despite the church services to strengthen faith and the *pati* to add to enjoyment, I cannot help feeling that a great dullness had descended. By comparison with 1934, village life was drab. I was not surprised to find the young people eager to move away to the towns. Making a living without any skills except an acquaintance with pidgin might be precarious, but the casual labourer was now amid the bright lights in the place where things happen. He also was not oppressed by loneliness, for, apart from new friends, relatives from his own and neighbouring villages were always on hand. The Wogeo quarter of Wewak, for instance, contains more than half a dozen families.

ARGUMENT OF THE BOOK

The account of Wogeo history over the past half century may have given the impression that the rest of the work would be devoted to a study of the principles of social change. This is not so. I am going to deal rather with the practices, attitudes, and structures of the period when European contact had barely begun. Further, for convenience I shall be writing mainly in the present tense, and the description of life in 1934 will be set out as though that is how everything would continue.

I shall begin by analyzing the role of the headman. Unlike his counterpart in most New Guinea communities, initially he depends for his title on birth, and the offspring of an old leader is alone eligible for the succession. The father passes on a knowledge of various esoteric rituals, notably the magic to control the extremes of weather, excess of rain and excess of sunshine, either of which, through flood or drought, can result in the destruction of the food crops. Almost as significant is the rite performed after someone has died to discover whether a sorcerer was responsible and, if so, which one. Thus although the heir may be ignorant of the black arts — and he himself always insists on his innocence — other people believe that he must be familiar with the names of those who regularly practise them. Hence after appointment to office there is always the possibility of his employing such services for private ends. It follows that these supposed powers of causing famine and bringing about sudden death are important sanctions backing up his authority.

But birth alone is not sufficient — to achieve the topmost heights the headman has to be gifted by nature with the personality traits generally admired, such as diligence, liberality, organizing ability, judgement, and tact. I shall explore the respective weight to be given to the characteristics inherited as of right and those that have to be earned. We can then decide whether the most renowned of the headmen inspire more fear than respect or vice versa.

When we turn to the lower ranks we shall have to consider the ordinary person's relations not only with the headman but also with equals. The village is small, with the residents tightly knit together by links of consanguinity and affinity. They combine for many everyday tasks and are at pains to point out that accordingly internal quarrelling would for obvious reasons be foolish, possibly a disaster. Then parents also instruct the children from the earliest years that open dissension between relatives is contrary to the dictates laid down by the culture heroes and hence immoral. Yet people recognize that anybody may still harbour grievances against a neighbour and become vexed. They insist that he should conceal his feelings and continue to show all the outward signs of goodwill, but they admit that mental suffering may result unless he has some kind of emotional outlet. The most quoted proverb is, 'When cross with your wife you should smash a pot; otherwise you'll be out of temper for a month.' Usually what he does is to have recourse, in secret naturally, to disease sorcery — magic to inflict minor ailments like toothache or a gastric upset — and then to rest content in the conviction that at some time in the not too distant future the offender will pay for his alleged misdeeds, though without having suspicions about whence the blow came. If the injured party has suffered a really deep wound to his pride, however, he may instead be driven to destroy some of his own most valued property, ostentatiously yet without any overt reference to the culprit. The latter, if sensitive, goes into retirement by temporarily moving to relatives domiciled in some other village.

The bonds of kinship, and those created by marriages, extend more widely than among ourselves, and the inhabitants of the same general locality also count themselves as related. They exchange visits and gifts of food at frequent intervals and are ready with help for undertakings demanding extensive collaboration. Conflict with them is therefore just as impolitic and is equally condemned as being at variance with proper practice. Trivial misdemeanours call forth performance by stealth of the familiar disease sorcery, but where a distant cousin or an affine has committed a serious offence the man wronged is permitted to seek a mildly violent type of redress. The bigger ceremonies, held two or three times annually, provide the occasion. For a brief period of ten or fifteen minutes, just before the festivities begin, the normal rules of conduct are in abeyance, and those attending engage in a round of brawling, individual against individual or group against group according to the circumstances. Weapons are barred, but sticks and stones may supplement fists. Afterwards, when the headman has declared the return to order, those who have taken part explain that now their rage has vanished. Purged of grudges, they no longer nourish resentments. At the same time, a person tried beyond endurance, as, for example, by a wife's adultery, may not be prepared to wait so many months for his revenge. Abandoning all discretion, he beats the wooden slit-gong lodged beneath the clubhouse of his village and loudly reviles the malefactor. This hammering away at the hollowed-out log is ostensibly to summon an audience, but there can be little doubt that the expenditure of so much energy brings relief in itself. Whether or not the episode is now ended depends upon the support at his command. Usually if he is young or a nonentity the headman tells him he has done enough, and he desists from further action. But a leader's approval, always given to outstanding figures, or even his withholding comment, encourages companions to rally round, and together they set off for the house of the accused. There is no direct confrontation — they merely repeat the performance, with further beating of the gong and a second flow of insults. Sometimes they also demand compensation, to which, if it is forthcoming, the relatives of the wrongdoer will have contributed. Humiliated, he generally keeps out of the way for some months.

In the final section I shall turn to politics. Pitched battles with arrows and spears, arising as a rule from frivolous causes, sometimes take place between troops of hot-headed young men from different districts, but a headman always intervenes to prevent bloodshed. Normally he prefers the common Melanesian practice of fighting with food, putting down rivals by overwhelming them with gifts of pork, vegetables, nuts, and fruit. The obligation incurred by the recipients takes months or even years to fulfil, and in the meantime the donor can treat them as inferior.[10]

Only at rare intervals does raiding occur, when a powerful leader organizes an expedition by his followers against someone he considers to have been presumptuous. The object is to kill the alleged guilty party and to do as little harm as possible to others, though it can happen that relatives standing in the way get themselves slain more or less by accident. So careful is the choice of victim that retaliation by means of a counter raid seldom, if ever, takes place. The vendetta is not a Wogeo institution, and oral records provide no instances of the destruction of any village or the annihilation of the inhabitants.

2 Place and People

Wogeo, located at 3°S. latitude and 144°E. longitude, is the largest and most western of the Schouten Islands, which lie from fifty to eighty kilometres off the north coast of Papua New Guinea between Wewak and the mouth of the Sepik River. The group is not to be confused with another of the same name in Geelvinck Bay to the west off Irian Jaya. Schouten, the European discoverer, was Dutch, and he therefore should be pronounced *scowten* not *shooten*. He made his voyage, with another navigator, Le Maire, in 1615–16. Several of the Schouten Islands are active or quiescent volcanoes. Bam (known locally as Bwem) at the eastern end of the chain is in frequent eruption, and on some others there are hot springs.

Properly speaking the designation Wogeo is incorrect as formerly it was used only by the mainlanders, and the people of the island called their home Wageva. Nowadays, however, they bow to fashion, and the registered title of their co-operative is the Wogeo Development Society. The spelling adopted on navy charts, and in consequence by the government and the missions, is Vokeo, but for this there is neither justification nor excuse.

The island is twenty-five kilometres in circumference and rises in the centre to over 700 metres. On the east and south sides a flat plain some 150–200 metres wide intervenes between the foothills and the sea, but the west and north are steeper, and at some points the slopes end in cliffs. The soil, mostly weathered basalt or limestone, is rich, the rainfall heavy, and the temperature consistently high. The uncultivated areas are in consequence clothed in dense forest.

As elsewhere in this latitude, the two main seasons are dominated respectively by the southeast trade winds and the northwest monsoons. The former blow steadily from June to September, the latter intermittently, though occasionally with near hurricane force, from November to April. In between, light variable breezes alternate with periods of calm. The monsoons bring more rain than the trade winds, but horticulture proceeds without any well marked rhythm — there is no special time either for clearing or harvesting — and crops grow equally well whether planted in January or July, April or October. A monthly calendar enables the leading men to plan festivities ahead,[1] but the years go by uncounted, and nobody knows how old he or she is.[2]

The people are typical Melanesians, with dark brown skin and fuzzy hair. The average stature is below that of most Europeans, and the head is long rather than round. In 1934 the majority of the senior men wore the traditional dress, consisting of a bark corselet covered with a length of beaten barkcloth that passed between the legs and ended in a front flap. They shaved the forehead and pulled the back hair through a wickerwork cone ornamented with dog's teeth and small cowrie shells obtained by trade with the mainland. The youths, on the other hand, preferred a cotton loincloth and shorter hair. The women without exception clung to the fashions of the past. From a waistband flounces of pandanus or sago-palm fibres descended back and front leaving the thighs bare.

THE SETTING

Ridges radiating from the three central peaks (Gwadabi, Yanasora, and Ilodap) divide the island *(vanua)* into five districts. There is no general word for such an area, but each has a name. Wonevaro lies at the southeast corner and, proceeding clockwise, then come Bagiau, Ga, Bukdi, and Takul. Relations between neighbouring districts have always tended to be edgy, though hostility is to some extent mitigated by intermarriage and the consequent ties of particular individuals related as consanguines or affines. The inhabitants of districts separated by one in between are, by contrast, likely to be friendly. In 1934 the Wonevaro residents had been on excellent terms for years with those of Bukdi, a harmony which continued till 1949, when, as we shall see later, a dispute arose over charges of sorcery. Similarly, Takul was linked with Bagiau and Ga.

Wonevaro (population in 1934 approximately 270) has five villages *(malal)*, Bagiau (pop. approximately 210) four villages, Ga (pop. approximately 120) one village, Bukdi (pop. approximately 200) three villages, and Takul (pop. approximately 130) two villages. All save those of Bukdi and Takul were earlier built close to the water. The north coast is so rugged, and so lashed by gales during the monsoons, that till recently the settlements there nestled in the foothills. Now these also have moved down (1974). The usual number of people in a village is between sixty and seventy, though three have fewer and Ga twice as many.

Inevitably I became identified with the Dap folk and when elsewhere was treated much as they were. Thus Gol, and to a lesser extent Bukdi as a whole, became my second home. Contacts in Bagiau and Takul remained more formal, except in the case of those men whose acquaintance for one reason or another I made an effort to cultivate.

In the majority of the villages the most imposing building, which if the terrain permits stands in the centre, is the men's club *(niabwa)*. It is higher than the dwellings *(luma)*, with the floor resting on stout hardwood piles three metres tall, thus permitting assemblies to gather underneath. The dimensions also exceed those of the houses of all save the main headmen. Usually the length is about eight metres and the breadth five metres. Great attention is paid to the construction, and the thatch, always of excellent quality, extends downwards to shade the walls. Entry is by a notched log or a ladder, alongside which stands a beautifully carved wooden slit-gong. If the settlement lacks a club the reasonable assumption is that the old one has recently tumbled into ruins and as yet insufficient food has been accumulated for the feasting that must accompany the replacement.

The essential purpose of the club is to provide storage for the sacred objects of the community — the flutes representing the spirit monsters of the male cult, the dancing masks, and the bones of famous ancestors — and a haven for those who, following on contact with the supernatural or substances held to cause pollution, are in a state of taboo.[3] Yet, if only incidentally, it also serves as a meeting place and a dormitory. Here the males gather after the day's work to smoke, chew betel, gossip, plan the morrow's tasks, and receive visitors. Sometimes they ask the women to bring across the evening meal. The younger householders, unless they are going on a fishing expedition by torchlight, return eventually to their dwellings, but the youths and older men stay on to sleep.

Except in Bukdi, where level ground is scarce, the ordinary houses are arranged in two clusters at opposite ends of the club. They vary in size according to the social status of the owner and whether he has many dependants. Those of the headmen may be almost if not quite as large as the club, though they are never as lofty, and decorated with carvings of men, crocodiles, and fish on the gables and paintings on the outer walls. At the other end of the scale, those of elderly couples whose children have all left, or the

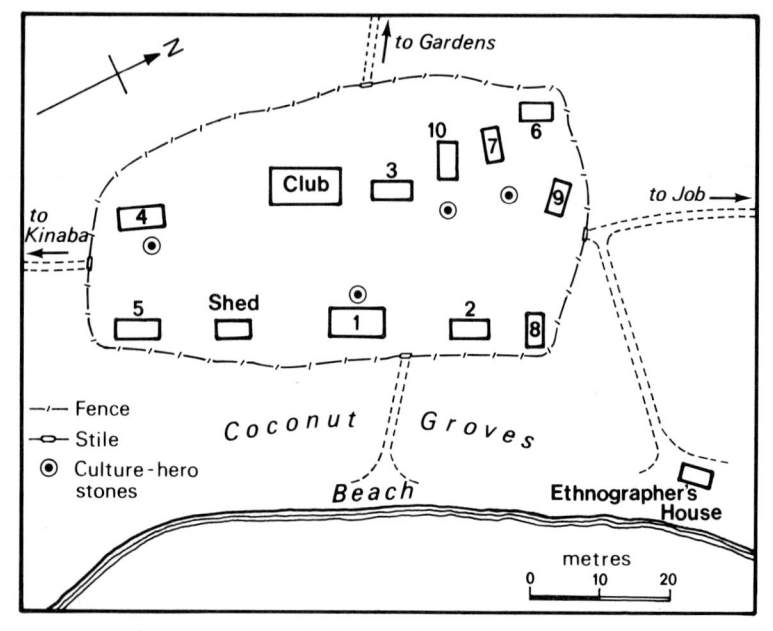

Sketch Plan of Dap Village

House 1
Cluster A; Marigum, his three surviving wives, the wife of a son absent in employment, and his unmarried children.

House 2
Cluster A; Waru (related to Marigum), his wife, and his child.

House 3
Cluster A; Tafalti (Marigum's eldest son), his wife, and an aged female dependant.

House 4
Cluster A; Sawang (Marigum's half-brother's son), his wife, and his unmarried brother.
Aligned with Cluster A; Sakum, his wife (Marigum's half-sister's daughter), and his child.

House 5
Aligned with Cluster A; Kalal, his wife (Marigum's half-sister's daughter), and the wife's son by a deceased husband.

House 6
Cluster A; Jaua (Marigum's half-sister's son), and one of his wives (Bagasal's adopted daughter). The house is wrongly located to enable the wife to be near her aged father.
Aligned with Cluster A; Wiap (Marigum's cross-cousin), and his wife and child.

House 7
Cluster B; Bagasal, and his unmarried son absent in employment.

House 8
Cluster B; Sabuk (related to Bagasal), his two wives, and his children.

House 9
Cluster B; Wiawia (Bagasal's brother), his wife, his children, and his mother-in-law.

2 Place and People

newly married without as yet a family, are only half the size but follow the same architectural style. All are raised on piles a metre or more high and have a verandah in front and the ends rounded to form apse-like extra rooms. The thatch is made from leaflets of the sago palm, the walls from spathes of the black-palm, and the floors of the outer covering of the trunk of the black-palm. In 1934 the people had not taken over nails from Europeans — such innovations would then have been too expensive — and the timbers and roof covering were lashed in place with creepers or hand-twisted cord. Ordinarily the two side rooms under their half-cone roof are filled with such objects as fishing tackle, spare cooking pots, and piles of firewood; but if the need arises the householder clears out such gear to accommodate a widowed sister or other close relative or even, should he have two wives, the one less in favour — or the less aggressive. The collection of the building material and the construction work demand extensive co-operation. The owner is obliged to feed his helpers each day and to entertain them at the end with a feast. Neighbours and other relatives offer their services not so much for the sake of the reward but because they know they are creating an obligation which the host will later on have to return in kind. In the tropics unseasoned timber and thatch soon decay, and houses have to be renewed every few years.

The man has the responsibility for providing shelter for his family. Usually if he is a polygynist each wife has a part of the house to herself, where she cooks at her own fireplace and sleeps with her children and older unmarried daughters, though he may feel obliged in the interests of domestic peace to relegate one of the women to an apse room. A few husbands, disturbed by continual squabbles, even think it advisable to put up separate dwellings for their spouses. Close kin of either sex may enter the house freely, but distant kin and strangers await an invitation. As a rule the men prefer to take visitors to the club.

Everyone avoids the area immediately behind the clubhouse, where objects prepared for ceremonies and other sacred paraphernalia are disposed of, and the members of each sex group also keep away from the place in the bush reserved by the other as

---

House 10
Cluster B; Gris (Bagasal's son absent in employment), his wife, and his child. For reasons later explained, I have elsewhere changed Gris's name to Gireno.
Cluster B; Sabwa (related to Bagasal), his wife, and his child.
Cluster B; widow of a relative of Bagasal (she is Marigum's sister), her widowed daughter (and this woman's children), and her unmarried children.
The small circles outside houses 1, 4, 7, and 10 indicate the position of upright blocks of basalt representing culture heroes.

a latrine. The different family units have the exclusive right to a section of the shore, but trespass is dismissed as of no consequence, and the people pull up their canoes above high-water mark anywhere and walk about or sit as they please. In very hot weather they may prepare, cook, and eat dinner on the beach.

In front of the dwelling of every villager of importance stands a columnar block of basalt from 30 to 75 centimetres high surrounded by many flat stones half buried in the ground. These are linked to culture heroes with whom the householder has a special association, a bond given as the reason why he builds on that site.

Horticulture provides the bulk of food supply. Taro *(Colocasia esculenta)* is the staple, with yams, sweet potatoes, many kinds of bananas, numerous greens, and sugar-cane as subsidiaries. Tillage is by the slash-and-burn method, and after each harvest the garden area must lie fallow for upwards of a decade. The digging stick remains the chief implement, though axes and knives are essential for clearing. In times of feasting when extra stocks are needed the people seek the giant taro *(Alocasia macrorrhiza)*[4] in the bush, and they may also prepare sago. Fruits include two varieties of breadfruit, mangoes, Malay apples, papayas, and oranges. Nuts are important, especially coconuts, Canarium almonds, and Pacific (or Tahitian) chestnuts *(Inocarpus edulis)*. The men do not eat the purple-husked Okari nuts *(Terminalia kaernbachii)*, but women and children consume them freely, and they are also in demand for trade with the mainland.[5] Cultivated drug plants include tobacco, the areca nut, and betel pepper. The last two are ingredients of the betel mixture, which most of the islanders chew.

Sea foods and pork furnish the animal protein. The islanders catch fish by every conceivable method both from the reefs and offshore, and occasionally they take turtles; but they kill their domestic pigs only for special events, never to form part of a daily meal. They organize hunting expeditions for wild pigs as opportunity offers, or inclination dictates, yet probably the total amount of meat consumed does not average more than 50–100 grams per person daily.

Food may be roasted directly on the fire, steamed or boiled in a clay pot, or baked on hot stones in the typical Pacific-island earth oven. The last is always used for pork and, because the taste is said to be superior, when a company of guests has arrived.

Canoe voyages between Wogeo and the nearest of the Schouten Islands, Koil (locally Kweil), are comparatively frequent, and intermarriage by no means uncommon, but contacts with the islands further away, where the language is slightly different, and with the mainland, where the various tongues can be counted by the dozen, were sporadic in earlier times. The Wonevaro and Bagiau residents fitted out a fleet of overseas canoes every five or six years and set sail for purposes of trade with various island villages and others of the New Guinea coast. On the outward journey they carried a cargo of local specialities — Canarium almonds and Okari nuts, fishing-nets, and small woven baskets. These items they exchanged for clay pots, women's large carrying bags, pipeclay as a cosmetic, bamboos to be made into flutes, and such ornaments as cowries, shell rings, bird-of-paradise skins, and crests of the Goura pigeon *(Goura victoria)*. After the lapse of a couple of years the mainlanders arranged a return voyage.[6]

SOCIAL STRUCTURE

A pair of exogamous matrilineal moieties called Tarega and Kilbong, the chicken hawk and the flying fox or bat, divides the Wogeo community into halves. People refer to these units as *tina*, literally 'mother',[7] but although fellow members say they have the one blood *(dara-ta)*, they do not regard themselves as related in the genealogical sense unless they know of a connection or can reasonably infer it. The rare marriage that takes place within the moiety arouses criticism, though nobody ever condemns the guilty pair in their presence. It is argued that in the past the leaders might have punished such transgression with death, and several examples are quoted in support, but these could well be legendary. The elders accept that promiscuity before marriage is normal but insist that moiety incest is reprehensible. They point out that although the man may escape any supernatural penalty, the single girl who fails to confess her fault and then becomes pregnant runs the risk of suffering grave difficulties during labour, the direct result of intervention by agencies from the other world. The young folk are inclined to ignore the warning — as are their seniors when arranging adulterous affairs — and in fact cases of moiety incest seldom give rise to much comment unless the couple have openly courted scandal.

Manifestations of rivalry, so often encountered in Melanesia accompanying a dual organization, are not part of the Wogeo system. Instead, the situation is reversed. A father is permitted to chastise his son, and paternal uncles their nephews, but contemporaries belonging to opposite moieties have ordinarily to treat one another with respect. The regulations are only relaxed, and then briefly, on certain ritual occasions; otherwise a Tarega man who strikes a Kilbong, or a Kilbong man who strikes a Tarega, loses his good name unless he hands over a pig or a collection of valuables as compensation.

Reciprocal duties are also laid down. Thus a father ought to seek someone from his own moiety for the initiation of his son, and at death the grave-diggers are also supposed to come from outside.

Compared with the Polynesians, and, indeed, some Melanesians, the Wogeo are poor genealogists. A few people can give the name of one of their great-great-grandfathers, but the majority are unable to go further back than four or five of the eight great-grandparents, although they may be able to enumerate the entire list of all the great-grandparents' descendants. Despite moiety membership following the female line, people remember men's names better than those of women, and there is thus more chance of a person's identifying his great-grandfathers than his great-grandmothers. Yet everyone counts his kinsmen by the hundred. He is convinced of his relationship with the entire population of his district and with many of the residents of other districts, always more than half the inhabitants of the island. A supposed connection between two of the seniors is sufficient for their sons and daughters to say they also must be kin.

The more important a man is, the greater the advantage in claiming a link with him. By this means the least significant householder can bask in the reflected glory of an acknowledged leader. The latter in turn is pleased to accept the compliment, thereby ensuring himself a following. Almost every person I asked, no matter where domiciled, said he was related to Marigum. Such self-styled kinsmen may have exceeded 600. Kawang had a circle just as extensive.

The kinship terminology is of classificatory type, modelled on the pattern known as Iroquois.[8] The terms for siblings are applied to the parallel cousins, but there is a special term for cross cousins; the term for father is applied to his brothers and the term for mother to her sisters and the father's sisters,[9] but there is a pair of alternative terms for the mother's brothers; and the son and daughter terms are applied to the brothers' children and, if a woman is speaking, the sisters' children, but a man applies the pair for mother's brothers to his sisters' children. The maternal-uncle and uterine-nephew words are therefore reciprocal. This is so also with that for grandparent and grandchild. The terms are extended to embrace all the people held to be kin regardless of whether the bonds are real or hypothetical.[10] So ideally relatives of a person's own generation are either siblings or cross cousins;

those of the first ascending generation fathers, mothers, or mother's brothers; those of the second ascending generation grandparents; those of the first descending generation sons, daughters, or, if a man is speaking, sisters' children; and those of the second descending generation grandchildren. In practice manipulation can occur. Neighbours who happen to be cross cousins usually prefer to think of themselves as brothers, as do younger uncles when in the company of older nephews. I have also known youths who called an older half-brother 'father' and women who called their husband's older children by a different wife 'brothers' and 'sisters'.

Europeans keep their kinship ties alive in part by exchanging gifts at Christmas and offering presents on birthdays. The Wogeo maintain theirs in similar fashion, except that with them the giving is continuous. When the women are dishing up at mealtimes they call the children to carry this or that platter of food to such and such a relative. 'Here, this is for your grandfather Uvisi: tell him you asked me to send it to him,' says the housewife. The youngster trots across the street and offers it with some such remark as, 'I don't like to think of your being hungry, grandfather, and I asked mother to let me bring you this to eat. Sit down and taste it. It's cooked just the way you like.' If the weather is fine the woman may also send baskets of choice bananas or bowls of vegetable stew accompanied by almonds to relatives living further away. Dap is made up of only twelve households, and often as many as six or seven containers go to kin in Mwarok, Kinaba, Job, and Bariat. Correspondingly, scarcely a sunny day passes without at least four or five baskets coming in (in wet weather everyone stays at home). The same sort of thing happened in my own establishment consisting of the two lads Dal and Gris. I issued them with rations of rice, meat, biscuits, tea, sugar, etc., but these they often gave away and ate instead supplies contributed four or five times weekly by their mothers, aunts, sisters, and cousins.

Such proceedings cannot be interpreted purely in terms of economic benefits except in so far as they provide nourishment for those temporarily short on account of illness, misadventure, or compliance with religious taboos (a woman while menstruating, for example, does not prepare food for her husband and children). More often than not each housewife cooks a surplus in order to give to people who already have an abundance, while simultaneously these folk also cook more than they need with the aim of bestowing in their turn donations which in the literal sense will be just as out of place. Fortunately the pigs are there to eat the left-overs, and nothing is wasted. The explanation for the constant trafficking is social — it sustains the network of consanguineous ties and helps to preserve it as a living reality.

In many societies each kinship term has associated with it a distinctive stereotype of behaviour; so a person may expect the men classified with his father to act according to one set of rules and those classified with his mother's brothers according to another set. Perhaps the father and paternal uncles will have the specific duty of finding him a wife, the maternal uncles of teaching him magical spells. Where this is so he has differing attitudes towards the two sides. Again, the father's sisters may be schooled into being at all times critical and severe and the mother and her sisters into being lenient and accommodating; or warmth may be the keynote of the parallel-cousin relationship and formality the keynote of that of cross cousins.

Wogeo has no such fixed and prescribed routines. Admittedly a man inherits his father's estate, not that of his mother's brothers; and the members of the parental generation, with the advantage of age and experience, have a certain authority and the privilege of giving orders — though this does not mean that the young people invariably obey. Further, the moiety division implies a code of mutal politeness for cross cousins. But otherwise the canons imposed on all kinsfolk are basically identical regardless of the category to which they belong. In particular the bearing of the patrilateral kin is scarcely distinguishable from that of the matrilateral kin. All relatives are expected to be considerate, understanding, sympathetic, forgiving, trustworthy, generous, loyal, and helpful; should one of them be accused of wrongdoing the rest are under the obligation of hastening to his defence and pointing out, or inventing, any extenuating circumstances; should one of them have a grievance against a stranger the rest must combine in exacting punishment; and should one of them be killed the survivors have the responsibility for taking vengeance. Kin stand by each other, united in good fortune and also in the face of affliction and disaster. Indeed, the code is so unyielding that if anybody forgets himself and harms a close relative the latter is obliged to keep silent and avoid attempting reprisals. The only course open to him for calling attention to the fault, though without naming the offender out loud, is to make a great show of destroying some of his own property. In an extreme case it is said that he might kill his mother or sister, though I never heard of anyone's having done so.

With a kinship system so dispersed and pervasive, there can be no room for the casual friend. If two men develop a warm regard for each other, and in consequence spend a good deal of their working and leisure time together, they take pains to find out exactly how they are related — with less than a thousand total population to choose from, related they always must be, usually in half a dozen different ways. In answer to an unlikely comment they would point out that, as brothers, naturally they share their tasks. Here we have the explanation of why the anthropologist is so frequently adopted into a family. It is part of his job to be cordial to everybody and infinitely patient, as well as charitable in his judgements, benevolent, and well-intentioned; above all, he is eager to accept intimacy (a list of qualifications not intended to be exhaustive). Where the concept of friendship is unknown, how can he be fitted into the community except as a kinsman?

The closest the Wogeo go to deliberately choosing a comrade is in their institution of blood-brotherhood. Usually the pair *(wasabwai)* enter into the relation in a formal ceremony during their initiation, when they are at the age of puberty.[11] From then on they are expected to be 'closer than true siblings', ready to grant any request big or small. At the same time, they are of most help before marriage. They should belong to opposite moieties, and in youth, when sexual promiscuity is normal, each can arrange assignations on the other's behalf with the girls of his own division.

Occasionally adults who have no true siblings may also decide to become blood-brothers, though without going through the rite. The mutual assistance is then of value in the various economic tasks. When I had been on Wogeo for about six months Kalabai, a young man from Job, suggested that we two should become *wasabwai*. I accepted gladly, and from then on, without any prompting, he took charge of all my travelling arrangements. On my last night on the island, when practically the entire population came to say goodbye, he sat alongside with his arm around my shoulders. During 1973, by means of a letter dictated to one of the literate juniors, he sent word of his continuing goodwill and hopes for my return. Unfortunately he was taken ill soon afterwards and died during the following January. In accordance with his request, the body was dressed for burial in the clothing I had sent. In 1974-5 his widow and sons made a special point of inviting me to meals.

Blood-brothers are always from the same district. In other districts, and on the different Schouten Islands, a man has partners. The word is *bag*, which is also applied to a rest platform, seat, or bed. The idea is that partners sit together — perhaps too, that when visiting they provide one another with accommodation. Generally the sons of partners become partners themselves. As with blood-brothers, they must belong to opposite moieties. Their hospitality facilitates travel, and they are further tied together by exchanges of foodstuffs on important occasions. The one gives a pig perhaps to supplement the other's offering at a festival, and the appropriate return follows a year or so later.

Overseas trading is also carried on through partnerships with people from villages on the New Guinea coast and from further Schouten Islands. The mainland word *lo*, or sometimes *tauve*, is in this instance preferred to the Wogeo *bag*.

The social structure as described so far, leaving aside for the moment the moieties, may be said to be based on kindreds, the people whom a person recognizes as his cognates.[12] A kindred is always centred on a single individual or a set of full siblings, and the links are traced through males and females. The members, though all united with this person, or the siblings, need not be related to one another; often they are strangers. If a man's father and mother were before marriage unrelated, for example, then his two pairs of grandparents, despite their being part of his kindred and sharing an interest in him, would also be unrelated. In a small community such as Wogeo the kindreds of different people necessarily overlap. A child's kindred is therefore never double the size of that of either of his parents.

A kindred differs from a unilineal group such as a moiety in that it is ephemeral. The newly born members of the moiety continually replace those who die, whereas each person or series of siblings is the focal point of a unique kindred, which exists only for as long as he or they remain alive. A society in which there are unilineal groups and no kindreds can be represented diagramatically by a figure neatly divided into segments; a society with kindreds alone is more like hundreds of circles endlessly intersecting.

The affines, although as such forming no part of the kindred, fit comfortably into the scheme.[13] They include the person's spouse's near kinsmen and also the spouses of his own near kinsmen. One term covers the parents-in-law, their brothers and sisters, the sons-in-law and daughters-in-law; and another the wife's brothers, the husband's sisters, the sisters' husbands (man speaking), and the brothers' wives (woman speaking). The rest are referred to by terms for the cognates. Thus a man calls his brother's wife 'mother', and she replies by speaking of him as 'son'. The father's and mother's brothers' wives are also 'mother' and the

2 Place and People

father's and mother's sisters' husbands 'father'. The children of the spouse's brothers and sisters are called 'son' and 'daughter'.

Affines are obliged to treat one another with deference and honour, but otherwise their behaviour resembles that of people bound together by ties of consanguinity. They are dependable and at every turn ready with support. It is said that a person runs to aid an affine accused of an offence, runs to aid him also should he be demanding satisfaction for an injury; moreover, the responsibility for avenging a killing rests as heavily on the affines as on the kin.

According to Bernard the word *warowaro* is the equivalent of 'kindred' as here defined. 'The term means all a person's relatives, his kinsmen as a whole,' he wrote in a letter dated 17 July 1973. Obviously it would be presumptuous of me to argue on questions of language, and I can only agree on this having always been the commonest usage. But I have an impression of formerly hearing *warowaro* applied on occasion more loosely, as, for instance, to those of a man's kin and affines who were by chance gathered together when some job had to be done — some of his kindred would be there, some absent. The derivation is from *waro*, a tough forest liana that can present an almost impenetrable bar to progress. I would judge the implication to be that those who are related belong together.

As is well known, the principles underlying group formation are likely to colour the dogma relating to conception. Many societies with patrilineal descent over-emphasize the role of the father and insist that the womb is simply a vessel, a sort of flowerpot, in which the seed planted by the man can grow. Correspondingly, many societies with a matrilineal bias maintain that the woman is wholly responsible and that her husband merely opens the way for the free passage of the infant at birth. The Wogeo by contrast hold the father and the mother both accountable for pregnancy, a belief suggesting that the bilateral kindreds may be of greater significance than the unilineal moieties. Yet there is no official doctrine on what exactly takes place, and speculation is rife. Three views are current — that the conjunction of semen and vaginal secretion (each called *jabejabe*) results in the formation of the embryo, which is nourished till birth by the blood that would have been lost in menstruation; that the blood contains the seed and the semen the food; and that the semen coagulates the blood and seals it in the womb, where it develops into the foetus.

The people may go on repeating over and over again that each kinsman and each affine gives his backing without stint as a matter of course day in and day out, but I must insist that they overstate the case. If a person's kith and kin number 500, probably some 150 will be adult males. He may be glad to accept a helping hand from as many as this when things have gone terribly awry, perhaps because he has been accused of murder and his life in consequence is under threat; but on ordinary occasions collaboration on such a scale is unnecessary. Housebuilding and the construction of a large canoe for overseas voyaging could require the presence of sixty or seventy people for some parts of the work, though the average task, like clearing forest for a new garden, is better done by a dozen at most. Often for planting, fencing, and fishing the labour unit is smaller still, not more than three or four.

My fellow villagers, when I argued with them about the real situation, were prepared to admit grudgingly to a charge of misrepresentation. Yes, perhaps they had told me what ought to happen at the expense of what actually takes place, they said. They wanted me to realize that distant relatives are ready to come along but agreed that normally the closer relatives suffice. Here they had in mind genealogical propinquity, though their language, unlike those in some other parts of Papua New Guinea, lacks an expression defining precisely who the near kinsmen are.[14] A speaker may include a third or fourth cousin to whom he is attached and omit a second cousin he actively dislikes. The demarcation is thus a blurred zone, not a sharp line.

This concession does not go far enough: it ignores geographical propinquity. Residence after marriage is most commonly patrivirilocal, and a man's father's brothers' sons are likely therefore to be his next-door neighbours, whereas his mother's brothers' sons, his father's sisters' sons, his mother's sisters' sons, and his brothers-in-law may be living at a distance of several kilometres. Men who come from the one village can scarcely avoid each other's company. They have to take the same path to the gardens, which usually are not more than a few minutes' walk apart, they fish off the same reefs and beach their canoes on the same stretch of shore, and in the evenings they assemble in the same club. True, physical proximity does not lead to extra formal privileges and extra mutual responsibilities; but inevitably those who are constantly together end up by activating the potentials of their relationship more often than do those who meet only by making the effort of a long walk. A man who would like a couple of helpers for an afternoon finds it easier to ask those from across the street in preference to his cousins or affines who live in another part of the island. Naturally he also approaches the person within earshot for the temporary loan of some tool or utensil. My nephew Jaua, for example, worked during my stay much more frequently with Waru and Wiawia from the two adjoining houses than with his brother Simukan, who had left temporarily for the village of Job, where he and his wife were looking after her aged father (the old man should have gone to live with them in Dap, but he was stubborn and refused to move).

I am not saying that the residents of the housing cluster or settlement are always, or even usually, alone; but it is a fact that they carry out much of their daily labour either by themselves or with the minimum of outside help. This week an uncle, a cousin, or an affine from elsewhere joins with them to make a garden, next week a different relative, perhaps a daughter's son or a daughter's husband, and the following week still another. Throughout, the nucleus is relatively unchanged, always allowing that on any given occasion somebody may be absent reciprocating assistance offered previously or anticipating that to come in the future.

The questions to be settled are, who live together and why? The answers demand a brief digression into the subject of land tenure.[15]

The mountainous country in the centre of the island is common property, and anyone in the district is free to hunt there, gather forest products, and fell the timber without let or hindrance. The flat areas on the coast and the foothills behind, however, are tied up with the villages and even more with the separate clusters of dwellings at either end of the centrally placed clubhouse. The folk from a distance speak of the Dap ground, the Kinaba ground, the Mwarok ground, and so forth, but closer examination reveals a clear division into halves, one for each of the component units. In Dap there is thus one segment for the cluster where Marigum lives and a second for the other cluster. These territories are cut into blocks of varying soil type, aspect, and drainage. The householders of the cluster own some jointly and from time to time make their gardens together, but the rights to the majority are an individual matter, and each man regards a separate series as his private property. Various people own in addition a few blocks scattered through the cultivation areas of villages where they do not live. At least half of Marigum's neighbours, although their main holdings are concentrated within the one Dap division, have small parcels in Kinaba, Mwarok, Job, or elsewhere; furthermore, some of the residents of these settlements claim small parcels in Dap. How does this interdigitation come about?

A man divides the bulk of his agricultural land among his male children, usually round about the time they reach puberty. The firstborn receives the most, but none can be ignored, not even a good-for-nothing. But fathers also like to give ground as dowry to at least the eldest daughter, although they may not be able to afford more than a small plot on which an almond or breadfruit tree is growing. On her death this passes to one of her sons. Headmen, however, richer than other people, can sometimes afford enough blocks to support a female child's entire family. They then expect the husband to join her in patriuxorilocal residence. In due course this dowry land descends to the sons, who, like male offspring in other households, also inherit the father's estate in his place of origin. Generally they arrange to split up, and while some stay in the mother's village to cultivate the areas that were hers, the rest go to live in the father's natal home and take over those derived from him.

Jaua and his brother Simukan are examples. They owed their membership of Marigum's cluster to the fact that their grandfather Jaran, Marigum's father, gave his daughter Fein, their mother and Marigum's half-sister, an extensive acreage in Dap. The husband Danug was from Mwarok, and when he died the sons also inherited the land there. Faithful to his mother's memory, Jaua remained in Dap till his death, but in 1937 or 1938 Simukan decided to transfer to Mwarok to look after the other heritage.

Occasionally a man who has been helping a cousin or a brother-in-law to clear a patch of bush may accept the offer of a garden plot, which after the harvest has been gathered reverts back to the donor. Later the recipient makes a similar gesture in return. But in general each householder prefers to cultivate the strips that belong to him outright. As might be expected, he likes to live in the village near at hand, thereby avoiding a lengthy journey to work and saving his wife the labour of carrying heavy loads of produce over great distances. The result is that the majority of the males remain for life in the place where they spent their earlier years. They build a house near the father's, just as the father himself and his forbears did in their turn in the past. By this means not only is convenience served, but they also retain the sentimental and religious ties with their own culture heroes commemorated by the pillars of basalt in front of the houses. Most of the birth members of the housing cluster are thus either agnates or, because nobody can trace his pedigree far, believe themselves to be agnates. Although Waru and Marigum refer to one another as brother and belong to the same cluster — the two dwellings stand side by side — neither is aware of the name of their common ancestor or of how many generations have elapsed since he was alive. The same is also true of Bagasal and Sabuk of the second Dap cluster. But in addition there are usually, perhaps always, two or three nonagnates, the descendants of female agnates of the men forming the nucleus, daughters whose fathers were able to furnish a lavish endowment. The shallowness of the local genealogical memory is in this instance also of significance in that it accounts for these women's seldom being from a generation more remote than that of the grandparents. Once the names of great-grandparents have been forgotten it comes to be taken for granted that the link must have been fully agnatic.

In my earliest publications about the Wogeo, going back to 1935, I spoke of the persons born into a cluster of houses as forming a patrilineal clan or patrilineage.[16] This was wrong. Later, with second thoughts, I described them as a descent group. If no longer grossly inaccurate, this was misleading. Recruitment is not by descent from a distant ancestor, unilineal or cognatic, but by filiation, being someone's offspring, usually the father, occasionally the mother, and hence inheriting that person's rights in land. Cumulative filiation down the years has the effect of creating what are putative descent groups, but this is incidental, a by-product, and has nothing to do with the local ideology.

Nowadays, unfortunately, the residents of Papua New Guinea, brown and white alike, have developed a mania for the word 'clan', which they employ indiscriminately for every type of localized unit irrespective of the criterion, essential for the anthropologist (though I temporarily forgot it), of a belief in unilineal descent from a common ancestor. So Bernard in the letter on nomenclature from which I have already quoted said that the vernacular expression for 'a family or a clan' — by which he meant the people of a cluster — was *dan*. The literal meaning is 'water', said to be here a euphemism for semen. In 1934 *dan* was applied not only to the residents of the half dozen houses at each end of the village but also to such assemblages as a man and his descendants, a headman and his followers no matter where domiciled, and the members of a household, who need not form an elementary family. A speaker who wished to be precise when referring to cluster residents gave the name of the leading man and his village. He talked of 'Marigum's *dan* in Dap', for example, and of 'Kawang's *dan* in Gol'.

Groupings resembling this of Wogeo are common throughout Melanesia. There is perhaps a myth of founding brothers, acknowledgement of a leader, stress on inheritance from the father, and a ready welcome for husbands living uxorilocally, whose grandsons if not sons become fully incorporated.

Although such units are localized, and the observer can actually see them before his eyes, the collective membership rarely if ever acts alone as a self-proclaimed entity when weighty political matters or important economic and religious undertakings are in train. What usually happens is that a few individuals put forward valid reasons for standing aloof or joining another faction, while simultaneously certain relatives from other places insist on participating.

As was mentioned, the obligation to exact vengeance when somebody has been murdered does not rest solely on the shoulders of the men of the local group; ideally the dead person's kinsmen from elsewhere and also his affines are concerned just as much – the agnates and nonagnates, the near kin of the spouse, and the spouses of the near kin. Whether or not on a particular occasion a certain relative will respond depends on his private interests, sympathies, and prejudices. Further, the aim of the members of the avenging party is to strike down the actual killer either by sorcery or violence, and they are not prepared to accept anyone else as a substitute. Of course, relatives who come to his aid should he be attacked are in danger of being slain, but this is only because they are obstructive. Spearing them is extrinsic and has no effect on the real issue: the original blood debt remains.

Similarly, the culprit is not content to call on just the neighbours for protection: he hopes that all his kinsmen and affines will be there. But again reactions are bound up with personal factors. R. F. Fortune wrote of a newly married man who a few days after the wedding accompanied the other residents of his village in an attack on the settlement whence the bride had come and also gave instances of warriors asserting that they had not long before made their sisters widows and their wives brotherless.[17] Whether such boasting was based on fact is another question.

The Melanesian situation is clearly in no way comparable with that described by M. Fortes for the Tallensi and other African peoples.[18] 'When a lineage is found as a corporate group all the members of a lineage are to outsiders jurally equal and represent the lineage when they exercise legal and political rights and duties in relation to society at large,' he said. 'That is what underlies the so-called collective responsibility of blood revenge and self help.'[19] It would be inaccurate to speak of the members of the cluster in Wogeo or like groups from other parts of the Pacific as jurally equal; only the leader, and he rarely, ever claims to be speaking as the representative of the rest.

2 Place and People

In the classical African lineage system everybody belongs to but one group or series of groups. If confrontation occurs, as in a feud, each has his pre-ordained place, and the question of divided loyalties does not arise. But kindreds, with their appendages of affines, inevitably overlap, as was indicated, and after a Melanesian killing a number of people may find themselves in a dilemma. If they are related to both the slayer and the slain, should they join the protectors or the avengers? Whatever they decide will in their own eyes and those of some other people be wrong. One way out is to remain neutral, another is to secure some sort of a compromise.

A word must also be said about leadership. The office of headman is ascribed; that is to say the title (*kokwal*, or sometimes *kokwal malal*, *kokwal* of the settlement) descends by hereditary right, though not necessarily to the father's firstborn — an additional requirement is that the heir must be his mother's eldest son. As an established headman will certainly have several wives, there are always two or three youths from whom he may choose. Once decided, he teaches the boy a corpus of mythology relating to the culture heroes, with the magical ritual enshrined therein, and the correct procedure for performing a number of rites and ceremonies. The information takes time to master, and not until satisfied does the parent name the lad officially as his successor. This occurs at a big food festival *(warabwa)*, when the father decorates the boy with a rich collection of boar's tusks, the insignia of rank, and has the men of the cluster hoist him to the top of two poles, to which he has to cling while reciting a spell, supposed to have the effect of confirming his renown and carrying it to the limits of the known world, or more specifically to all the Schouten Islands and the adjoining New Guinea mainland.

Should the favoured son be still a child, too young for instruction, an elderly father may ask one of his brothers, or sometimes a sister, to act as a trustee. This person stores the heritage away until the boy has grown to early manhood. The formal proclamation through the hoisting on the poles, however, can only be organized by a real headman. The parent before his death arranges this with another leader.

The ideal is two headmen to a village, one for the residents of each cluster of dwellings. But the reality may be otherwise. One or both may have died before a successor was appointed. In 1934 Kinaba and Job, the settlements on either side of Dap, lacked leaders, although Marigum was expected to see that the deficiency was remedied in the near future.[20] Then even headmen properly installed can differ significantly in temperament, ability, dignity, wisdom, and energy; further, a man approaching old age has difficulty in continuing to exercise influence. By my 1948 visit Marigum had become blind and was dependent on a daughter who led him by the hand.

The population of the average village is, as I said, between sixty and seventy. The clusters therefore, are unlikely to contain more than thirty-five people made up of six to ten adult males and their wives and unmarried children. These few households form a hard core of followers for the headman in their midst. At the same time, each member includes among his kindred headmen from other places, and to these also he owes allegiance, though, as he is in their company less often, he may be casual in showing it. The more forceful the leader, the more he acts as a magnet. In 1934 Marigum overshadowed the second Dap headman, a toothless ancient named Bagasal, whose relatives in consequence seldom paid him the respect due to his office. The Kinaba and Job villagers, lacking headmen of their own, also tended to tail along behind Marigum.

Other title holders are the headmen of the beach *(kokwal wole)*, one for each cluster, and the elders *(ngaro)*. The headman of the beach, always a close relative of the headman of the village *(kokwal malal)* and often his half-brother, possesses the ritual knowledge for carrying out the initiation ceremonies, and on these occasions he therefore takes charge; the elders, by virtue of their seniority and supposed good sense, act as intermediaries between headman and followers.

3 Headmen

Circular boar's tusks imported from the mainland are the symbols of rank, and a headman when officially proclaiming the heir invests him with a pendant consisting of half a dozen strung together and a pair of armbands each adorned with one or two. The youth wears such decorations at subsequent festivities, as may his brothers and half-brothers; but from then on the father seldom bothers to do so. I never saw Marigum at any time with a single tusk. On my enquiring the reason, he replied that everyone knew who he was without his flaunting a special marker. This was in line with his general attitude: he considered that calling attention to himself by outward show would be ill-mannered.

Followers treat their headman with deference rather than veneration. Unlike the Trobriand Islanders, another community with hereditary leaders, they do not feel called upon to crouch in his presence, and the language has no honorific terms. On meeting him casually, however, they pause for him to utter a greeting and open the conversation. Again, if he approaches a group those present wait until he is comfortably seated and are later careful not to break up the gathering till he is ready to move. Anyone called away unexpectedly murmurs an apology. They also refrain from interrupting him and avoid coarse jests unless he gives a lead. All stand aside to allow him to go in front when he joins a party setting out for the cultivations or a visit to another place. He works much harder in the gardens than anyone else, as I shall explain in a moment, but in the village seldom has to carry out odd jobs. His kinsfolk willingly repair the thatch should the roof of his house develop leaks, fetch coconuts if he is thirsty, and come forward to haul his canoe out of the water when he has been fishing.

Most well-established headmen have a gracious disposition and carry themselves with a natural dignity, though there are exceptions. Wakera of Ga was notoriously querulous and much given to scolding his followers for alleged laziness. If annoyed he was also inclined to bluster. Janggara of Gol, by contrast, was something of a comedian, eager for a joke even in the middle of a ceremony. Once while calling up the spirit monsters *(nibek)* from the other world to attend the initiation of a batch of youths he had us all roaring with laughter at his antics, which some might have thought scandalously inappropriate. He was pleasant in every respect, easy and informal, and I always enjoyed his company. At the same time, when angry he could be terrifying till his rage was spent, as a rule within the hour. Kawang, ordinarily conscientiousness and courtesy personified, if crossed was more apt to harbour his wrath till the moment when he could crush his victim with withering scorn. Marigum in a bad mood sulked.

Headmanship goes with generosity. To win approbation the leader must be open-handed to all. He keeps a free house and distributes food, betelnut, and tobacco not only to his own villagers but to visitors from further afield; he inaugurates the bigger feasts and provides the bulk of the supplies; and he is ready with a contribution when his followers arrange small gatherings for a family celebration. Of necessity therefore his gardens and coconut and areca-palm groves are extensive, a good deal larger than those of other people, and he owns many pigs. This means that he has to spend much of his time tilling the soil and erecting fences to prevent destruction of the crops by domestic or wild animals. His followers are willing to help if called upon — on occasion too when he has made no specific request — but he is there toiling almost every day. A traditional saying runs that a stranger can easily discover who is the headman by looking for the person with dirty hands and muddied feet or, alternatively, the one who smells of sweat. Concentration on gardening reduces the hours available for fishing, and it was a rare event for Marigum or any of the others to take part in an expedition or carry a pronged spear along the beach.

Greed over food is always deprecated — parents train children to control their appetite — and people expect a headman to exercise temperance and discrimination. It is said that at a feast he should leave the most succulent taro, the slabs of lean pork, and the strips of white fat and be content with the bones, advice that Marigum at least faithfully observed. 'The host should see that ordinary folk depart with full bellies; he himself holds back and tightens his belt.' Certain foods also are for magical reasons taboo. Thus headmen abstain from deep-water fish because these 'swim at the bottom of the ocean far below the surface' and so might endanger renown. Garfish are favoured — 'they leap high in the air.'

Several villagers described the ideal headman. They stressed that wealth is essential to support his liberality and that therefore he is usually to be found in the gardens, often late in the afternoon when other householders have gone home. He does not remain aloof or give himself airs of superiority; instead he mixes freely with both the elderly and the young, chatting and exchanging betelnut and tobacco. He is neither loud mouthed nor quarrelsome and even when rebuking a wrongdoer is brief and to the point, not constantly repeating himself and nagging. It is also an advantage for him to be a good speaker, capable of explaining a train of thought clearly. "We say that a good headman is like the father of a family,' was Wiawia's summing up. 'He is the one over all, but before giving orders he considers his children and enquires what they think. He may be stern to keep them along the right road, yet he is also understanding. At the back of his mind he has to be thinking of what will be best for everyone.'

Any islander asked in the 1930s who were the principal headmen would without hesitation have named Marigum and Kawang. If he belonged to the housing cluster of either of them, or was a close relative, he might have added that these two groups have always supplied the main leaders, a statement backed up by corroborative myths. Thus a Marigum supporter might have referred to the story of Mafofo, the founding culture hero of Dap, who allegedly made the first trading voyage to the New Guinea mainland.[1] 'The obelisk representing Mafofo stands even now in our village, and that's why Marigum's forefathers right back into the past, and now he himself, have commanded the canoe party,' he would have concluded. Similarly a Kawang supporter would have told the tale of Goleyangayang, hero founder of Gol, which is named after him, holding the first great food festival *(warabwa)*, the prototype of those of today.[2]

People from other places dismiss these claims as pretentious and without foundation. They point out that the residents of Falala in Bagiau have a myth relating how their founding hero Mwanubwa inaugurated expeditions to the mainland, thereby entitling his successors to direct the arrangements.[3] Who can say whether the Dap or the Falala villagers are speaking the truth? They also give a reminder that to fit out a fleet in any one of the remaining districts — Ga, Bukdi, or Takul — would be impossible on account of the ruggedness of the coasts and the wild seas that beat upon them. As for Goleyangayang, they add, he may have started festivals, but this does not mean that entertainments organized in Gol since have necessarily surpassed those of other places. For that matter, the founding hero of each settlement on the island was responsible for some one custom now practised everywhere.

The evidence, while not conclusive, seems to support such arguments. Headmen of an earlier age universally admitted to have been famous were resident in such villages as Job, Bariat, Bwanag, and Kwablik. I agree that a person's views about previous generations are apt to be untrustworthy in that he may see his ancestors in a light more favourable than they deserve, but I checked the accounts over and over again with informants from different localities. Then again the now much vaunted Jaran, Marigum's father and predecessor, cannot have been in his younger days so overwhelmingly prominent. He was driven from Dap, as I heard in another context, and forced to take refuge for some years on the far side of the island. We shall be hearing the story presently.

The reasonable conclusion is that invariably two or three headmen tower over the rest, but who they will be at any given moment nobody can accurately forecast. The mythology furnishes little guidance, for interested parties make a habit of distorting or suppressing differing versions to validate present conditions.

Thus although Wogeo leadership is ascribed, we must realize that birth by itself does not ensure distinction. The basic qualifications, as I have pointed out, are being a headman's son, a mother's firstborn son, and passing through a formal proclamation ceremony; but personal factors over and above these are clearly of importance. The most obvious are a well graced manner, force of character, stamina, vitality, perseverance, industry, a flair for organization, astuteness, amiability, a persuasive tongue, and perhaps a degree of low cunning. In other words, the successful Wogeo leader, apart from his hereditary right, must be the same sort of individual as a big-man in those areas of Papua New Guinea, and Melanesia generally, where titles are wholly acquired.[4]

Three grades of headmen may be separated out — the widely renowned like Marigum and Kawang; those of lesser fame such as Janggara of Gol (Kawang's opposite number), Wakera of Ga, Kaman of Bagiau, and Mangora of Takul; and those of not much more account than their own elders, unimpressive perhaps because of their callow youth or advanced age, perhaps for lack of fundamental drive. In this last class were the remaining handful from Wonevaro — Bagasal of Dap, Fandum and Kauni of Bariat, and Wakalu of Mwarok.

Headmen regard polygamy as their special privilege, and while all have at least two wives, some, like Kawang, support as many as five. A large household is in itself a mark of superiority, and, in addition, each woman is an extra worker to share in maintaining the garden acreage. Further, a plural marriage creates ties with an extensive body of affines. Usually one of the spouses is herself the offspring of a headman and her mother's firstborn daughter. The husband would have been betrothed to her beforehand and the wedding in consequence celebrated with a food exchange, as we shall see in a later chapter. This woman is potentially the leader of the members of her own sex within the housing cluster and the wider village. If she has a commanding personality, takes over the direction of the communal tasks of the females, such as parts of the cooking when a feast is being prepared, and makes food permanently available so that her husband is never embarrassed when unexpected guests pay a call, she earns the title of *mwaere*, an honour bestowed by outsiders, not the neighbours. In the Wogeo of 1934 there was but one *mwaere*, Marigum's second wife Yam. She was almost as outstanding as he, with poise and a great deal of natural authority. She was not remotely in awe of her husband, was prepared when the occasion arose to argue with the men, and if necessary did not hesitate to give orders. She could make an entire crowd cringe when she chose but also had a gift of setting strangers at ease immediately by exercising her considerable charm. Almost alone of the women she would call on me unaccompanied and engage in long conversations. Like Marigum she was a constant gardener, but within the settlement other people took over the household chores and filled her water-bottles, chopped her firewood, and swept up the mess in front of the dwelling left by the domestic pigs.

The term applied to the headman's family, *nat damwa*, literally 'people of the forehead', draws attention to the position they to some extent share with him. 'He is the crown of the head,' the villagers explain, 'and his children, more particularly the eldest sons and eldest daughters of the various wives, are almost as important. They are at the top too, for it is their job to show us what he wants done.' The *nat damwa* are always prominent when the bigger enterprises are afoot, and inevitably they play a major role in the ceremonies. The headman arranges an initiation rite as each of the males comes of age, and the other members of the community then seize the chance to push their own sons forward into adulthood.

Parents are always warning the children that fighting with close relatives is wrong, and if two brothers or cousins from the same village come to blows an adult intervenes to drag them apart. Usually he gives them a knife each and sends them off in different directions with advice to vent their anger by chopping down a sapling or hacking at the trunk of a large tree. It is regarded as specially blameworthy to struggle with the *nat damwa*. Certainly the elders fear incurring the headman's displeasure, but they also seem to consider that harming his offspring might be sacrilege. 'The headman is like a shrub, and his sons and daughters are the main shoots growing from the stem,' I heard an old man caution his grandson. 'Just as cutting them away exposes the bush to the winds, so your hitting this boy may lead to a great wrath blowing down on us. You see, grandson, we'd feel unhappy and ashamed. Remember the boar's tusks and that you mustn't provoke those entitled to wear them.'

Soon aware of their privileged position, the *nat damwa* come to dominate their companions and are not above bullying them into submission. Everybody accepts such conduct with indulgence, although it is directly contrary to the precepts so often repeated in the households of lesser men. One afternoon when Yam's only daughter, then aged about two, had made another little girl cry, a bystander turned to me and remarked with a complacent smile, 'There, you see she's just like her father and mother; she doesn't listen to a word she's told. I'll be bound she'll have the same sharp tongue as theirs when she grows up. Why, she's a proper headman's daughter already.' Yet only a few hours before this same man had slapped his own small daughter soundly for throwing stones at a playmate. Dal, Yam's elder son, already had undisputed sway over the youths of the place. The older people agreed that he had learned to have his own way and would thus be well suited to succeed when his father came to nominate him.

HEADMEN AND RITUAL

As I said above, the headman's son before his formal appointment as heir must be an adept in the special knowledge appertaining to office. Some of this is concerned with welfare, some with destruction. At first sight an observer might assume that as at the moment of the young man's proclamation during the food festival, when the villagers lift him up on the two poles, he recites a spell to bring about the enhancement of his reputation, that this rite is the most vital. Indispensible it is — achievement and renown go together — but those concerned with the weather are still more significant. I would argue that in the societies of Papua New Guinea, and Melanesia as a whole, where honour is hereditary the titles are based on control of rain, sun, or wind or all three together. The Trobrianders are an example.[5]

The common problem in Wogeo is too much wet, leading to bodily sensations of chill, and, in the countryside, to landslides and water-logged cultivations where the plants smother under layers of mud. Accordingly, the ritual most highly esteemed in its positive form, and most greatly feared in its negative opposite, is that bound up with clear blue skies and accompanying warmth. 'The sun makes the gardens flourish: it causes coconuts to fill out, and taro to swell, and the bananas to ripen,' Marigum once told me. 'What about showers,' I enquired. 'Were they not just as essential?' 'In moderation,' he answered; 'but steady downpours, with cold, their usual partner, are mostly a hindrance to growth.'[6]

A simplification it may be, but there is some truth in the statement that, as in many parts of hot dry southern Africa the tribesmen accept as their chief the man who inherits the magic to conjure up storm clouds, so the residents of Wogeo, plagued by an over abundant rainfall, accord headman status to the person who acquires the magic for sparkling sunlight. Their word for weather magic, not surprisingly, is the same as that for 'sun', *varang*.[7]

Droughts also occur, though at long intervals, possibly not more often than once every three decades. I learned in 1975 that the last of such disasters had taken place in the late 1930s. My informant was a man of considerable experience of the world outside Wogeo. He had served for the full term in the northern fleet of the Royal Australian Navy, from which he received a pension, until national defence passed to the control of the Papua New Guinea government; he was also the first island councillor, a post from which he resigned early in 1974. Who was responsible for the lack of rain, I wanted to know. 'I was only a child, but people have told me Marigum,' came the reply. 'He'd been on a trading expedition and I believe ran into trouble with the villagers near the mouth of the Sepik – possibly some of them had failed to treat him with proper courtesy, but I don't know. Anyway, he was angry and determined to see that the rascals should suffer for their offence. That meant taking things out on the entire region, us islanders included, although we'd done nothing wrong. I suppose his rites weren't capable of making exceptions. It was very bad here, and everyone was hungry. The gardens on the flats and in the foothills shrivelled up and burned, and the ground was as hard as rock, no good for a digging stick. I remember my father and uncles clearing areas for planting deep in the mountain valleys. The pools close to the houses also dried up, and the women had to fill their water-bottles from the springs way back in the bush. In the end Marigum had pity on us and made magic to bring the rains back.'

Headmen have command, in addition, over gales, unwelcome because they also interfere with the food supply. The men cannot take the canoes out to sea fishing, and the women's journeys to the gardens for vegetables are both unpleasant and dangerous on account of the uprooted trees and the risk from falling branches.

The fact that a headman who is displeased may use his powers to cause famine is never far from the surface of the people's consciousness. When events go against one of the leaders they begin voicing their alarm. Over and over again during a quarrel between Marigum and his eldest son Tafalti, and after Kawang's youngest wife had run away with a lover (incidents to be dealt with at length in later chapters), those on the sidelines expressed horror lest in the near future there might be nothing to eat — and, equally important, nothing to give away. Again, the Bagiau residents developed increasing qualms each day of a heavy storm. They whispered that here was Kaman, the headman of Falala, paying them out with high winds and deluging rain for concentrating on gathering the almond harvest instead of taking time off to reroof his dwelling. What next had he in store for them?

The most dangerous type of sorcery, that to cause death, is also thought to be, if not a monopoly of the headmen, well under their control. A sharp line separates this from the sorcery of illness and more or less trifling upsets, and as the latter is practised universally there will be an advantage in our digressing to consider it first.

MISFORTUNE SORCERY

Nothing in Wogeo happens by chance, and success and failure are alike determined by the action of nonhuman agencies. The islanders see the natural environment as basically neutral but open to manipulation, by the forces of white magic when the ends are productive, by those of black magic if the aim is to hurt, hinder, or destroy.[8] In order to thrive a householder must exercise the skills available to the fullest extent and put forward his best efforts, but all the insight in the world, even when coupled with Herculean labour, counts for little without that extra something derived from the supernatural. He is well-advised also to take common-sense precautions against accident and discomfort — for example, when setting out for a day's fishing in the open ocean he should make sure that the outrigger of his canoe is securely fastened and furnish himself with some sort of covering to prevent painful sunburn, against which even brown skins are not immune. Yet here, too, an enemy may have invoked the supernatural beforehand to nullify his prudence.

Everybody can list a score or more of common ailments such as headache, toothache, boils, indigestion, nausea, diarrhoea, fainting attacks, sore throat, bronchitis, strained muscles, and fever. None of these is likely to be fatal, and we would say that the infection is bound to disappear of its own accord if the patient agrees to stay in bed and perhaps restrict his diet. But to the Wogeo the cause lies in a mild form of sorcery, differing from that leading to death, and relief demands the performance of beneficent magic to counteract the evil.

Each of the diseases has an associated ritual system, with spells to induce the complaint and spells to cure it. All members of the community, from the most powerful headman to the humblest villager, inherit from their forbears at least one of the systems, and in some instances three or four. They also do not hesitate to publish the fact, though they maintain secrecy about the actual words to be recited and the names of any herbs required. So all can say which of the householders from round about are able to bring on headaches and administer the remedy, which bring on toothache, which boils, which indigestion, and so forth.

The only legitimate use for the darker of the rites is to protect property located outside the village, when they are referred to as *bwab*. So a man who owns an almond or mango tree some way off in the bush, or a distant grove of coconut or areca palms, carries out the magic nearby and then puts up a cautionary sign, such as a twist of ginger stalks or a dried sago leaf knotted in a particular way, indicating that trespassers meddle at their peril. Most people heed the warning, and petty thieving is rare.

But the same rites, now known as *muj*, can also be employed with less justification to satisfy personal grudges.

I have already said that close relatives, especially those who are neighbours, are mutually dependent. No one can exist in isolation; he needs help not merely for major undertakings but also in lesser tasks. For him to fall out with his kinsmen or affines is therefore tantamount to doing himself a personal injury — he loses both the goodwill and the assistance of which he is so sorely in need. An additional consideration is the firmly held belief that breeding discord in the inner circle is immoral. Irritations there are, nevertheless, as the anthropologist (private confidant of every resident in the village) quickly becomes aware. The more frequent the contacts, the sharper the friction is likely to be. This man has a hidden grievance – whether genuine or imagined is of no consequence – against a brother for being too persistent in demands for aid in clearing new ground, that one against a cousin for borrowing a newly sharpened axe and returning it blunt, another against an uncle for delaying the transmission of secret information, still another against a single girl from across the way for repelling his advances. I think it would be correct to say that nobody in Dap, or any other settlement, is wholly satisfied with the behaviour of his fellows – he is convinced that they all have at some time let him down, been selfish or unfair, neglected his interests, or presumed on his good nature. The upshot is that in a fit of bad temper he is apt to relieve his feelings by performing his magic to make them unwell – and is the better for it. Naturally he does so behind closed doors, for to arouse their mistrust would be as dangerous as accusing them openly. Concentrating on the efficacy of the rite, he assures himself that they will now pay the price of their shabby conduct or deceit. Subsequent events seem to bear him out. Wogeo is not a healthy place, and sooner rather than later the victims are bound to be overcome by illness. On occasion the magic to produce one disorder may result in the visitation of another, but for this an excuse is ready to hand. He probably forgot to recite part of the spell or omitted an essential herb, or a different sorcerer may have forestalled him, and the effects of the two systems became mixed up.

Various kinds of annoyances also have their rituals, which in similar fashion can be directed against persons held to deserve punishment. There are spells to cause sterility, miscarriages, and labour difficulties; to weaken garden fences so that the pigs can force an entry and eat the taro; to afflict the crops with blight; to persuade fish to avoid a certain canoe; and to drive a domestic animal into taking to the bush. To the owners these spells appear to be just as effective as those for sickness. Some women are sterile – and some men, though the Wogeo would not agree – some miscarry, and some suffer during childbirth; pigs from time to time break into gardens; taro plants for no apparent reason droop and die; everyone on occasion has bad luck when fishing; and pigs have been known to wander.

What of the victims against whom the magic is directed? Usually the sorcerer, to disarm suspicion, goes out of his way to be pleasant to the very people who have provoked him most. They are therefore unaware of his being an enemy. Far from worrying themselves into imaginery sufferings, they carry on with a clear conscience unperturbed by thoughts of any future pains or frustrations.

The sorcery of disease and misfortune, whether *bwab* or *muj*, can thus be considered a peacemaker. It not only prevents stealing but also allows men who imagine themselves to have been injured to secure redress to their own satisfaction without in fact doing harm to anyone.

When a man feels out of sorts it does not as a rule occur to him to make a mental inventory of all those he may have wronged whether inadvertently or on purpose; rather he consults an appropriate specialist — a headache doctor, toothache doctor, boils doctor, indigestion doctor, or whoever is needed. The latter recites his incantations and brews a potion for the patient to drink; and the members of the family, now confident, await the improvement. More often than not the sickness runs its course — or nature does its work — and within a few days recovery is complete. Faith in the efficacy of magic is therefore confirmed. The magician receives a small fee only when he and the patient belong to opposite moieties.

Prolonged illness leads to the calling in of other specialists, more particularly those with a reputation for rapid cures. Sometimes the sufferer moves to a distant village in the hope perhaps of more skilful treatment, perhaps of defeating the unknown sorcerer by escaping from his immediate vicinity. If everything fails, and complications set in, people conclude that the diagnosis must have been incorrect and neglect of the cleansing ceremony is the cause. The patient probably delayed too long in hacking his penis to rid himself of the pollution caused by contact with the supernatural or with women.[9] If this operation also fails, and death supervenes, then most clearly not misfortune sorcery but the lethal kind *(yabou)* was to blame.

DEATH SORCERY

I am doubtful whether even in the past any headman would have boasted of knowing how to kill with magic, and certainly today the more important of them aim at giving the impression that they are too big to stoop to such underhand practices. They like it to be assumed that when they consider someone should be eliminated they say so openly and have their followers run him through with a spear. The Dap villagers concurred with this view so far as Marigum was concerned. 'He doesn't have to bother with *yabou* as long as we have weapons,' they insisted. Yet they often added as a rider that probably every other headman on the island had at some time resorted to it. The Gol villagers expressed similar opinions except that to them it was Kawang whose record was clean and that of Marigum and the rest suspect. Thus when a death occurs the relatives are prone to believe a headman from somewhere else must be to blame.

In accounts of this kind of sorcery given without any definite case in mind people say that the practitioner takes two assistants, usually his apprentices, and follows the victim, male or female, till the latter is alone in some isolated spot. The assistants suddenly spring from behind and hold their hands over his or her eyes, whereupon the sorcerer advances reciting a spell. Within a few seconds the man or woman falls to the ground unconscious with the eyeballs rolled upwards. They then straighten out his or her limbs, remove the clothing, and batter the joints, ribs, spine, and jaw with stones. Next the sorcerer takes a knife and a pointed instrument, perhaps a piece of palmwood cut from the tip of a spear, perhaps the spine of a stingray. First he cuts the ligament under the victim's tongue to prevent the speaking of anyone's name and then plunges the point into his or her side till it penetrates the lungs. He may push it right in and leave it, or he may withdraw it, extracting some vital organ in the process, and insert it in the anus, urethra, or vagina. He now applies herbs to the gaping holes in the flesh and recites further spells, and the wounds disappear leaving not so much as a drop of blood. He also places various leaves over the mouth and eyes as a further precaution against his being recognized. Then he calls the assistants, and all move into concealment to watch what the victim will do. They make a loud noise to arouse him or her. If he or she is aware of being naked and gropes for the missing garments they know they have succeeded and that he or she will remain unaware of what has happened. They accordingly go off to bathe, smear charcoal under their armpits as a protection against the ghost, separate, and return to their respective villages. But should he or she stagger about in bewilderment, that is a sign that the sorcery is not working properly, and everything has to be repeated.

The victim, ignorant of fast approaching doom, resumes his or her journey or finishes the interrupted task. For the rest of the day he or she feels perfectly well, but as night draws on his or her temperature rises and the hidden bruises and cuts begin to ache. By the next morning he or she is really ill, with pains in the joints, chest, and back and possibly bladder trouble or acute diarrhoea. The other persons in the household may suspect *yabou*, but so effective is the magic of concealment that their questions meet with a sharp denial. No cure is known, and death within a few days is inevitable.

Not everyone dies suddenly, however, and fatal illnesses that go on for months are as common in Wogeo as among ourselves. Despite the absence of the classical symptoms, the relatives ascribe these also to *yabou*. Even succumbing to snakebite or a serious accident is attributed to the same cause. Snakes if left to themselves move out of the way when anyone approaches, or they remain still, so people argue; if instead a reptile acts contrary to its nature and attacks, then obviously a sorcerer must be directing it (in a period of forty years three persons have died of snakebite). Similarly, hundreds of men climb almond trees in safety, and the only acceptable explanation when somebody breaks his neck by trusting to a branch that proves rotten is that a sorcerer has determined to kill him. The problem is not why did he fall — no one when so high above the ground disregards the danger — but who took the necessary steps to see that he would perish. How in these circumstances the rites of *yabou* can be made to operate is not clear, but the islanders are in no doubt that they do. The loss of somebody in the prime of life, unless by outright violence, is irrefutable evidence that the black arts have been invoked. So firm is this conviction that autopsies are unheard of. When you know positively that there are internal injuries, not to mention foreign objects present, it would be silly to go to the trouble of looking for them, particularly when the dissection would be so unpleasant.

Irrelevant though this conclusion is to the people at large, we as disinterested outsiders can reassure ourselves that the beliefs concerning *yabou* sorcery are a figment of the imagination. It is inconceivable that the Wogeo islanders should be more skilled surgeons, or hypnotists, than anyone from the West, able to make incisions and instantaneously close them up again without the aid of a needle and sutures, able also to force someone into dying against his or her will. At the same time, there is always the chance that a few individuals may believe that they can perform the miracle. If so they probably indulge in controlled dreaming and fantasy.

Fire and water, specific against death sorcery in many parts of Melanesia, are in Wogeo of no avail, nor are there any amulets or charms to give protection. Yet people do not live in a constant state of terror. A wave of alarm sweeps through the district when anyone dies, and for a few weeks the journeys already planned are abandoned, and little else is talked about, but things soon return to normal. In the ordinary course of events the villagers go about in small groups, and a man compelled to visit the cultivations by himself is careful to take the family dog along to give warning of the presence of strangers. Such measures stem more from habit than deliberate forethought.

THE INQUEST

Headmen are the only persons who can carry out the ceremony to identify the sorcerer guilty of a particular death. There are two methods, 'to ask the bamboo' *(sua maratigi)* and 'to ask the spears' *(yiwo maratigi)*. Most headmen are familiar with both, but some favour the one and some the other. They have to work in pitch darkness for fear lest the ghost, which must be present to make the revelation, will be too ill at ease to attend — like spirits everywhere, those of Wogeo abhor daylight — and they invite only a few of the seniors to participate.

In the bamboo rite the performer takes a feather from the decorations on the corpse, a stone from the spot under the house where the grave will be dug, and a Cordyline leaf. These he rubs on the floor where the body lies exposed before stuffing them into a long bamboo, which he plugs with a leaf stopper. The mourners then depart, leaving the place empty. He pushes the bamboo through the wall and over it recites a spell to force the ghost to take up the end inside. The other end he rests on the membrane of a hand-drum set upright on the ground. Further spells follow, and much rubbing of the bamboo with herbs. Finally he places his hand lightly upon it while in a whisper inaudible to the men present he asks the ghost a series of questions, each so phrased that it can be answered with a plain yes or no. 'Did someone kill you with *yabou*?' 'Where did the sorcerer come from — the north?' 'The west?' 'Was he from Takul district?' 'Does he live in Bwanag village?' For 'no' the bamboo remains motionless, for 'yes' it moves up and down, thereby tapping the drum.

The other method requires three spears, which the headman in charge ties together firmly in the shape of the letter H. To the cross-piece he then fastens the bone of one of his ancestors. He asks four of the elders to arrange themselves so that the weight of the frame can rest on their upturned wrists. When they are ready he grips the bone and mutters the spells to conjure up the ghost. The questions come next, and this time for 'yes' the spears swing sideways.

In both instances manipulation is easy, though the headmen with whom I talked about the matter all reiterated that the ghost took control and gave the replies. Most people accepted this explanation, but one or two were sceptical, including Jaua. He had been present at three inquests, during one of which he had helped to

3 Headmen

hold the frame. There was no doubt about its swinging over, he was prepared to agree, but he believed that the expert, in this case Marigum, had given it a nudge. 'Who could tell? The night was so black you couldn't see what was going on. Like everybody else, Marigum had already guessed who the sorcerer was, or he had inside information, and the business with the spears was nothing but a pretence to allow him, if this became expedient, to bring the man's name forward. He knew we'd believe what we were told. Mind, I'm not denying that this was the person who'd done it: it's just that I don't believe a ghost would take hold of the spears and shake them.'

Once the headman is sure of the sorcerer, whether through unwitting or conscious fraud makes no difference, he can proceed to vengeance. Should he wish to have the man despatched directly, he must hold discussions with the village elders, possibly also with the leaders from the neighbouring settlements, in order to secure support. But if he elects not to run the risk and instead determines to rely on counter sorcery he may keep his own counsel. Though probably unacquainted with the correct *yabou* ritual, he will, nevertheless, as a leader and inquest specialist, be able to find someone whom he can ask to act on his behalf. The brothers and sons of the dead individual are not content till an important personage from another district expires, when they think that he must have been the culprit and now at last has met with a just reward for villainy and aggression.

4 Sorcery in Real Life

So far I have written about *yabou* sorcery in the abstract and largely ignored the social context. The notion that every death, except that of an infant or someone already senile, should be followed by an inquest to discover the guilty party, who is then killed, I now admit is the local ideal; in real life formal investigations are rare. The survivors, in doubt where the blame lies, therefore hesitate to go ahead with vengeance. Thus in 1934 five people perished, three men and two women, but the headmen made not one single appeal to the ghosts for guidance, and nobody attempted to move against any suspects. On each occasion the relatives began by insisting that a sorcerer was at work, and some of them even offered guesses as to who he might be, but after a lapse of time they came round to acknowledging that their judgement could have been at fault. They now suggested that perhaps the cause was to be sought in some ritual infringement. Mourners, menstruating and childbearing women, and men who have hacked their penis to rid themselves of pollution are all held to be in a state of taboo and hence dangerous to a person who comes into contact with them or their belongings. Normally they keep out of the way, but it can still happen that somebody by accident touches their clothing or unwittingly eats food they have handled.

Beliefs of this kind have a direct bearing on the well-being and continuity of Wogeo society. If each death were to lead invariably to retaliation the result would be chaos and a steady decline in population; but with sorcery ruled out in the majority of cases, so also is the obligation to seek vengeance.

The most interesting case with which I was personally concerned was that of Waki, widow of the Job headman Kaneg (who had died only a year or so before) and mother of Marigum's wife Yam, the island's only *mwaere*. She had exerted an influence on village affairs by virtue of her husband's eminence, her own dominating personality, which her daughter had inherited, and her affinal relationship with Marigum. So impressed was I that some weeks

4 Sorcery in Real Life

before her final illness I wrote in my diary, 'Here is one person whose death will certainly be avenged.'

At the start Waki's condition gave rise to no great anxiety. She took to her bed suffering from pains in the chest and fits of coughing, but everyone assumed that ordinary health magic would bring about a cure. Instead she grew worse and within a week was gravely ill, presumably with pneumonia (in 1934 I doubt whether any of the antibiotics had been discovered, but if so I knew nothing of them). Several persons mentioned the possibility of *yabou* sorcery and wondered vaguely who might be to blame, but as yet they did not press the matter. Less than a fortnight later she was dead. The moment the body was in the grave the subject came up again, now with the interest magnified. Seemingly nobody could speak of anything else. How evil sorcerers were, creeping about in the shadows to slay the unwary! We must all be careful to travel together and avoid being on our own! Whence could the blow have come? Could it have been a man from Bagiau, where, as was well known, so many were not to be trusted? Or was it not a headman from Ga transferring his envy of Waki's deceased husband to her? Takul was also worth a thought! But at least we were sure none of us from Wonevaro could have done the deed! We were so firmly bound to one another and had been so fond of Waki, from whose hand we had often accepted food. We could not possibly have harboured malice against her! Well, it was fortunate she had Marigum for a son-in-law. He knew all about the inquest rituals and once the mourning was over could announce who the sorcerer was and decide what we must do with him.

During the next few months I asked Marigum over and over again when did he intend to hold the ceremony, to which I expected to be invited. He promised to let me know but always produced some plausible excuse for delay. He was unwell and would wait till he felt better; the almond harvest must be gathered first; as soon as the weather improved; after the annual rising of the palolo worm *(Eunice viridis)*, due at the next full moon; the District Officer at Wewak might come to hear and be angry. I could not decide whether each postponement was a considered judgement, the result of continuing inability to make up his mind, or whether he had determined from the beginning to fob me and others off and take no action.

When about three months had gone by many villagers appeared to be less confident about the use of sorcery. They were discreet and held their tongue in the presence of members of Waki's family but among themselves were saying that they may have been over suspicious. Was it not a possibility that she had been careless in fulfilling ritual requirements? One or two of my intimates also whispered that they remembered hearing from their fathers years before of a probable intrigue between her and her husband's brother. This is the worst form of adultery and one of the few moral faults carrying a penalty of supernatural punishment. Marigum, by refusing the inquest, so these men averred, might even be aiming at saving Waki's reputation. If he performed the ceremony, and the ghost denied the practice of *yabou*, those familiar with the gossip would have their surmise about her misconduct substantiated. She must have died for her sin.

Yam, her sisters, and her only brother retained their conviction and in the December, when I left the island, were still reiterating that in the end Marigum would reveal the sorcerer's name and approve some form of retribution. At what stage they changed their mind I cannot say, but by 1948 they had accepted the majority view. Naturally, they made no mention of adultery but concentrated on the likelihood of someone set apart as ritually unclean having inadvertently gone too close.

The reactions after the other deaths of 1934 were similar. There was an initial insistence on sorcery, a view to which the immediate relatives clung tenaciously for longer than anyone else, though ultimately they also were prepared to offer as an alternative the theory of a religious prohibition thoughtlessly or accidentally broken. The dead person could have brushed against a menstruating woman, or she might without knowing have sat on his sleeping mat; or he could have been neglectful when he last hacked his penis, or another man whose wound was not fully healed might as a matter of pure habit have lent him a lime-pot. These were conjectures, and no method existed for checking which hypothesis was correct.

VENGEANCE

The only time performance of an inquest can be forecast with confidence is after the demise of a headman or some other person of note. (This does not include a *mwaere*, no matter how respected she may have been.) The prestige of the members of his cluster and of all his other kinsmen and affines then demands that they hold somebody responsible and take up arms to wipe out the stain on their honour. The coroner, if we may so speak of him, professes to be disinterested and genuinely in touch with the ghost, but, all the same, the name he produces is dictated by elementary prudence and common sense. He may not be aware that he is an imposter, but it seems certain that he always tries his best to avoid the risk of a counter offensive, with the consequent hazards. By such means, of course, he also gives satisfaction to the relatives, who have no wish to be killed themselves at the time or afterwards. If he cites a leader as the sorcerer, then assuredly it will be one without a powerful following on account either of extreme youth or advanced age. But he may pick on some dubious character already in bad odour, an habitual thief perhaps, a notorious lecher, or a simple misfit, one whose loss will be counted, even by his fellows, as more a blessing than an outrage.[1]

I recorded several accounts from the past, alleged to be authentic, of a sequence of sorcery, vengeance through ccunter-sorcery, further vengeance through counter-counter sorcery, and so on, always ending up with the triumph of an ancestor or close relative of the speaker. These can be described as wish-fulfilment dreams, glories of the imagination. I shall explain why at the end of the chapter. On the other hand, I never once heard any tales of sorcery succeeded by vengeance through violence and then a chain of still more violence. This is in marked contrast with what used to take place in the communities of the coast of mainland New Guinea, where often pairs of villages stood in the relationship of traditional enemies. A death in one of these led to killings backwards and forwards until the hatred flared into a pitched battle, with each side attempting to annihilate the other. The victors seized the valuables, drove off the pigs, and burned the houses down; the land they left untouched as they already owned enough to satisfy their needs. The vanquished fled to relatives living elsewhere and eventually were either absorbed or else drifted back one by one to the old site and rebuilt the settlement.[2] The difference in the reactions on the island and on the coast are to be explained by the fact that Wogeo has a small population and is isolated and self contained. Each resident is acquainted with all the rest, and if they carried on warfare against one another the effects would be devastating. In no time everyone would be dead.[3] But on the mainland some groups are always outside the limits of regular peaceful relations, with the members regarded as foreigners. What does it matter if such people are wiped out? No kinship link is severed, no moral precept violated.

The Central Highlands of Papua New Guinea present another picture again. Here already in pre-contact days the people were so numerous that agricultural land was in short supply. Expanding units, to push out the boundaries of their estates and provide themselves with adequate sustenance, were obliged to make attacks on the neighbours with the intention of dispossessing them permanently. Today, with the introduction of cash crops and a lowered death rate, unclaimed areas suitable for cultivation are scarcer and even more valuable. Armed clashes are thus as frequent now as formerly and just as bloody, and the national government is seriously concerned. So far riot police have not been able to impose more than a series of uneasy truces.[4]

MARIGUM'S DEATH

The sequence following on this event, in 1949, was reasonably typical of what goes on when the relatives are determined on an outright killing in revenge. The first news I had was contained in a letter from Father Meyer, at that time in charge of the island parish. He has kindly allowed me to quote.

> You know that your great friend Marigum died? I liked the old man and used to go and sit with him a while and talk. He was totally blind, and sure Dal was his pride. I found, too, that he did not like his son Tafalti [the eldest son by his first wife, Dal's senior by about ten or twelve years].
> Well, in August or early September 1949 Marigum was one morning found badly hurt and unable to speak. It was the so-much-feared ... *yabou* sorcery. Now, do not laugh Mr Hogbin; I know you do not believe in it. But it had gone too nice according to your description [in 'Sorcery and Administration', *Oceania*, vol. 6, 1935-6, pp. 1-32]. Marigum had left his house in the night for some reason. When they found him in the morning he was conscious but could not speak — but not because he did not want to speak. No, the reason was a sharp needle under the tongue so that the throat was swollen. Long sharp needles shot between the keybones had gone into the lungs [sic: Father Meyer's mother tongue is Dutch]. Needles were also in his upper arms and in his thigh. They told me a spear had been shot in his anus also. Some ribs were broken, also his arms. After a day he died. Two weeks later another man was killed in the same way in Falala.
> Dal got in a rage because of this. He sent word to the other side of the island to come for a talk about the trouble. The people of Kwablik, Bajor, and Ga [in the northwest] came from their side over to Mwarok. The people from Gol, Maluk, and Bwanag [in the northeast] came along the other side. When [the latter] reached Job the people from Dal were ready with spears, and there was a fight; but the old guys knew how to get out of the way (they themselves were without

spears). Dal's party rounded them all up in Dap and fenced them in. The others came on from Mwarok to Kinaba, but when they heard what had happened they swam out to sea and round to Taro [the mission station, with a New Guinean catechist in charge: it is located midway between Mwarok and Falala], where they went ashore and disappeared into the bush. Immediately the Dap party set out for Bajor, where they killed the old man Sami, who was blind. They kicked him to death. Some days later they killed the old man Mok in Ga (with a rope round his neck).

Dal told the people that he had licence to kill. The news soon reached Wewak, and the police officer made an investigation. He did not believe much about *yabou* and was sure he could never get anything about it from the natives. So in the court the two early murders were not mentioned, only the two later ones. For these 12 persons are now in gaol. How that is possible I do not know. Dal, who gave the orders, is free. Probably the people are afraid of him. If they told in court what he had done, he or someone from his family might kill them.

Now, about half a year ago the talk was going around in Wogeo that Tari of Mwarok, who is in gaol, had sent word to Tafalti: 'If I have to stay in gaol much longer I shall tell the District Commissioner everything.' Everyone is sure that Tafalti killed his father with the help of Tari and some others. (This Tari married Sale, the widow of your friend Jaua: she now stays mostly in Dap with Dal [her sister's son]).[5]

When you know the relations between Tafalti and Marigum you wonder whether it might be true. As a fact, the people are more afraid for Tafalti than Dal. And Tafalti does what he likes without any regard for Dal.

Dal is the man now. He claims to be the same big man that his father was; but he is not. I have seen the people of Kairiru when Marigum paid a trading visit there. He was already blind, but they still revered him. Everyone feared Marigum from Kairiru to Manam [two large islands respectively a little to the west and east of the Schouten group but not part of it]. Pigs were killed when he came, and there was dancing in his honour. But Dal has not authority even for his own island. People from the other side of Wogeo laugh at him. They say he is lazy, not a worker like his father. When at home he is always sleeping, and if not doing that he hangs around Wewak. He goes there for weeks at a time. The main reason, I guess, is that he is afraid that he will be killed too. He does not know that I know the real story. The whole thing was set out very cleverly for the court so that all the judge heard was: 'The old men were no good, sorcerers and so on.'

Well, if Tafalti was the man who did it, Dal has reason to be afraid.
I asked him if he knew about the gossip that Tafalti was the murderer of his father. He got very nervous and said no. But he was uneasy and went away as soon as he could. That made me sure he knew. Dal will not bring Tafalti before the court because he would accuse Dal of the other two murders. So they both keep quiet. For how long?
I myself was sorry for old Marigum. Even with his blindness he had authority. I went to the island a few weeks after his death, and the whole place was upset. No one went alone into the bush, and never without spears. Now all is quiet again, but I am sure something is working under the surface.

Further details emerged during 1974–5. A survivor from among the killers, Jangir of Falala, approached me spontaneously, and I sought an interview with three others, two of whom I knew well (the only one still living whom I missed was Tari, temporarily in Wewak recovering from an illness which had meant a stay in hospital). A couple of men from Gol who had been in their late teens at the time also volunteered information.

Naturally, I do not accept that Marigum was attacked by a *yabou* sorcerer. The symptoms described point to a cerebral haemorrhage. It was night, and he was over 80, blind, alone, and outside the house. A fall from the verandah, which was a full metre above the ground, would account for his broken ribs and arms.

Dal was away on Koil Island, the nearest of the Schoutens, staying with the relatives of his second wife, whose father was a headman there. He returned at once and arranged the funeral, for which he killed many pigs to feast all the residents of Wonevaro district and relatives from Falala in Bagiau. Nobody spoke of anyone from other places being present, but I would have expected a few from Gol, although Kawang was already dead.

My informants were positive that Dal must have conducted an inquest, and Jangir said he had heard that the method adopted was 'asking the bamboo', necessarily carried out before the burial. But as all denied being present — and there was no reason for them to lie — I am not sure. Dal could easily assert that he had done so.

Once the more rigorous part of the mourning was over — and by then the second death had occurred in Falala — Dal sent two of his younger followers round the island to summon everyone to the meeting at Dap in the succeeding week to discuss sorcery in general and these two cases in particular. Then the day before this assembly was due to take place he called in several of the seniors, men mostly in their late thirties or early forties — though two were older — and disclosed that the murdering scoundrels had proved to be the elderly headmen Sami of Bajor and Moga, originally of Ga but then living at Jug in Bagiau (Moga is the correct spelling of Father Meyer's Mok). They could not have acted themselves as both were crippled with rheumatism and hardly able to walk — Sami, in addition, was blind — but they had thought up the plan and then employed agents to execute it. Considering their disabilities, they were unlikely to attend the meeting, so Dal ordered these seniors to cross the mountain unobserved by anyone coming to Dap by the ordinary route and put them to death by whatever means were convenient. The fearless warriors hastened to obey. Under the leadership of Tari, they first beat and kicked Sami till he expired and then proceeded to strangle Moga by fixing a rope round his neck and dragging him through the village till he choked.

While the killings were taking place Dal harangued the crowd in Dap on the wickedness of sorcery, a matter on which nobody would have wanted to contradict him. He threatened to thrash them all one by one and as an earnest of his intention lashed at two young men from Ga, Yamuna and Marewawere, kinsmen of Moga, whom he alleged had assisted at Marigum's slaying.

The relatives of Sami and Moga were not prepared to accept the charges and, once back in safety at home, announced their intention of reporting the story at the government station in Wewak. Dal, fearful of being hanged, decided to forestall them. He took a passage in the first available schooner and informed the District Officer that the warriors had misinterpreted their instructions. He wanted them only to bring the sorcerers before him so that he might exhort them to change their ways; he had not spoken of an execution. The members of the raiding party must have been so consumed with passion, he said, that they went further than intended.

The officer held Dal in custody till the boat went out to seize the others. The court later dismissed the case against him, presumably on the ground that he was not present when the deaths occurred. It is also possible that these henchmen shielded him by withholding the truth lest their families might suffer. Tari received a sentence of five years, the rest of four each.

It is hardly unexpected that in 1949 so many islanders should have in their hearts such strong feelings against Tafalti. He hated his father, as we shall learn presently, and fifteen years before had been in bitter conflict with him. But Dal could hardly have brought an accusation against a half-brother. Relatives, as I have pointed out, are trained to live together in peace.

A quarter of a century onwards all this was forgotten or suppressed, and I would like to know why. Tafalti had died in January 1974 just eleven months before my return in the December. Although a pagan till almost his last hour – and by that time less than a dozen remained – he had in his later years, when no longer harassed by his father, enjoyed universal respect. His nephew Bernard was sincerely attached to him despite the fact that he could extract no information about the incidents here described – he had sought leave to go home in sympathy after the death of Tafalti's wife in 1973 and was also responsible for the subsequent conversion. Of course, Tafalti had had nothing to do with Marigum's dying, Jangir reiterated in answer to my doubting enquiry after his recital. A son kill his father? Quite impossible!

Why did Dal pick on Sami and Moga? I cannot be certain, but it is worth noting that they fulfilled the conditions set out earlier. Both enjoyed the title of headman, but neither had been notable for his achievements; moreover, in 1949 they were too decrepit to exert any influence at all – Sami could not see, and Moga, a widower, had abandoned the village of his birth to live with his daughter and son-in-law in Jug. It was improbable therefore that their kinsmen and affines, however eager for revenge, would resort to the traditional weapons to achieve it, and Dal could be reasonably confident that a feud would not develop.

Dal survived for less than a decade. He contracted leprosy and died in 1958. Sixteen years afterwards these relatives of the victims were still speaking of his fate as a just retribution.

KAWANG'S DEATH

The unusual feature on this occasion was the allocation of blame not to an outsider but to a man originally belonging to the same village though no longer resident there.

Kawang, younger than Marigum, predeceased him by about three years. He died, as far as I could tell, late in 1946. The heir, a man of barely twenty-two, whose initiation I had attended when he was nine, had not yet mastered the necessary ritual for an inquest. Possibly relevant also was his colourless disposition. Kawang had been at some trouble to train him as a successor (p. 160), but, like the other members of the family, he was an adopted son and lacked the temperament for becoming a proper headman (presumably Kawang was sterile, for although he had five wives, the latest

4 Sorcery in Real Life

a young widow with three children by her first husband, he fathered not one offspring). The Gol villagers, however, were unanimous about the identity of the sorcerer, and other people agreed with them. They fixed upon Janggara's younger half-brother Kajug, a person against whom they had long cherished hatred — in fact, since 1934, when he persuaded one of Kawang's wives to elope with him. The pair remained in hiding in the bush till eventually his sister's husband Kaiaf gave them shelter in Bariat. They lived here till the beginning of the next year, when they fled to Wewak. He took employment on a neighbouring plantation and did not return to Wogeo till 1942, just before the Japanese occupation. Then, although he made visits to Gol from time to time, he stayed in Bariat under Kaiaf's protection.

Adultery with Kawang's wife was a serious offence in itself, and setting up an establishment with her doubled the affront. I made no public comment one way or the other but was convinced that fear lest I might intervene alone restrained him from giving the word for Kajug to be killed, a view that received ample corroboration in 1974–5. The islanders were perhaps the more shaken by Kawang's apparent acceptance of his humiliation. If he would only flare up, they said, his rage might subside; but while he stayed silent there was always the chance of his turning against everyone and bringing on flood rains or drought, with consequent famine. 'We're upset because we're scared lest he should curse the crops and so starve us to death,' one man lamented.

The long absence on the plantation did nothing to lessen Kajug's unpopularity, nor did he seek on his return to ingratiate himself. He engaged in a dispute with his brother Janggara and became conspicuous as an adulterer although he had now married a second wife. It was probably inevitable that when Kawang died Kajug's name should be the first to spring to mind as the sorcerer.

A year passed, and still Kawang's relatives took no steps to avenge him. At that point Marigum decided to accept the obligation. The two of them had been close partners *(bag)*, and he felt that his continued silence might cast a slur on the office of headman itself. He called up several of the Dap seniors and others from villages nearby and told them to cut down Kajug forthwith. These men took up their spears and lay in ambush alongside the path at the edge of his garden in Bariat to catch him on the way home that evening. But before leaving he happened to climb an areca palm to collect a bunch of nuts and saw them waiting below. Although they closed around him, in the ensuing scuffle he managed to escape after plunging his bush knife into Jaua, who was leading the attack. The wound did not prove immediately fatal, and actually Kajug died first, according to the general consensus as a result of sorcery paid for by Marigum.

WAKERA AND UMBE

Another case of unpopularity giving rise to a sorcery charge and ultimately to homicide was that of Umbe from Job, who met his fate in early 1933.[6] His parents had died during his infancy, and a couple with two older sons had adopted him and brought him up. He married at the usual age and, I gathered, lived in normal amity with his wife. A year after his murder I found it difficult to decide why people had reacted against him so intensely. The characteristic most often mentioned was his unsociability. He always worked by himself, seldom took part in any of the larger undertakings, and almost never went to the club in the evenings to talk and smoke with the other men. He was also gruff in his speech and sometimes short tempered. But the elder foster-brother Kera maintained that his behaviour was always suitably fraternal and that he never refused assistance when this was needed. Kera added further that he neither bragged about possessing *yabou* nor threatened anyone with it. A final point was that gossip had at no time linked him with any married woman.

When late in 1932 Wakera, one of the Ga headmen, lost his son and heir, a promising young man in his mid-twenties, he intimated that Umbe was the silent killer. Whether he informed Kaneg, the Job headman, who still had a few months to live, I cannot say, but the feeling was that he must have done so and secured approval for carrying out revenge. The villagers repeated over and over again that he could hardly have ordered the striking down of one of Kaneg's followers without some assurance first that there would be no reprisals. Armed men from Ga, accompanied by three or four of Wakera's relatives from Jug and Urawo, made the assault and speared Umbe while he was in the bush. They returned to their homes unharmed, and on the subsequent discovery of the body Kaneg gave orders for it to be buried where it lay instead of in the village.

Marigum, when I talked the slaying over with him, denied that he had been in Wakera's confidence but said he would not have attempted to divert him from his purpose. 'I might have helped him, for Umbe was a thorough knave and earned his fate,' he went on. 'He was well known as a sorcerer and responsible for many deaths here in Wonevaro and on the other side of the island. We are not safe as long as such men remain alive.'

Kera admitted anger at the treatment his brother had received, especially the burial in the bush, but felt too much alone for a protest. Now my enquiries gave him an idea for paying the Ga folk out. Unknown to me, he informed them I was making an investigation and intended on my final departure to place the facts in the hands of the District Officer. The police would then arrive to arrest them, and probably they would all be hanged. They became more and more anxious and at last waited on me in a body to find out what I was going to do. It took some effort on my part to reassure them that my lips were sealed. Shortly afterwards Wakera tried to make his peace by offering Kera two pigs as compensation.

SORCERY ON THE ROAD

One other incident of the 1930s demands a brief reference. On this occasion two men through sheer mischance acquired a reputation as sorcerers. It all happened not long after Waki's death, when the residents of Wonevaro were on edge and still mindful of how vulnerable they were to further attack.

One morning Waru's wife Mujewa went off to the gardens in the foothills behind Dap. She was expecting him to join her within a few minutes, but a neighbour called him over, and he stayed talking. Afterwards she related how when walking along the path thinking of the day's work ahead she became aware of the dog bristling and sniffing. She screamed *'Yabou!'* at the top of her voice, turned, and raced back to the settlement. She saw nobody, and the animal had probably caught the scent of a pig, but everyone concluded that swift retreat had saved her life. I accompanied the half dozen men, all armed, who went off to investigate whether the intruders had left any trace of their presence. The path was muddy, but we saw no strange footprints, and although the forest growth was so dense that to force a way through would have required much slashing with a knife, not a twig was broken or cut. My companions shook their heads and insisted that sorcerers are adept at covering their tracks, but I felt sure it was a false alarm and that Mujewa's disturbed state of mind, the result of the recent death, was the reason for her fright.

The news travelled around the district, and that afternoon someone from Bariat arrived in Dap to inform us that earlier in the day he had come across two men from Takul making their way through the Wonevaro bush. They had said they were hunting (in my view they must have been keeping an assignation with a couple of the young girls), but probably they were returning from the vain attempt on Mujewa. The villagers agreed, and three days later I heard one of them stating that before she ran away she had seen the pair trying to conceal themselves. Waru was so convinced of their guilt that he promised to report them when next the District Officer made a patrol.

SORCERY IN EARLIER DAYS

I can vouch for the truth of everything said so far. All the actors concerned with the exception of Umbe were well known to me, and I was present at the time or on the scene reasonably soon afterwards. In the cases I heard about from the past, however, the details of each incident seemed to vary according to who was holding forth. Everyone who spoke made a practice of glorifying his own ancestors and denigrating their opponents, and I found it difficult, even impossible, to be certain about anything. The stories are of value for charting present-day rivalries, but they cannot be used as accurate reconstructions of former happenings. I shall quote but one example as an illustration.

Kera of Job gave the following account of a series of episodes from his youth about two generations before. One of the headmen of Dap, Kintabi, the father of Bagasal and Wiawia, came to hear that his wife and a headman from Job, Barok by name, were having an affair. In great indignation he called his relatives together, and they all marched against the adulterer. On reaching Job, Kintabi smote the slit-gong outside the club house and began hurling insults at Barok. The latter, instead of remaining silent or slinking away, as in decency he should have done, took up a weapon and sprang against his accuser. Bystanders dragged them apart, and both retired, Kintabi back to Dap, Barok to a hut in the gardens away from the settlement, where shortly afterwards he died, the victim of sorcery procured by the injured husband. I queried whether really his wounds had been fatal, but this Kera dismissed. He was sure that the death was Kintabi's handiwork and sorcery had been employed, not necessarily by him but by someone engaged to do the job.

Barok's kinsmen were now angry with Kintabi and determined to pay him out, Kera went on. As none of them knew how to perform *yabou*, they had to ask Jaran, Marigum's father, the other Dap headman to arrange for his death. Jaran agreed and had him killed by a sorcerer from Takul.

I checked the facts as given by Kera with the other Job elders, who agreed in general terms as to the correctness of the account. Then I approached Wiawia. He made much of Kintabi's encompassing Barok's death but described as ridiculous the Job claims of getting their own back through the agency of Jaran. Kintabi had survived Barok by many years, he assured me.

Next on the list for questioning was Marigum. He confirmed Wiawia's assertion that Barok died first but maintained that indeed Jaran had caused Kintabi's demise, not, however, on account of pleas from Job but rather as punishment for another adulterous liaison. Kintabi, so Marigum told me, had seduced one of Jaran's wives. Then after Kintabi's death his younger brother Bwo wanted revenge. Through relatives he approached some warriors from Ga and urged them to come to Dap, surround Jaran's house during the night, and spear him when early in the morning he set foot outside. But Jaran also had kinsmen in Ga, who warned him of what was being planned. Accordingly he fled in good time with his wives and young children — Marigum had barely reached puberty — and took refuge for a few years with a partner in Bwanag in Takul district. Marigum concluded by affirming that later on, after the return to Dap, Jaran invited a sorcerer to kill Bwo. Nonsense, exclaimed Wiawia when I passed on the information for his comment: Bwo lingered till at last he became senile.

In an earlier chapter I mentioned that the concept of jural equality for the members of the kin group, so strongly emphasized in much of the African literature, is in Melanesia unknown. In the Pacific persons seeking revenge concentrate their efforts solely on the man judged to be the enemy. No other victim will serve, not even a son or a brother. When Jaran departed for Bwanag his firstborn Gerobo, Marigum's half-brother, was already married and elected to stay on in Dap, where he lived in perfect safety. The decision seems extraordinary, a disregarding of family loyalty, but according to reports he detested his father as much as Tafalti was to do some forty years later. In due course we shall learn why.

This incident led to three adventitious deaths. The first was that of Jaran's sister's son Sarewo, resident in Ga, who fell before the warriors' spears as he tried to prevent their setting out; and the other two were of his cousins Bari of Bariat and Lang of Kinaba, who suffered a similar fate when they blocked the road to Bwanag. The motives for these men's intervention are clear. Mindful of their obligations as close kinsmen of Jaran, they felt in duty bound to do their best to protect him (nobody could tell me whether Gerobo was smitten with feelings of guilt at their example). They perished because they were hindering the achievement of ends felt to be legitimate, and the warriors were under no illusion that a balance had now been struck. The attack on Jaran would have persisted had he not escaped to a powerful protector.

5 Marriage

We have noted that the members of the small community seldom quarrel, in part on account of their early training, in part because of their mutual dependence. Further, if they do have a grievance, disease and misfortune magic are available as a hidden, and therefore harmless, means of securing satisfaction. Reference in the last few pages to sexual jealousy, however, suggest that this can be a potential cause of open conflict. Wronged husbands, it would appear, do not invariably abide by the accepted convention that at all costs peace must be maintained. This hint I propose to follow up. As a starting point I want to investigate the general subject of marriage, particularly since betrothal, and the union itself, at times give rise to disputes not only between parents and children but also between the relatives of the bride and bridegroom.[1]

REGULATIONS

These are simple. The moieties are exogamous, and in addition a match is forbidden between persons who are related as 'close kin', interpreted in this context as 'those who regularly work in company'. 'If a boy is accustomed to taking food from a girl's hand, then he thinks of her as a sister and would not want to make her his wife,' people say. This automatically excludes the daughters of the men of his housing cluster; but which of the cousins from beyond are barred depends on the way he and his parents have been treating them. Familiarity and warmth of feeling have a bearing on the problem, and we know that while some second cousins come into the category of near kin, others do not. Occasional matings between first cross cousins are recorded and give rise to only slight condemnation. There is no prohibition as such on the girls from the cluster at the far end of the village, and provided the formal requirements are satisfied the wedding can go ahead.

Dap provides a series of examples of marriages between kin, including, if the strict letter of the law were applied, one of incest

5 Marriage

(see Marigum's Genealogy).[2] Kintabi,[3] a member of the second cluster, headed by Bagasal, had two spouses, Marigum's full sister Makwa and also Mwal, the daughter of Marigum's half-sister. Naturally, the children of both women, like their father, belonged to Bagasal's group. Thus when Bagasal's younger son Gireno[4] took as his bride Makwa's eldest daughter Mareta he was guilty of an infringement of the rules. This must have been prior to 1926, for their only offspring Keke was in 1934 about eight years old. By then the scandal was, if not forgotten, in abeyance. Their relatives offered as excuse that, although Kintabi and Bagasal were of the one cluster, they were ignorant of the identity of their common ancestor. Then in 1974 I learned that Kulbob, the son of Kintabi and Makwa's son Bo, had not long before wed Elizabeth, his second cousin, the eldest daughter of Dal, one of Bernard's sisters (she was Kulbob's father's mother's brother's son's daughter).

Usually the young people have a major say in choosing their mates. The men of the two families concerned may insist on airing an opinion, but the boy and girl are not obliged to accept the advice, and those with sufficient strength of character treat it with indifference or derision according to their temperament. The accumulation of wealth for bride-price, a common Melanesian practice, is unknown, and the peripheral kin are therefore not caught up even to the extent of contributing to the wedding expenses.

A headman likes to pick a suitable partner as the first spouse for each of his children, the girls as well as the boys, a year or two before they are old enough to entertain settled views, but if when the time comes either of the parties rejects the other he has no alternative but to abandon the plan. Men lower down the social scale cherish a similar ambition with respect to their eldest sons and eldest daughters, yet here also the chances of compelling couples to set up a household against their will are negligible.

In ordinary families the younger sons and daughters have as a rule to engineer an elopement. The girl's father and brothers, and perhaps an uncle and cousin or two, make a great show of disapproval in a noisy protest, but this is largely, and sometimes wholly, a token, adherence to a convention, and unless the bridegroom is really unsuitable they soon cease complaining and accept the match with equanimity if not positive rejoicing.

Such freedom, coupled with lack of concern by wider groups, is probably to be explained by the ephemerality of the personal kindred. Only when a community is made up of perpetual corporations, such as lineages or clans, can symmetrical ongoing exchanges of women, or asymmetrical exchanges of women against goods, be readily organized.[5] To achieve the required balance the elders then insist on retaining firm control.

BETROTHAL

A headman seeking a future spouse for his heir tries to confine himself to the eldest daughters of the wives of equals. His aim is to find somebody of high rank, and the idea of the union creating or cementing an alliance between two circles of kinsfolk would not occur to him. Few girls of the right age are likely to be available — there may not be one — and often he has to look in a distant village or even another island, as in 1948 Marigum was obliged to do for Dal's second wife.

For their other offspring headmen, and also fathers of lesser consequence, must be satisfied with the lower ranks of society. The final choice is justified on grounds of either sentiment or reciprocity, depending on the circumstances. Thus a man searching for a fiancée for his son aims at securing a girl who shares an ancestress born in his village. Later the new husband and wife, both descended from this same woman, may be persuaded to keep her memory green in the place of her birth by promising to name a daughter after her.

Matters are more complicated when a man wants a husband for his daughter. He now tries to select a matrilateral cousin, a mother's brother's son's son. By this means an old debt is discharged — that incurred when the girl's father's father accepted as his bride the young man's father's father's father's daughter. A glance at the accompanying genealogy will make the argument clear. The affiancing of the maid Wanai to the youth Malagun was a delayed repayment for the bestowal by his great-grandfather Igaru of the girl Ilu on Kabai, Wanai's grandfather. Lala, her father, explained the engagement as follows. 'Yanai's grandfather gave his daughter, my mother, as wife to my father, and I am now evening things up by promising my daughter as a bride for Yanai's son. A person's good name suffers, as you know, when he fails to return the equivalent of a gift.' It is obvious that he saw the transaction purely in terms of individual persons. Igaru sent his daughter not to a family, kindred, housing cluster, or village but just to Kabai; and now Lala, Kabai's son, was making a settlement with a single direct descendant of Igaru.

Simultaneously the boy's father undertakes to relinquish the land that came as dowry with her grandmother.[6] In this instance Lala intended to endow Wanai with the plot he inherited from his mother Ilu, who had received it from her father on the occasion of her marriage. An area lost to Igaru's immediate successors would

5 Marriage

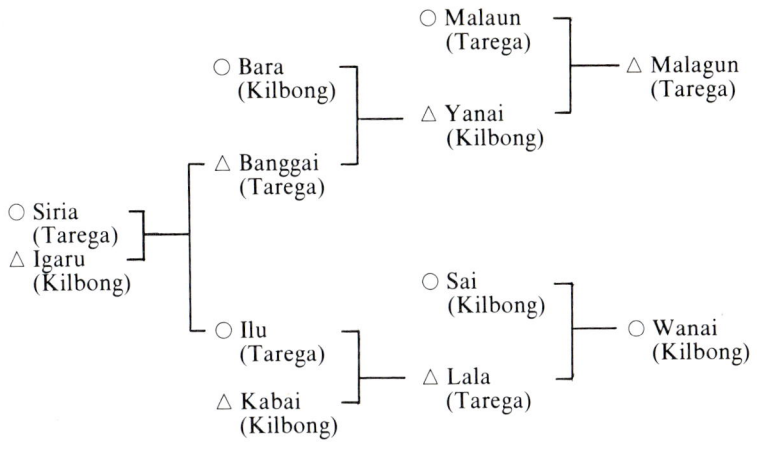

```
                         ○ Malaun
                           (Tarega)      ┐
         ○ Bara          ┐                ├── △ Malagun
           (Kilbong)     │                │     (Tarega)
                          ├── △ Yanai    │
         △ Banggai       │    (Kilbong)  ┘
         (Tarega)        │
○ Siria              ┤
  (Tarega)           │
△ Igaru              │
  (Kilbong)          │
                         ○ Sai
                           (Kilbong)     ┐
         ○ Ilu           ┐                ├── ○ Wanai
           (Tarega)      │                │     (Kilbong)
                          ├── △ Lala     ┘
         △ Kabai         │    (Tarega)
         (Kilbong)       ┘
```

△ represents a male   ○ represents a female
A linkage after names indicates marriage.
The matrilineal moieties, Tarega and Kilbong, are shown in parentheses.

Genealogy

thus revert to one of their progeny, Malagun's son, after the lapse of three generations.

A father whose maternal uncles' grandsons are already married, or as yet mere children, ought by rights to offer his daughter to one of the other men of the correct moiety from this same village whence her mother came. Only if these also are too old or too young is it accepted that he may look elsewhere.

I learned many of the details about betrothal from talks with Marigum about what he would eventually undertake for Dal. At that time, in 1934, it was too early to think seriously about the matter, he said; to bind a lad when such a long period must elapse before his marriage would be futile. Stupid parents who act prematurely often find themselves for one reason or another left lamenting – the girl may perhaps have died or fallen a victim to some crippling disease. The appropriate day would be when Dal began to grow a beard. The girl should be younger, still a child but showing the first signs of approaching maturity – at the stage when her relatives were saying, 'Yes, her breasts will soon be starting to fill out.' He expected to be able to provide the eldest daughter of one of the wives of a headman, but if this proved to be impracticable he would be satisfied with somebody whose father could offer a large area of land as a dowry. (Dal was first married in 1945, when he was about 29: I do not know whether a betrothal took place, but the bride was not a headman's daughter. She had three children; Bernard and two daughters. The second marriage, this time to a high ranking girl from Koil Island, took place three years later.)

Marigum went on to point out that he would entrust the negotiations to an intermediary, thereby avoiding loss of face at a refusal and embarrassment should he wish to continue social relations with the girl's father. The go-between must be a man of judgement and discretion, able to overcome the objections that on these occasions are inevitable. 'We Wogeo dislike the thought of losing a daughter and always try to keep her with us: parents refuse at first even when satisfied that the match is a good one,' it was explained. ' "No, no, no!" the father says. "My daughter is too young as yet for me to contemplate her leaving; and, supposing she were older, what close relative has she in Dap to support her in trouble? And who would look after her brothers if they should become ill?" ' Such arguments must be answered with skill and the suit pressed till every quibble is silenced.

After the betrothal the girl pays frequent visits to her future parents-in-law, who give her various jobs, supposedly as tests of her upbringing. They also take the opportunity, if they are wise, to throw her and the prospective bridegroom into one another's company in order to break down their reserve. Wiawia was critical of his elder half-brother Bwaiak, who had arranged his marriage — their father was already dead — for not inviting the girl to the house beforehand. Had Bwaiak taken his responsibilities seriously, so Wiawia maintained, the agonizing embarrassment of the first formal meeting would have been avoided. He was only vaguely aware of the plans when, on his return from a day's fishing, Bwaiak called him to eat the supper his 'bride' had prepared. Instead of going home he retreated to the club, where he remained, pleading sudden illness, till well into the night. At last Bwaiak came across and, berating him for a fool, ordered him to meet the girl and take the food. 'I almost vomited with shame,' he told me.[7] 'Yes I went; but for a long time we didn't allow ourselves to be alone together. People tried to make things easy by joking about our being man and wife; yet, left to ourselves, either she or I ran away. I've seen the same situation develop elsewhere: if the boy and girl aren't familiar they're always shy.'

Should the father have overestimated the girl's age, the young man may grow tired of waiting and elope with someone else. If he is the son of a headman the parents of the betrothed do not offer objections, for in such circles polygyny is usual, and they see no reason for complaining that their daughter will have to share his attentions. But an ordinary villager may face resentment.

5 Marriage

The leaders hold that they alone are entitled to large households and other people should be content with one spouse. The man may abandon the girl, though I recorded many cases of his refusing to do so, with the result that the earlier arrangements had to be cancelled.

The coming-of-age ceremonies of an affianced girl are more elaborate than usual. The honour of the future bridegroom's family is also at stake, and his father likes to make a lavish contribution towards the accompanying feast. Till recently a formal debate between some of the unmarried men concluded the celebrations. The girl's brothers and cousins called those of the boy 'thieves' for taking her away, and the latter retaliated by boasting about what they proposed to do. 'Nobody was really angry, and her kinsmen objected only because they were sorry to lose her,' Jaua explained. The custom has been abandoned owing to the absence in employment of so many who would have taken part.

A large gift of food for the girl's feast may serve in itself as a proposal. Thus Pantob, lacking the courage to ask so important a man as Marigum outright for the hand of his daughter Sanum on behalf of an orphaned nephew Kakameri, offered a couple of pigs when she first menstruated.[8] To begin with Marigum was furious at the effrontery and refused to take them. He would in due course attend to the nuptials, and outsiders need not be free with suggestions, he said. But then the headman from Kakameri's cluster stepped forward and stressed the suitability of the match. Sanum's grandmother had come from Mwarok, Kakameri's village, he indicated, and a return now would be appropriate. (The woman had been espoused to a man from Falala, where a daughter, Sanum's mother, had been born.) Marigum retired to his house grumbling but after an interval ordered some of his followers to bring Pantob's offering across to where the food was set out, thereby acknowledging acceptance and consent. The match proved to be unfortunate for Sanum, as we shall see.

A few days after the feast the girl's relatives decorate her and accompany her to the new home. The father is supposed to be still reluctant to let her go, and in consequence the mother has to fix the date. Ostensibly he is so upset that he prefers to appoint some senior man as his representative. Each woman in the party carries as a present for the couple some household utensil, perhaps a basket, carrying bag, platter, cooking pot, or water-bottle; and she herself bears on her head a package of clothing from her mother and a palm spathe to serve as a bed. She arrives therefore with a full trousseau. The bridegroom's relatives present food to the retainers, who eat it at once and return. They do not take a ceremonial leave of the girl, but generally all are in tears. The young man may be present throughout but as a rule keeps well out of sight.

Today difficulties may arise if the husband is absent in employment. No one expects the young wife to be chaste, and after a series of affairs she is apt to grow impatient and run off with a boy of her own choosing. Her parents always withhold their approval, and in most cases she comes back to wait for a further period. When the husband does arrive he may decline to accept her, especially if she is now notorious. Her only chance then is of marriage with a widower.

Many villagers expressed sympathy for the particularly attractive girl Mor, whose affianced husband Bwaga, a close relative of Marigum, had been away for several years in one of the mainland towns. She had already eloped twice, and then in 1934 news reached us in Dap that she was now in hiding with a third man, Kajikmwa of Job. Marigum at once strode off there, followed by one or two kinsmen who happened to be on the spot. He beat the wooden slit-gong in the centre of the village to call the people together and proceeded in a loud voice to announce his grave displeasure. Mor was promised to Bwaga, he shouted, and Kajikmwa's brothers had better see that she was back with her parents by nightfall. If she was still absent after sunset he would demand several pigs as compensation. 'Hurry and bring her to her father,' he concluded. The brothers started out at once, and late in the afternoon poor Mor, looking thoroughly miserable, was at work with her mother and sisters.

My own intimates, including those related to Marigum, were unanimous in condemning him for wanton interference. They admitted the slight to his honour as the reason – an injury to Bwaga, a near kinsman, was the same as an insult to him personally – but was it likely, they asked, that Bwaga would accept as wife a woman who had given such proof of her preference for other men? No, he would refuse her. Then she might bear two or three illegitimate children and never fine a husband.

I recorded information about over thirty betrothals, and of these seven were broken off. In some instances the man ignored the girl until at last, in desperation, she went back to her parents, in others she repelled his advances and fled, refusing to return. People account for the high incidence of failures by pointing to the interval between the initial promises and the wedding. In the earlier stages the boy and girl are too immature to know their own minds, and consultation with them would be useless. A person ought to respect the wishes of his or her parents, it is agreed, but

5 Marriage

when marriage is in question the seniors would do well to take the feelings of their offspring into account — are not the youngsters more directly concerned? If a battle of wills takes place the rule that members of adjoining generations should normally avoid explicit reference to sexual matters in one another's presence helps to prevent an open breach, but a boy or a girl who is resolute can always carry the day.

The behaviour of Sawang, one of Marigum's nephews, was typical of that of men determined to reject the girl selected. He had been betrothed in the normal way to Kugi, but when the parents sent her to Dap he disdained to notice her. His uncle reproved him in private and in public, but he was unmoved. Eventually she left in disgust. Her mother brought her back once, but Sawang departed on a protracted visit to kinsmen living elsewhere as soon as she set foot in the village. Later, when she eloped with a man called Wukala, Sawang's near kinsmen attempted an exchange. Let Wukala have Kugi, and they would accept his fiancée, Marigum offered on their behalf. This girl's parents agreed to the arrangement, but Sawang was even less enthusiastic. A few months afterwards he eloped with Bara, a widow some years older than himself.

Equally characteristic was the case of Wanang, a girl indifferent to the man chosen as her husband. Her mother and brothers took her again and again to the house of her betrothed's parents, but repeatedly she seized the first chance to escape. In the end they had to bow before her determination.

A betrothed girl who forms an attachment with someone else is well advised to demonstrate clearly and unmistakably before eloping that she will have nothing to do with the man her father has in mind. Foolishly, Sanum, Marigum's daughter mentioned above, delayed running away with a lover, Bwareo of Job, until the marriage to Kakameri had been consummated. Naturally, the latter considered her action an affront and resolved to compel her to come back. He beat the slit-gong in his own village of Mwarok and announced his intention, rounded up a few of the men present, and went on to Dap to enlist further help. Marigum and some of his kinsmen joined in, and they all marched off to Job. This time Kakameri and Marigum both struck the gong. Shouting wild threats against the residents, they insisted that somebody go at once and, by force if need be, drag Sanum to her husband's house in Mwarok. Much alarmed, several men made their way to the place where the guilty pair were in hiding and urged the woman to leave. She wanted to stay, but Bwareo, fearing Marigum's anger more than that of Kakameri, would not agree.

Weeping bitterly, she allowed herself to be led away. Nothing would persuade her to go to Mwarok, and the men had to be satisfied with seeing her creep into her father's dwelling in Dap. Marigum let her stay for a few days and then told one of the older women to return her to Kakameri. At a slightly later stage she met Bwareo and again begged him to run away, but he declined on the ground that he would have to face too much ill feeling, an explanation held by others to be eminently reasonable. He might have consented, some of the villagers assured me, if she had made the effort immediately after her first-menstruation feast and convinced Kakameri that she would never live with him. Certainly Marigum would have expressed indignation at the flouting of his wishes — that was to be expected — but ultimately he might have come round to accepting the situation.

After a few months, when the marriage appears to have some chance of developing into a successful partnership, the girl's father gives two pigs to the boy's parents, a present known as 'the ladder' or 'the flight of steps' *(gwaba)*. It serves to ratify her right to 'go up into' their house and also helps to ensure her status. Should the mother-in-law scold her she can now shame the woman into silence by a reminder that as she has filled her belly with the pork she ought in return to be more understanding and tolerant.

It is to be noted that the transfer is not a bride-price in reverse, a sort of husband price. The girl's uncles may contribute, but if so they offer no more than a few vegetables and a bunch or two of bananas. Further, in the unlikely event of an early divorce the *gwaba* gifts would not be returned.

Little ceremonial accompanies the presentation except that the donors make a clear distinction between the food for distribution and the share for the boy's parents. The following is an account of the proceedings after Sole, the daughter of Kaman, a headman of Falala, married Marigum's eldest son Tafalti, Sanum's full brother.

Kaman notified Marigum two days in advance of his intention to send the pigs, together with five baskets of taro. During the interval the Dap villagers gathered green drinking coconuts, areca nuts, and betel pepper and also took packages of tobacco to Marigum's house. On the day appointed many of the Falala residents attended Kaman, and in addition some of his kinsmen and affines from elsewhere came. These people between them contributed but one more basket of taro and half a dozen bunches of bananas. Arrived in Dap, they set their burdens down in front of Marigum's house and immediately began singeing the pigs and

5 Marriage

carving the carcases. They placed on one side what was called 'the short pieces' *(dubu)*, consisting of the back and ribs, and piled the rest, 'the long pieces' *(niubelalaba)*, and the other food on his verandah. The Dap folk, who, apart from Sole, had hitherto taken no part, now advanced with the coconuts, betel mixture, and tobacco. Kaman and his retinue remained chatting for a brief period and then departed, taking the short pieces back with them. Marigum at once divided the pork they had left, together with the vegetables and bananas, among the villagers present.

That evening Kaman's family baked the other pieces, and in the morning his son and a daughter-in-law carried them once more to Marigum. They chose an hour when most of the householders were already busy in the gardens and sneaked into the place as quietly as possible. Fifteen minutes later they were gone, this time with packages of dried fish. Marigum would have been entitled to keep this pork for himself, his wives, and his children but preferred to hold back only a small portion. The remainder he distributed as before.

The bridegroom's parents are not obliged to make any return but usually do so to avoid a charge of meanness and gain a little extra prestige. They make a single presentation without separating the short from the long pieces.

ELOPEMENT

Betrothal may be the dignified method of entering wedlock, but at least three-quarters of the population have to make their own arrangements. Such persons, younger sons and daughters from ordinary households, describe themselves metaphorically as 'merely urine' by comparison with their elder siblings, the 'real semen', who in consequence are the prime concern of the parents. For the most part they drift into matrimony after a lengthy courtship.

When a boy and girl have been lovers for some months one or the other hints that perhaps a permanent union might be a good idea. Waru confessed that he had not thought seriously about marriage until one day a companion enquired did he propose staying single much longer. 'The words made me consider the question, and I decided to take a wife,' he continued. ' "Why not Mujewa?" I asked myself. I knew her well, we'd played together as children, and we'd been having intercourse for ages. What's more, for all that time I'd never heard of her going with anyone else.'

The bulk of the women approach the new state with the same casualness, though three of them told me they had waited for the man they fancied to return from overseas. (At that stage, as I have said, no one could write, and the exchange of letters was impossible.)

An impression of cold calculation is perhaps conveyed by the maxims stressing the folly of selecting a promiscuous woman. 'Never wed a girl who accepts your advances easily: she will yield just as quickly to others,' and 'If you want a faithful wife, choose when proposing the girl who has always replied "no" ', are two such. Doubtless the popularity of the sayings can be accounted for by the men's dislike of being laughed at. All wives are prone in the end to adultery, they freely acknowledge, but precautions are advisable if one is to avoid becoming a cuckold immediately after marriage.

People say that the occasional sudden union not preceded by courtship is likely to be the result of pique. Jaua, on our overhearing the girl Sakat vilify the youth Rais, remarked casually that he supposed the boy had rejected her advances. 'You'll see, she'll be off soon persuading someone else, trying to show that Rais is of no importance to her. But he must have been or she'd not now be so bitter. Listen to her! You'd think, wouldn't you, that he was a thorough rogue.' Three days later she did go off, significantly enough with a man suffering from ringworm.

Similarly when Mwaibo suddenly married the girl Lae the villagers pointed to the fact that Doma, with whom his name had long been associated, had instead wedded one of his close kinsmen. They surmised that he must have determined on a quick runaway match to prove his indifference. Lae, whose reputation was not above suspicion — rumour said that she had had an abortion — was, naturally, eager to accept him.

Apart from fidelity, the only quality receiving constant mention in discussions about the model wife, as distinct from lover, is industry. The seniors warn the young men never to choose a woman known to be lazy, even when she is good-looking, and I heard one old fellow telling his grandson that it would be better to pick someone with a skin infection. The smell could be ignored, he reiterated, for, lacking temptation, she would be bound to be a good worker.

Only when a boy and girl belong to different clusters in the same village are her parents prepared to welcome him as the bridegroom at once. If he comes from another place etiquette compells them to object no matter how socially acceptable he may be. Normally therefore young couples are obliged to elope.

My own observations confirmed the account by Waru of what usually takes place. First the man needs a confidant, someone pre-

5 Marriage

pared to offer advice and shelter for a few days. This person, who is always a member of the opposite moiety — 'You are ashamed to speak about your marriage with those from the same division as yourself' — must be married and possessed of a house of his own but is never a near kinsman. The blood-brother would act but, as a contemporary, is rarely able to fulfil all the conditions. The prospective bridegroom tells his plans in detail and then collects the girl, who will have stocked her carrying bag with food and fresh water, and at nighfall the two make their way to the garden hut or cave where they have decided to hide. The girl's parents, unaware of what is afoot, assume to begin with that she must be visiting relatives, and not until the boy is reported missing do they realize what has happened. The father and his adult sons, and perhaps, if they are on the scene at the time, his brothers, nephews, and brothers-in-law, proceed to the boy's parents' house and demand that they compel him to send her back. 'Her choice may have been sensible and the bridegroom a good worker, but it isn't customary to approve of him yet,' Waru went on. 'No, indeed! They're always angry. "What your son has done is wrong," the father shouts. "He's stolen my daughter, whom I expected to send to another man. She must return at once." His supporters back him up, exclaiming, "We too have been ill-used. Who'll look after us if we're sick should our sister — or niece — be here with a husband? Did this thief offer us one of his sisters in exchange? He did not! Very well then, our sister — or niece — must come home. If she's to marry at all her spouse will be from her own village so that she can always be near at hand." ' The man's parents and any other relatives present listen politely but point out that no girl is willing to stay single for life simply to please her brothers and that their kinsman is no seducer but in every respect worthy. He will be eager to work for his father-in-law and brothers-in-law, who will thus gain an able helper.

The girl's relatives, having had their say, retreat empty-handed. The confidant now has the duty of discreetly sounding out public opinion. He discusses the incident with some of the seniors to find out whether they have any objections. If not — and unless the girl is already betrothed or the boy is an undesirable, nobody is likely to be at all disturbed — he fetches the pair and takes them to his dwelling. The bridegroom, abashed because his parents have on his account been forced to accept loud reproaches, generally keeps out of sight for a few more days. Then one evening he brings his bride to the family home. The neighbours and other relatives present sufficient mats, pots, and household utensils to form a trousseau, and the mother-in-law sets aside a corner of the fireplace for her to cook and a garden from which she can gather vegetables.

The bride's relatives rarely ask for her return a second time, but she and the husband avoid personal contact with them for the space of two or three months. By then it can be assumed that they will have calmed down, and the couple take baskets of the choicest foods supplied by his mother and make a visit. At first the atmosphere may be chilly, but the barriers of reserve soon disappear. A few days later her mother returns the call, also with food. Usually she hands a few dried fish or some other delicacy to the confidant as an acknowledgement of his services to her daughter.

Ideally the bridegroom and bride should now confirm their new relationship by eating a ceremonial meal in the presence of both sets of parents and siblings and any other kinsfolk who care to attend. In actual fact the pair generally refuse, offering as excuse that they would be seriously embarrassed. When performed the rite is carried out twice in different houses, one from each cluster of the bridegroom's village. The two sit side by side on a mat, and a brother of the husband, or another close relative, presents him with, in this order, a coconut, a taro corm, a fish, and a platter of vegetable stew. The husband begins by opening the coconut and drinking half the liquid. The remainder he hands to his wife, who finishes it. He then eats half the taro corm and half the fish, and she has the other half. The stew they merely taste, and afterwards each person present takes a few mouthfuls. The meal concludes with the company chewing betelnut together. 'The wedding is now complete, and the boy and girl are joined for good.'[9]

People deny that the girl's father and brothers feign their short-lived opposition, and certainly the anger in such displays as I witnessed appeared to be genuine. The men reserve the animosity exclusively for the bridegroom, absolving her from blame, and speak as though he had carried her off against her wishes or even been guilty of rape. They agree that too many insults would be undesirable, but they sometimes threaten to abduct his sister or cousin as a bride for one of themselves. Sometimes they demand compensation though fully aware he will refuse unless he lives so far away that the wife cannot easily remain in constant touch with her parents. In these circumstances he might in pre-contact days have handed over a pig: today the payment of a dollar or two suffices.

The reason for the outburst is said to be affection. The members of the family are so united that inevitably the girl's departure prompts those left behind to direct their annoyance against her ravisher. 'The father and brothers hate the thought of her being out of sight and not coming when they call. Only after reflection do they realize that she would hardly have gone unwillingly.' The lack of resentment when bride and groom are from the same settlement serves as endorsement for such an explanation. Even then he may keep in hiding for a few days, though on his emergence the new affines, who, of course, are also close kin, greet him warmly.

There are occasions, nevertheless, when the anxiety turns out to be well founded. An unscrupulous young man may trick a girl into an elopement without any intention of marrying her. After a sexual orgy lasting a few days he sends her packing on the pretext that he is not prepared for such implacable resistance. Neither she nor her father has a hope of securing redress.

A detailed study of marriage from the woman's side would be of great interest, but I am able to quote the statement of only one of them. 'Yes, I was sorry to leave my parents and my brothers,' she assured me. 'But I wouldn't have been able to stay with them always. I wanted a husband and a house of my own. And as it was my husband he was to be, why shouldn't I do the choosing? It was unpleasant to know that my relatives were making a fuss, but I comforted myself by thinking, "Well, they're not angry with me, so I can put up with it. Besides, they'll soon come to their senses and simmer down."'

MARRIAGE BY CAPTURE

Men suffering from physical disabilities often have difficulty in persuading anyone to elope. The girls say of a person with ringworm, for instance, 'He brings the flies. And how can he expect us to tolerate the smell?' After such unfortunates have been repeatedly turned down they may seek the headman's approval for requesting some of their companions for help in kidnapping a wife (*veine kalarafeti*, literally, 'pulling, or dragging, a woman'). The effort is rarely a success, and the woman runs away.

Wiap, the most wretchedly ugly man in Dap, is said to have suffered rejection by thirteen women — I cannot swear to the accuracy of the count — before deciding to beg the villagers to capture Yar of Bariat for him. He obtained Marigum's grudging permission and that evening set several bunches of areca nuts and a package of tobacco before the men gathered in the club. They agreed to do what he wanted and the next morning carried the girl off from a garden where she was working with an elderly couple to whom she was related. The man ran to Bariat, beat the slit-gong, and told the assembled villagers what had occurred. Kauni, the headman of the cluster where Yar's parents lived, went off at once to Dap to demand an explanation. But he was years younger than Marigum and lacked the self confidence to stand up for the rights of his followers. Fortunately for herself Yar was able to handle the situation alone. After telling Wiap at great length what she thought of him, she strode off home. He subsequently married a woman equally disfigured by ringworm.

6　Husband and Wife

The newly married pair are keen to move into their own house, but at least two years must go by before they will have accumulated the food required for the feast with which the workers are customarily rewarded. In the meantime they live with relatives, usually the man's parents, either in their own corner of the main part or in a room in one of the apses. They are glad to accept such hospitality but still look forward to their independence, and the final removal is a great moment for everybody.

Labim and his wife were obviously excited when they showed me over their new residence in Bariat the day after its completion. 'This is our own, and I can now feed my guests,' he declared with pride as he pointed out the details. 'You must stroll over one evening.' 'Yes, come and eat with us,' the woman added. 'You'll be able to tell me whether the soup is properly prepared: my mother-in-law tells me constantly I never cook it right.'

Yet the Wogeo dwelling lacks privacy. The walls are so thin that almost every word spoken can be heard by the neighbours, and the couple therefore leave intimate matters for discussion when they are gardening.

Care of the house is women's business, and a wife is expected to sweep the floor twice daily, morning and evening, keep the water-bottles filled, and maintain the supply of firewood. She also does the everyday cooking of meals — men rarely take an active part except during feasts — and it is her right to serve the food. Only when menstruating is she obliged to keep in the background. She advertises her condition by putting on a dun-coloured skirt, and the neighbours come to the rescue with supplies.

Husband and wife share most other types of work, though each has separate tasks. In horticulture he cuts down the trees (which later both combine to burn), clears the ground, erects the fences, and plants the banana suckers; and she sets the taro shoots, tobacco seedlings, and greens; keeps the plots free of weeds; digs up the ripened taro corms and brings a load daily from the garden to the village: in gathering forest products he strips the trees and she collects the fallen fruit and nuts: and although he catches the fish, she brings home mussels, clams, and other shellfish from the reef. Both making clothing, too, but each is responsible for his or her own garments. Men alone hunt, however, and work with wood. They build and thatch the houses, construct the canoes, and carve the platters and food bowls; in former times they made the stone tools.

Toiling for common ends, the man and woman soon learn to understand one another's point of view, and before long they discuss many of their concerns together. He frequently asks her opinion before choosing a plot for new gardens. With most of the carrying to do, she dislikes going far afield, whereas he is more inclined to pick a spot where felling the timber will not be too difficult. A wise husband often pretends to have set his heart on a remote block when in reality he is interested in one only half the distance, Jaua told me. By a graceful show of yielding he then succeeds in having his own way and acquiring a reputation for taking his wife's wishes into account. The two of them may also consult on such questions as whether or not to offer a pig to a kinsman holding a feast or what attitude to adopt to relatives engaged in a quarrel.

At the same time, the man is the senior partner and has the final authority. Thus he manages the family property, including that part of it nominally belonging to the woman. Should he wish to offer a pig towards someone's feast he is free to choose an animal given to her in childhood, though she then expects him to favour her kin rather than his own. (The removal of these beasts to her new home is rarely practicable, and she usually leaves them in the care of a brother and sister-in-law, who can them claim a choice joint as a reward for their trouble.) Again, although the land the woman receives at marriage from her father passes back into the keeping of her kin should she die childless, the husband for as long as the match endures cultivates it as an integral part of his estate. The sole qualification is that he may not use it as a dowry for their daughter. The first person with this right is the son to whom it passes by inheritance.

The man also exercises discipline, and the wife's relatives do not complain if occasionally he strikes her to enforce obedience. Traditionally mothers advise their daughters, among other things, to accept a blow or two in good part. 'A wife must have no mouth for her husband, nor must she sit with head averted' — that is, she should carry out orders without answering back and if struck

Marigum's house in Dap. He is standing at the entrance.

Keke teaches her cousin Gwa how to make a string figure.

The clubhouse at Dap. Kanakula is standing in front alongside the wooden slit-gong.

Men and women preparing the hot stones for an earth oven during a feast.

Marigum, Dal, and Jauon.

Yam preparing taro for the evening meal.

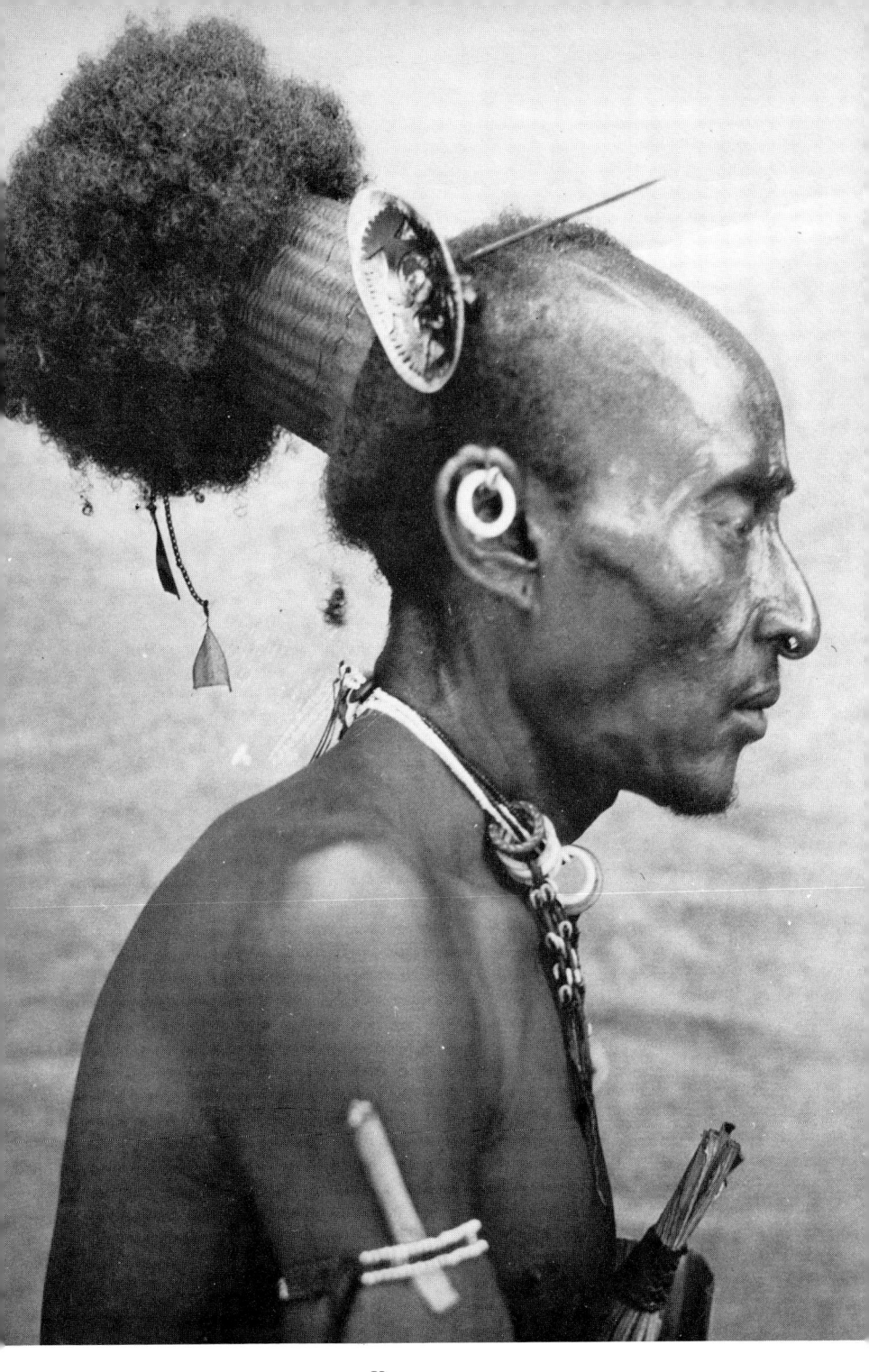

Kawang

Jaua

Sale

Kalabai recounts the details of a fight to his father and mother

Kalal

Kalal strikes the Dap slit-gong

Tafalti

Magar

Jaua, on the right, directs the distribution of Pacific chestnuts and coconuts at Marigum's *walage* in Dap. Kalaua is on the left, Sawang in the centre.

The dance in Bwanag to open Kawang's *warabwa*

The women's dance in Gol. The platform where Kawang later displayed the *warabwa* food is on the left.

Dance in Ga at Wakera's *warabwa*. The orchestra of hand-drummers is on the right.

Ballet of the nut collectors in Ga

Erecting the platform for the food display during Kawang's *warabwa* (Gol village facing south)

Pigs lying ready for the performance of magical ritual to create an abundance of pork during Kawang's *warabwa* (Gol village: the ethnographer's house is in the centre background)

The ritual fight preceding the final stages of Kawang's *warabwa*. One of the two masked figures *(tangbwal)* can be distinguished in the centre of the mêlée. (Gol village facing north: the clubhouse is in the background, the ethnographer's dwelling on the right in the centre.)

Wakera performing the *kinaba* rite during his *warabwa* in Ga

A *tangbwal* spirit monster

Janggara, in the background on the left, despatches the *nibek* monsters, represented by bamboo flutes, back to the spirit world at the conclusion of Kawang's *warabwa*. In the foreground one man lights a torch while two others stand ready with bow and arrows; slightly behind on the right the members of the orchestra hold hand-drums or wooden sounding-boards; and behind these again the flautists stand in two rows facing each other. The remains of the display platform can be seen on the left in front of Janggara. (Gol village facing north.)

refrain from sulking. Brutality arouses censure, nevertheless, and the man who so ill-treats his spouse that she feels obliged to run to her father and brothers for protection may find that he has to pay compensation before they will allow her to return. When Kakameri hit Sanum with a burning log she at once fled to the shelter of Marigum's house, whereupon the latter despatched a messenger to say that she would remain with him till the erring husband sent him a pig. A myth tells how, when a man had thrashed his wife, his parents were afraid lest they also might be killed in revenge, but no one could recall an instance from real life.

It is the sisters' duty to warn their brother should he be guilty of undue harshness. His wife can easily bring him to a final judgement, they insist. She has only to touch his clothing or handle some of his food during her periods, and he will fall a victim to a fatal wasting disease (the symptoms described are similar to those of tuberculosis, which is comparatively common). He may be grateful but is more likely to deprecate such counsel. 'Yes, yes, a woman who is menstruating can kill her husband with a finger, I know that. Why, she could also cut off his head while he's asleep, couldn't she? But to retaliate with murder for a slap would hardly be reasonable, don't you agree?' Jaua replied when his sister Wurun remonstrated with him. 'I expect you're right, but you shouldn't be too certain. Always bear in mind that a wife is not to be trusted like a sister,' she answered. At that stage I interrupted to enquire had she actually heard women threatening such dire vengeance. Indeed no, she reluctantly admitted, but the danger was still real. 'This is merely the talk of sisters afraid for their brothers,' Jaua laughingly protested. 'Wives don't do such things. You know, we husbands are no more concerned about their menstruation than we are about their gardening knives.' It is true that at no time was any widow accused, even behind her back, of deliberately encompassing her husband's death.

Men in general maintain that nagging women are more of a problem than cruel husbands. Several lamented that although often deafened with shrill scoldings, they were themselves innocent of even breaking their wives' skin with a cuff or a blow. The chief trouble with the other sex was an over long memory, they went on. It is the nature of females never to forget anything, and the most trivial arguments can lead to a recital of grievances going back to the time of the wedding.

Such complaints are probably overdone, and I would describe only a few housewives as shrewish. Yet it is a fact that women do not hesitate to speak their minds, and when annoyed they may take the entire village into their confidence. 'Come along, don't keep me waiting till the sun's overhead,' they call across the street loudly if ready for the garden first; and some even dare to summon the husband from the sacred precincts of the club to mind one of the children or help with a household task.

Laziness and work left undone are common causes of squabbles, and family jars may also arise through the difficulty of making an accurate estimate of time. The husband, if hungry, becomes annoyed if his dinner is delayed, and the wife may be disappointed if he comes home late. Again, in the early months of married life the man is apt to scold his wife for her imagined inexperience. He jumps to the conclusion that she may perhaps be unused to large-scale catering and hence have difficulty in judging the amount of food required. His great fear always is of guests rising from their dinner unsatisfied.[1] The pre-marriage homily of the bride's mother lays great stress on this point, with its instructions to see that the bellies of visitors, especially the husband's brothers, are stuffed full.

Neighbours on good terms with the couple generally intervene and try to laugh them out of ill humour. Sometimes the husband and wife refuse to listen and start destroying one another's property. He may smash a pot — which he has later to replace — and the wife may reciprocate by breaking a fishing-rod or tearing some of his garments to shreds. If reconciliation does not take place speedily she will probably threaten suicide and select a rope for the purpose. So blatantly does she indicate her intention that bystanders can easily prevent her from coming to harm, but as a rule the display is so effective that it brings the husband to ask pardon.

Jaua returned one evening from a fishing expedition and was disappointed at having to wait for something to eat. He made a few pungent comments about his wife Sale's lack of consideration and ended by hitting her around the shoulders with his open hand. 'You're so cruel I won't live with you,' she sobbed as she collected her belongings and left the house for Job village, where her brother lived. That night and the next day Jaua joined my table, but the second morning, as Sale was still absent, he went after her to Job, entered the brother's dwelling — he was not present — and struck her once more. 'Come back to Dap at once and see you cook this evening,' he told her as he strode away. Relatives persuaded her that she had been foolish, and at about noon she crept quietly back. Jaua addressed her as though nothing had occurred, and for a few days all went well. His anger was not far below the surface, however, and at the end of a week when she was tardy in obeying his order to gather up some breadfruit he struck her across the face with a stick, drawing blood. Two women from next door rushed in and took her away, and he walked off into the forest.

An hour or two passed, and Sale, saying she felt better, returned to her own house. Ten minutes later she emerged in a bright new skirt with a rope in her hand — she was swinging it round and round — and took the path to Job. The women at once ran to the beach, where a group of men were fishing, and urged them to follow. They caught her tying a noose in the rope, one end of which she had already thrown over the lowest branch of a tall tree. They brought her back, and for the next few days the women kept her under observation.

Jaua was unimpressed and went around with feathers in his hair in an attempt to make her believe he was having an affair with some girl. 'Sale's an idiot. This is the sort of thing women do, but no one of them has ever got to the point of actually killing herself,' he scoffed. Soon the villagers, Marigum especially, began expressing disapproval, and at last he decided to make his peace with a gift — a string of beads begged from me. One of his own ornaments would have served, he explained, but she would be better pleased, and hence less inclined to bring the subject up again, if he gave her something she had not seen before.

SEXUAL LIFE

People take it for granted that young couples will want intercourse frequently, and for the first few months newlyweds are encouraged to be together as often as possible. Decorum prevents the pair from sharing a bed unless they occupy a separate room — if they have to make do with a corner of the family dwelling the husband continues to sleep in the club — but when garden work is in progress the seniors make opportunities for them to slip into the forest during the midday rest. One posture favoured necessitates the woman's supporting some of the man's weight as well as her own on the small of her back, and the villagers look to see whether young wives show any sign of a bruise. Much to everyone's amusement a bride in Kinaba was disfigured for several weeks by a rash near the base of her spine. Her husband's vigour, so it was said, prevented the skin from healing.

Yet faithfulness is a rare virtue, and so many cases of adultery became public during 1934 that I reached the conclusion that few husbands or wives married for more than two or three years could boast of an unblemished record. The striking fact is, however, that people when speaking in a general way about extra-marital intrigue without anyone particular in mind always maintain it is wrong. They compare the adulterer with a thief and say he ought to have reserved his genitals for his wife's enjoyment. As for the paramour, she is like a receiver of stolen goods, a person who accepts a joint of meat cut from a pig killed without the owner's permission. Should she also be married they may add she is making free with something that is no longer hers to give. My suggestion that couples might come to a mutual arrangement scandalized some of the villagers. 'But adultery is evil, and we cannot condone misdeeds,' they scolded with great display of assumed integrity. Each one when later I taunted him with his own conduct offered some barely plausible excuse, as, for example, that his wife had so harried him with unfounded suspicions that he determined to give her something to worry about, that she was at the time set aside on account of suckling taboos, or that this other woman had drawn him in with magic.

The innocent partner is both hurt and angry. 'I'd have given it to her more often if she'd only asked me,' one wronged husband lamented. He was also irritated by the thought that his fellows might be laughing at him, though as a rule it is only the unsuspecting cuckold who is a figure of fun.

The husband who has established his wife's frailty reprimands her severely and gives her a beating; sometimes he turns her out of the house. If so she goes for a few days to her kinsfolk and then prepares a dish of his favourite food as a peace offering. The assumption is that acceptance indicates forgiveness, and in the morning she sets about her work as usual. A wife with a straying husband must be content with scolding him and afterwards leaving him alone. He also expresses his contrition with a gift, probably a new skirt obtained from one of his sisters, and eventually, within a week or two, she returns to her own fireside.

In Malaita, one of the Solomon Islands, where adultery is condemned even more keenly, wives are subject to such stringent regulations that a husband seldom has cause for jealousy. A Malaita woman never speaks to anyone, apart from her husband and brothers, unless somebody else is present, and a chaperon accompanies her everywhere while she is away from home: a Wogeo woman, on the contrary, is entitled to hold conversation with whomsoever she pleases and grows restive if kept under surveillance. 'You men do as you like, so why then must I have a companion?' she exclaims. Many husbands are as a result a prey to chronic suspicion and inclined to make accusations of infidelity on the flimsiest pretexts. Some of them actually carry out magic to bring evidence to light. It was no accident I am sure that my description of a mediaeval chastity belt was greeted in Malaita with distaste and in Wogeo with approbation. No less than a dozen men requested me to order one from Australia.[2]

Incidents similar to the following, which took place within the first week of my 1934 stay, occurred several times. Kajikmwa of Job had been in the forest and on his way back took a path leading through a patch of scrub that Kaiaf and his wife Mango of Bariat were in process of clearing. Kaiaf was out of sight, but, as is usual in such circumstances, Kajikmwa stopped for a chat and a smoke with Mango. When he had finished his cigarette he rose to leave, and at that moment Kaiaf approached from the opposite direction. Assuming that the meeting had been prearranged, he strode over and slapped Mango on both cheeks. Only with difficulty did she convince him of his mistake by insisting that she could have had no prior knowledge that he would be temporarily absent.

A month later our old acquaintance Kakameri of Mwarok subjected his wife Sanum to ill-treatment for innocently speaking to a young Takul villager named Yarong — he merely asked for a light for his cigarette as he passed her in the road. A few seconds later, when he was already on his way, he heard her scream and, turning, saw Kakameri, who had been following, hurl a tomahawk at her. She was stunned though by good luck not fatally wounded. Yet when Yarong stepped back to help her to her feet Kakameri ordered him to desist. 'Leave my wife alone, you man of fornication and trouble — I saw the two of you arranging to meet. Go, eater of excrement, go back to where you belong,' he stormed. Argument was useless in the face of such passion, and accordingly Yarong went home and reported what had occurred to the headman of his housing cluster. The latter first sought confirmation of the facts and then told him to send his sister to Kakameri with a demand for a dollar to wipe out the insult. She set out the next morning, but Kakameri possessed only twenty cents in cash, which he gave her. Yarong and the headman together subsequently went to Mwarok and asked for the remainder but had to be content with a basket of taro. (I repeat that in this period a dollar was a large sum: the monthly wage for a labourer was fifty cents.)

On still another occasion Jaua greeted Sale on her return from a visit to a distant village with a slap across the mouth. Women are always unfaithful when away from their husbands, he excused himself, and he had no scruples about administering punishment without positive evidence of impropriety.

The jealousy of some men, fortunately a small minority, reaches such pathological intensity that people avoid entering their houses. Wiap, the man mentioned above who tried to capture a spouse, never had a guest at his fireside during the whole of 1934. 'He's tied his wife's vulva to his belt,' the villagers used to say. 'Poor woman, he'd sew her up if he could. He beats her if a man sneezes in her presence for fear that the noise might have been a signal agreed upon for an assignation.' So fearful was he of letting her out of his sight that he rarely went fishing, and the household lived mainly on vegetables. If for some reason he was forced to be away he would set her a task and, on his return, closely question the village children concerning her whereabouts during each part of the day. He and the other three men of this type whom I encountered were all socially insignificant and of unattractive appearance. Wiap himself had the minimum of land under cultivation and no pigs; moreover, as was indicated, he suffered badly from ringworm.

Other husbands are philosophical and react only when confronted with incontrovertible evidence. Waru, perhaps more phlegmatic than the average, once remarked that all women had lovers, his own wife included. 'I want her to be true to me, but how can I stop her wandering?' he continued. 'I can't keep my finger in her vagina from sunrise to dark — as Wiap, that silly fellow, tries to do with his spouse — so I remain silent. Only if someone told me he'd run across her in the forest with a man would I make trouble.' Probably such persons are able to enjoy a fair measure of domestic peace, though their complacency may be a subject for jokes. People sometimes made fun of Wiawia behind his back for his trust and also his pride in his firstborn, who, according to rumour, was fathered collectively by the crew of a passing schooner.[3]

It is unlikely that jealousy is a male prerogative. As I said, a man commonly excuses misdemeanours with a plea that his wife was too suspicious. The underlying theme of many myths also is a wife's apprehension lest she should have been displaced. Her doubts are aroused when the husband on returning from work is not hungry — she concludes a rival must have fed him.

MARITAL AFFECTION

The prevalence of adultery raises the problem of whether Wogeo couples are devoid of fellow feeling. Certainly when in the presence of others they use no endearments, exchange no soft glances, and scrupulously avoid physical contact. Yet close observation reveals many examples of affection. Jaua and Sale, though they quarrelled so often, were a notable example of devotion: they had scores of private jokes, they often sat for an entire evening on the verandah alone playing with a litter of puppies, and he was constantly taking illustrations from books and magazines from my house for her to see. At the same time, he laughed off as preposterous the notion of an obligation to be faithful to her. One afternoon he came asking for tobacco. I gave him some at once and enquired why he wanted it. He replied that along the road he had just met a woman who insinuated that he might procure her a smoke and then meet her under a prominent fig tree in the forest not far away. Why was he risking his reputation in an adulterous intrigue, I wanted to know, especially as this woman was married to one of his near cousins? Had he not two wives already? Were these insufficient? He brushed my objections aside with the remark that the chances of discovery were slight as if need be I would be prepared to tell an untruth and back him up with an alibi. On my persisting he agreed that although in the early years of his married life he used to feel uncomfortable, that era was long since past. Would he prefer then to change Sale for someone else, perhaps the woman he was about to meet?, I needled. Of course not, came the answer: why was I being so obtuse? Could I not see the difference between a lifetime of marriage and a few moments of sexual indulgence? He hoped he was a good husband to both his wives, but nobody would want to bathe in the same water-hole all the time.

Mutual attachment is revealed most plainly in times of crisis. In childbirth the expectant father is almost as anxious about the mother's safety as she is, and if illness strikes a husband the woman shows every sign of distress. Bara, Sawang's wife, when he was suffering from pleurisy following an attack of influenza, sat motionless all night with his head pillowed on her breast; and Mujewa, Waru's wife, was equally attentive when he had an attack of dysentery. She left his side only to seek out various persons skilled in the magic to effect a cure. Matiti, who subsequently married Marigum, was an exception and continued to carry on an adulterous affair with him while her husband lay dying; but her conduct was still being criticized three years afterwards, though never to her face.

When an ailment proves fatal the survivor of the married pair is obliged by social convention to give way to an abandonment of grief, but it would be unreasonable to suppose that therefore the feelings expressed are not authentic: in most instances I am convinced they are. Nobody thinks that the widow, as in some communities, ought to make a show of attempting suicide, but many who are aged refuse every offer of remarriage and remain true to the husband's memory. A widely told folk-tale speaks of a bereaved wife as so desolate that she forsook her young children and followed his spirit to the world of the dead.

People take the oneness of spouses so much as a matter of course that, despite the admitted affection of siblings, they tend to assume when conflicts arise between a man and his brothers-in-law, and the woman's loyalties are in consequence divided, she will nearly always come round in the end to his point of view. They may well be right about couples who have been married for years and shared half a lifetime of pleasure and suffering, of satisfaction and disquiet; but I know of some young wives who were more inclined to consider their brothers' interests as paramount.

POLYGAMY

Men married for several years would all like to take an extra consort. Of the thirty-six husbands living in Dap and the villages nearby no less than thirteen maintained polygynous households. They were mainly persons of some consequence, though only Marigum and a headman of Mwarok, Wakalu, had more than two wives. The high infant mortality is the most usual explanation. Few women rear half their children, and a man with but one spouse has little hope of surrounding himself with a large family. A second wife also provides help in horticulture, thereby permitting the husband to keep up a good supply of food to distribute among his followers. Then in individual cases the attractions of youth must carry some weight. New Guinea women living in traditional surroundings use neither cosmetics to hide lines on the face nor supporting garments to conceal sagging breasts; hence they show their age earlier than men.

Though polygyny is so popular with members of the male sex, it can hardly be regarded as conducive to domestic peace and harmony. In only four of the thirteen cases were relations between the wives sufficiently tranquil to encourage regular collaboration in child care, housework, and gardening; and in five of the remainder they quarrelled so constantly and so violently that the husband was compelled to set up a separate establishment for each.

The villagers accept the situation, and several of them maintained that plural marriages invariably lead to discord. Were not the myths full of accounts of how in the time of the heroes co-wives were at odds with one another? The only way to minimize the risk was for the man to choose two sisters, and even then he could never be certain of avoiding trouble. Two of the four polygynous husbands whose wives lived in amity had, indeed, sought out a pair of sisters; but what about the other two, I wanted to know. The reply was that their spouses were exceptional.

The explanation for a severe gale that suddenly struck Dap was illuminating. One of the men who had taken shelter in my house remarked casually that Marigum had probably been neglecting Yam for another of his wives and this was her way of showing resentment. 'The wind looks like Yam's magic: how cross she is!' 'That's it — I saw him at work yesterday with Nyem,' a companion agreed.

Men who have remained monogamous often express smug satisfaction. 'We haven't many children, and our gardens are small; but the house is quiet, and that's pleasant,' they repeat. Yet the vindictiveness some of them displayed when a polygynist discovered one of his wives in flagrant adultery suggests a degree of envy. 'The silly fellow thought his one penis would satisfy two wives — as if it could! This'll teach nim,' a neighbour gloated.

The second marriage is almost always by elopement. The woman's relatives complain at length but seldom make a further demand for her return unless they have legitimate objections, as, for example, if the man is known to be lazy. The headmen of the housing clusters of the two may also make a demonstration, arguing that polygyny is their special privilege. A determined husband takes no notice, however, and brings his new bride back to the village. The first wife now makes a great commotion and at the earliest opportunity attacks her rival.

Wanang, the wife of Fandum of Bariat, when he eloped with Jongotaia sought the pair out in the garden where they were hiding and concealed herself nearby. After some time he went away to fetch betel pepper, leaving Jongotaia alone. Wanang sprang upon her, threw her to the ground, scratched her face, and tore her skirt. 'Bitch,' she spat — my report came from a chance passer-by, who dragged them apart — 'go before I kill you, for kill you I will if you enter my house.' That evening Fandum ushered Jongotaia inside before him, nevertheless, and announced that half of it was to be hers.

Sometimes the already established wife is so enraged that she inflicts grave injuries. Thus when Marigum ran off with Matiti, Yam almost killed her. She stalked the pair into the forest and after watching them embrace pounced upon the intruder with a gardening knife. 'Stealer of men with a vagina that's always itching,' she yelled as she made one deep gash after another. Matiti, with Marigum's assistance, managed to reach the nearest house, where she collapsed. He refused to leave her side till recovery was certain, and then he went to Dap in order to inform his followers of his intention to leave them forever. The older men, much alarmed lest in his anger he should use weather magic against them, begged Yam to accept a co-consort, and after much argument she allowed them to fetch Matiti. There was another fracas not long afterwards when Marigum persuaded Nyem, also a widow, to become his fourth wife (the first, Maijabra, had died some years before). Her sisters, fearing for her safety, begged her to reject the offer, but she declined, assuring them that Yam, once she had made her position clear, would be bound to calm down.

Occasionally the new wife becomes terrified at the show of opposition and, despite the man s promise of protection, runs back to her kinsmen. Sakma undoubtedly attracted the girl Jina, who did not hesitate to elope with him, but after his first wife Kabwas had given her three beatings and screamed threats of annihilating her she scorned all his entreaties and insisted on leaving. Wama, more original, chose public insult in a way of ridding herself of a co-wife. She waited till the village was full of visitors and threw a breadfruit in front of the woman. 'Stuff that up your vagina,' she yelled. 'That hole of yours is so big no man could fill it. Why, even this breadfruit will be lost.'

There are also times when the position is reversed, and the first wife packs her belongings and departs. She may return later, but if the husband still pays undue attention to his new bride she carries off the younger children and makes a home with one of her brothers. This action does not constitute divorce, which, as we shall see shortly, is unknown once there is a family, and as a rule the husband continues to clear garden land for her and bring her part of his catches of fish. She cooks his meals, too, and is ready to go with him to the bush for sexual intercourse.

Jaua was one of the men obliged to maintain separate households. He lived in Dap with Sale, his second wife; and the first, Salola, whom he had married in early manhood, occupied part of her brother's house in Mwarok with their two daughters. He always slept in Dap but often visited Salola and ate a meal with her every few days. When clearing ground for new cultivations, sometimes in Dap, sometimes in Mwarok, in both of which places he owned land, he also made a practice of putting up a fence in the middle and allocating half to each. He often complained of the inconvenience and lamented that Salola refused all his requests to come back to Dap. Few were sympathetic. The majority argued he had only himself to blame as Sale was so obviously his favourite. At the time of the second marriage, instead of allowing the customary fight, he warned Salola that he would hit her twice for every blow inflicted on Sale, and for a period lasting several months he never once ate the food she had prepared. She considered herself slighted and took the children to her brother's. After a time she went back but, finding herself still neglected, eventually persuaded the brother to make a spare room available for good.

Wives who agree on living together are supposed to be of equal status. Headmen, however, may have as many as four or five, one of whom is likely to be the eldest daughter of the consort of a headman. This woman will have been accustomed from childhood to deference and in consequence now takes the lead in all matters concerning the larger household, as, for example, when food has to be cooked for a feast. We know already that if of outstanding personality she earns the title of *mwaere*. But the other wives remain mistress in the affairs of their own families.

The women divide the house into sections, each with a fireplace and separate sleeping quarters. They also keep their utensils and other belongings apart and in the gardens tend their individual plots. If dinner is to be eaten at home, then ideally the children are also differentiated; for the most part those of the same mother congregate around her hearth. The father may take his food in the middle where he can converse with everybody and see all that is going on, or he may move out to the verandah and invite a couple of the boys and girls to join him. Often he remains in the club and calls for someone to bring his share there. The women either take turns to fill the basket he uses for snacks during the day, or else each puts in a little.

In very hot weather somebody may suggest dinner on the beach. The wives then pool their supplies, prepare the vegetables together, and cook in the one pot. At times neighbouring households may combine in this way for a sort of picnic.

Despite the divided dwelling, dissension is more frequent than concord, as I have indicated. Sabuk's matrimonial troubles were characteristic. His two spouses, Uj and Bagim, hated one another so bitterly that after some months, during which they had cut seventeen of each other's skirts to pieces and smashed nine pots — figures quoted by the neighbours — he persuaded the former to move into one of the apse rooms. The latter, as the younger and more recently wed, ought to have gone, but, a person of great determination, she refused to budge. Squabbles still occurred when the two were together, nevertheless, and they often came to blows over the allocation of gardens, each declaring that her plots were inferior or too full of stones. His ailments were another cause of disputes. He ate with them alternately, and each blamed the bad cooking of the other. 'That's that lazy good-for-nothing Bagim who always gives you food raw,' Uj announced when he complained of abdominal pains. 'Raw food yourself, you stinking hag. You've given him something putrid and are now blaming me for it — that's what's wrong,' came the reply. 'Speak once more, speak but one word, and I'll tear out your tongue, you faithless hussy with a gaping vagina,' Uj hurled back. Sabuk cuffed them both and sent them indoors.

Bagim's stock retort to abuse was that, as the mother of three children, she was at least not barren. This aroused Uj to fury, for she had had to adopt her only son. One day when they had drawn blood in their fighting Sabuk became so angry that he formally disowned the boy, who, he said, must go back to his true parents. His action was without precedent, but he imitated the ritual used when a child receives its name. He split the stalk of a ginger plant down the middle and passed it over the lad's head, simultaneously sprinkling him with the fluid from a green coconut. Although in deadly earnest at the time, after the lapse of a few days he welcomed the boy back from Uj's relatives, whither the two had fled. 'People try to separate me from my son, but they'll never succeed, no never,' he murmured in my ear.

The neighbours believed that every misfortune each of these two women suffered was the result of the other's black magic, but oddly enough they denied that either would visit her enmity on the children. 'What, inflict the son of her husband with disease? Never!' they insisted on my enquiring whether Uj was responsible for the illness of one of Bagim's sons. 'She detests her and wouldn't look after her family — yes, that's true. But kill them? Impossible!' Bagim herself did not appear to harbour suspicion, and when, to test her reaction, I counselled her to rest and leave the infant for an hour or two with Uj, the reason she gave for refusing was merely that Uj might neglect him. 'She's so lazy that she'd make him wait till tomorrow if he only wanted a drink,' was her answer. Uj did not appear to be interested and made no offer of assistance.

In households of this kind relations between a woman and her step-children are mostly polite but formal. Bagim, usually ready to bandy playful remarks with the small fry, was in general stiff in her dealings with Uj's son, and although she occasionally gave him titbits, she seldom asked him to run errands. Uj appeared to surround herself with a barrier when with Bagim's family and was clearly more at ease with other children.

The few co-wives who live amicably together provide a striking contrast. Far from differentiating their families, they seem almost to pool them. Tago's[4] house in Kinaba, one of the happiest on the island, revealed an example of such a sharing. His spouses, Sei and Su, were first cousins and demonstrative in their feelings for one another. At mealtimes the two sets of half-siblings usually sat on opposite sides, but otherwise I could scarcely sort them out.

The behaviour of mothers is reflected in that of their children. Karing and Manoua, sons respectively of Uj and Bagim, though of approximately the same age, were rarely together unless other boys were present; Yanag and Maganubwa, sons of Sei and Su, were inseparable.

DIVORCE

The most significant feature of Wogeo marital relations is that full separation never in any circumstances takes place after the birth of children. This is perhaps the more surprising in view of the absence of any payment during the wedding ceremony. While there is no absolute correlation between the presentation of brideprice and marriage stability, it is a fact that when wealth is handed over the recipients, afraid lest they should be called upon to make a refund, tend to bring pressure to bear on quarrelling man and wife to have them compose their differences instead of parting.[5]

The causes of new marriages breaking up include clash of temperament, preference for someone else, adultery too often repeated, laziness, and cruelty. The woman retains her dowry land, if any, but often she leaves the cooking pots and other household goods behind. A man who is sick of his wife ignores her. He refuses the food she sets before him and goes off to eat with relatives. Humiliated, she at length packs up her clothing and departs, as she also does when taking the initiative. In the latter event she simply walks out and goes back to her parents. The father may at first insist on her returning to the husband, but in the end firmness and resolution always win.

The arrival of an infant alters the situation in that the woman has no right to take it with her. She may be prepared to abandon her husband but apparently never the child, and treatment that before would have aroused her indignation she now accepts. Mera remained outwardly unmoved by her husband's infatuation with Rikoa. At the height of the affair he followed the girl everywhere, and even when he finally realized that she would not marry him he still refused to enter his own dwelling. 'Yes, it's bad for me because I can't get away. You see, I could never leave my son,' Mera answered when I expressed sympathy. As we have seen, ill-treatment must also now be tolerated. The only comment after the brutal Kakameri assaulted Sanum was, 'What a pity the marriage ever took place!' They had a child, and divorce was therefore out of the question.

Women with a family also resist any temptation to elope with a lover. Jagamwein, Waj's wife, was rumoured to be so fascinated by Salam, a handsome man several years her junior, that she rejected all other invitations to a casual liaison. After the two of them had been caught together in the forest for the third time she admitted to a cousin, whose husband came hotfoot with the story to me, that he had on several occasions urged her to fly with him to one of the other Schouten Islands, where they could remain till the scandal of their conduct had died down. 'But, alas, I cannot leave my babies: if I went away they would never call me "mother",' she lamented in unconscious imitation of the Victorian heroine of the once best seller *East Lynne*. Waj, righteously angry, thrashed her severely but never ordered her out of the house. He well knew that no one else would take the same care of the children.

DISSOLUTION BY DEATH

A polygynist with a dead wife faces few practical problems. The remaining woman, or women, has now to accept full responsibility for looking after him and the orphans. But a monogamous widower with a young family must consider remarriage almost as soon as he emerges from formal mourning. Of prime importance is finding someone who appears most likely to carry out the duties of a stepmother efficiently. His first choice, if such a person is available, is a sister or cousin of the dead woman, a relative who already treats the children as though they were her sons and daughters. Also ideal, and for the same reason, is the widow of a deceased brother. These preferences, from one point of view so obvious, may perhaps seem curious in the light of certain aspects of the kinship terminology. As was mentioned, a man calls both types of sister-in-law by the word for 'mother', and a woman calls both types of brother-in-law 'son'; moreover, extra-marital sexual relations with the sister of a living wife,[6] or the wife of a living brother, constitute the worst form of adultery. The explanation for the change of attitude is twofold — death has broken the family unit, thereby rendering the prohibition void; and the interests of the children must predominate.

Should there be no sister-in-law, the young widower looks further afield. He may have to be satisfied with a widow or a woman whose good name has been tarnished by scandal.

Elderly widowers seldom think of remarriage. They now depend for subsistence on their sons and daughters-in-law and to a lesser extent, because usually these live in other villages, their daughters and sons-in-law. A man with no surviving son may be forced to change his place of residence in order to live with a daughter. It will be remembered that this is what the murdered Moga, Marigum's alleged killer, had done (p. 62).

Considering how little the seniors can affect marriage choices, and the absence of bridal payments, it is scarcely to be expected that people would regard a woman as permanently incorporated into the group occupying her husband's housing cluster. On his death therefore his brothers are not obliged to reconfirm her position — they have neither the responsibility for taking her as an extra wife, nor, should one of them be single, is it assumed that he will necessarily wed her. In general she is free to do as she pleases. Most often, if she is still young, she returns to her natal village, where her brothers look after her till she finds another husband. The children needing care accompany her, though the boys, who inherit their dead father's land, go back eventually to take up residence with a paternal uncle. Kasule, originally of Dap, decided after her husband's death in Job that she would be happier in her birthplace, and thither she brought her two daughters and a son, Tabulbul, to live with her mother and a brother. The lad stayed till he was about eight, when he told me he had grown tired of walking backwards and forwards between the two settlements, which are a kilometre or so apart. Such arrangements would also have been followed had Kasule during this period married again (later on she accepted an offer to become Kawang's fifth wife). Tabulbul would have lived with his step-father for just as long as he chose to be near his mother.

Only a headman's widow is positively required to stay on in his village. Out of respect for his memory she is expected also not to remarry.[7] The brothers-in-law support her until the children are old enough to fulfil the obligation. Elderly widows of ordinary men generally remain where they have spent their adult lives, though some of them, when too old to work, may have to move to where a daughter is living.

A further word about the marriage of Marigum and Nyem will

be of interest. Her first husband had belonged to Bajor in Bukdi, but the union was unfruitful, and they adopted two boys, Ulbai and Sabwakai, the latter the younger son of Marigum and Yam. On the husband's death Nyem returned to Wonevaro, and Marigum asked her to become his fourth wife. 'We needed an extra worker for the gardens, and I also wanted Sabwakai back,' he intimated. The idea of regaining the companionship of her son also appealed to Yam, who raised much less objection to this match than to that with Matiti on the earlier occasion. Yet her manners were always scrupulously correct, and in the house she never interefered in the boy's relations with his foster mother. At mealtimes usually Nyem, Ulbai, and Sabwakai sat around one hearth, and Yam, Dal — if he was at home — and a daughter Jauon sat at another.

Sabwakai, by 1947 in his mid twenties, was a member of the crew of the canoe lost with all hands on a voyage to the mainland just before my second visit to Wogeo (Mot, the war hero, was drowned on the same expedition, p. 182, n. 4). Both women, Yam and Nyem, begged me with many tears to entreat the District Officer in Wewak to institute a thorough search to see whether he had been cast up on some deserted island.

7 Cases of Adultery and Theft

The one expression *mwang-tabo*, literally 'good-not', has to perform a double duty. It stands not only for 'bad' in the sense of unpleasant or technologically inadequate, as applied, for example, to inclement weather or poor workmanship, but also for 'wrong', implying disapproval, distaste, contempt, derision, or ridicule. When anyone uses it in criticism of unseemly behaviour, however, he leaves no doubt that his judgement has a moral basis. With scant regard for the truth, especially should his past be unknown to those present, he loudly proclaims that he neither has been nor ever would be guilty of such conduct. He may then add, as incontrovertible testimony, that the culture heroes uttered their condemnation in the strongest terms and left behind records enshrined in the mythology of the sufferings experienced by such of their number as yielded to temptation. Thus the hero Wonka and the woman he seduced, the wife of his blood-brother Mafofo, although they escaped when the angry husband attempted to burn them alive, were in the end obliged to hide their shame by emigrating to a place inhabited by foreigners, a dreadful fate.[1]

As might be gathered from the previous chapter, people deviate from rectitude most frequently in their dealings with other men's wives. I shall begin with this type of misdemeanour.

The headman seldom intervenes on his own initiative, but the unobtrusive presence is of profound influence on the attitude of his followers. They gain confidence from the knowledge that he will be ready with active support if appealed to, should they feel too weak to enforce their legitimate claims or resist the unjust demands of an opponent.

Culpability in adultery is reckoned by degree, and some forms are held to be worse than others. The most heinous is for a man to carry on an affair with the spouse of a close relative — or for a woman to commit an indiscretion with a close relative of her spouse — particularly a brother or someone else from the same housing cluster or village. As we saw with Waki's death (p. 56),

101

vice on this scale is supposed to bring about its own punishment. The injured husband, if he is wise, refrains from taking action against the offenders. Grievously sinned against he may have been, but only by sticking to the precepts relating to the bearing of near kinsmen can he hope to remain blameless. He must stay his hand and keep quiet, pinning his faith on retribution striking from the world of the supernatural.

At the other extreme is adultery with a comparative stranger from another district. Regarded as a matter of ethics, this is but a trifle; on the other hand, the practical consequences may be armed conflict.

ADULTERY WITHIN THE VILLAGE

Jaua cited Waru's behaviour after his wife's adultery with Tafalti, Marigum's eldest son, as approximating to the approved prototype. Waru was the medical orderly for his district and a year or so before had taken passage in a visiting schooner to the government station in order to replenish his stock of medicines. Communications were so poor that he had to wait for three months before he could return, and during this period rumour linked the name of his wife Mujewa with that of Tafalti. When the gossip reached Waru's ears, within a week of his arrival back, he sought corroboration forthwith from Jaua. The latter equivocated, denying that he had heard the stories, and warned that it would be stupid to raise the question publicly as there were no facts to go upon. Let Waru give Mujewa a thrashing if he wished, but he should do so in the privacy of the gardens, not in the village where the neighbours would hear. If Tafalti was really her lover he would then know of his discovery and be ashamed. Waru took the advice, and scandal was averted. His bearing towards his rival remained outwardly cordial, though he several times seized the chance when we were alone to denigrate Tafalti's character and attributes. The fellow was lazy and untrustworthy, he told me, not an active man of honour like his father. No wonder Marigum loved Dal more. The charge of disingenuousness might have been sustained, but, according to others, not that of indolence (p. 141).

Sabuk also avoided accusing Sawang, Marigum's half-brother's son, of intriguing with Bagim, the woman who so often fought with her co-wife Uj (pp. 95, 96). Yet he must have felt justified in inviting sympathy, for he attempted to burn his house down. The episode ended on a comic note in that the whole thing turned out to have been based on error. Sabuk is hard of hearing and on this occasion, as so often previously, had misinterpreted the most innocent of remarks. (A short time before, on observing two

7 Cases of Adultery and Theft

youths laughing, he had smashed the canoe on which he was working: he thought they were making fun of his clumsiness, though actually they were unaware of his presence and were amusing themselves by making up funny stories.)

Late in the afternoon when the men had all returned from work and were waiting for their dinners we heard a commotion and then cries from Sabuk's house. In a moment he emerged with a firebrand, which he hurled on the roof. Two bystanders jumped forward to hold him while a third hoisted a youth up to grab the torch before the sago-leaf could catch. Sabuk knocked aside those who were restraining him, dashed back into the dwelling for an axe, and now began chopping away at one of the corner posts. This time the whole crowd combined to disarm him. There was a tremendous hubbud, with him loudly weeping and everyone else shouting and yelling. At first we thought he had run amok, as some men do from time to time, but at length he appeared to grow calmer. When liberated, nevertheless, he strode away into the gathering darkness. A relative followed, while the rest of us tried to solve the puzzle. It appeared that on his return from the cultivations he had begun some job which he suddenly left to attack Bagim and savagely beat her. The kinsman, now back again, could tell us nothing. Adultery seemed to be the most likely explanation, but who could the man be? Nobody had the slightest idea.

A few days later we pieced the ridiculous story together. Sabuk must have been standing alongside when Wiawia, who lived next door, mentioned to his wife that the woman Bara was menstruating but there was no need that evening to think of a meal for her husband Sawang as Bagim had already sent him some food — Wiawia had seen her give the dish to a young boy to carry across to the house at the opposite end of the village. Someone undertook to explain to Sabuk, who still stayed away for another week. To all outward appearances his family affairs then reverted to normal. The other villagers refrained from seeking him out, but this they seldom did at any time — his deafness rendered him such a difficult companion.

Many years before, when Marigum was probably less famous than he subsequently became, his first wife Maijabra, long since dead, was unfaithful with one of the neighbours. He also made no open reproaches but instead set fire to his house. On that occasion the building was reduced to ashes and all the personal property destroyed. The lover at once made off for relatives living in another district.

Not all husbands have enough self-control to keep silent or

destroy their dwellings, and some overstep the mark and pour open abuse on the lover. This is most likely to happen if they catch the pair *in flagrante delicto*. Such a case occurred in 1933 not long before my arrival. Samara of Job became unsure of his wife and decided to set a trap. He told her he was going into the forest to collect cane to renew the lashings of his canoe outrigger and then concealed himself in a thicket just outside the village. Presently she emerged and went along the beach. He followed at a distance and, to his astonishment, saw her meet his own brother's son Karabase, her nephew by marriage. Obviously the rendezvous had been arranged, and the two sneaked into the bush. Samara crept along behind and burst upon them while they were in a passionate embrace. No satisfactory explanation was possible, and they fled at once, Karabase to Takul, the woman to her brother's in Mwarok. Samara went back to Job, beat the slit-gong and screamed his grievance. He mentioned his wife and Karabase by name and described in intimate detail what he had seen.

Two or three days later a young headman from Bariat, Fandum, who was closely related to Samara and hence to Karabase, set out for Takul and brought the latter home to make his peace. He spent the night in Bariat, whither somebody had now fetched the woman. Next morning all adjourned to Job, where the elders tried to find out which was the more at fault. She alleged that Karabase had pulled her against her will with love magic, whereas he asserted that he had yielded only after repeated overtures from her. No decision could be reached about who was telling lies, and after some discussion Fandum announced that Karabase must pay compensation. Within a few days the young man was able to scrape together four dollars, which he handed over for Fandum to present. But he was too ashamed to face his uncle and continued to keep well away from Job. Not long afterwards a recruiting schooner called in and made escape possible. Like so many wrongdoers of the present day, he signed on as a plantation labourer. Samara's wife returned to him, and when I made their acquaintance they appeared to have settled down together again.

Sufficient time had elapsed before my enquiries for people to consider the incident objectively. Most of them professed to be scandalized and insisted that had Karabase not gone away they would have ostracized him. This I doubt. They may have derided him behind his back, but it is unlikely that they would have taunted him to his face. Certainly the woman, his partner in transgression, escaped overt discrimination. Samara's outburst the villagers excused, arguing that his observing the culprits in the very act of copulation must have so aggravated him that he was

7 Cases of Adultery and Theft

beside himself with rage. All the same, he had reached the limit of what was permissible, and a further move against Karabase would not have been justified.

The only persons showing much sympathy for the adulterer were his elder brother and brother-in-law, who between them had provided the compensation money. The latter pleaded youth as vindication. The main fault was neglect of precautions against discovery, he said. I was unable to decide whether this man was guided by the loyalty due to an affine or was a cynic by temperament.

A further case of adultery within the housing cluster came to light some four or five months after my reaching the island. This time the person dishonoured was the headman Fandum, just mentioned. The offenders were his second wife Jongataia and his half-brother Kaiaf.

One afternoon after some heavy work fencing a new plot Fandum left the gardens while his two wives were still planting taro shoots. He started out for Bariat but when half way turned into the bush to collect a supply of betel pepper. He was himself fully concealed but caught a glimpse of Kaiaf and Jongotaia through a gap in the bushes as, on hearing voices, he looked towards the path. What they were saying sounded suspicious, and, going nearer to listen, he found they were arranging an assignation for the following day. Immediately he took a short cut to the village, where he began beating the slit-gong. When the people had gathered he gave a long harangue, though without mentioning names, on the falseness of wives and vileness of brothers. Next morning Kaiaf was missing, and so also was one of the larger canoes. The villagers concluded, rightly as it turned out, that he had paddled to the island of Koil some twenty kilometres distant.

Dap was agog with the news. Everyone sympathized with Fandum and some decided they would that evening send him gifts of food as evidence of their commiseration. What a pity Jongotaia already had a child, they went on. If only there were no infant he could have divorced her. A woman who caused trouble between brothers ought to be sent away before she created further mischief. As for Kaiaf, he was a disgrace. The enormity of what he had done would not be forgotten in a hurry, and for the time being he was better out of the way. After a week, however, Fandum sent word for him to come back and accept a reconciliation.

Kaiaf wasted no time and appeared the next evening. The other Bariat headman, Kauni, then took charge. As was appropriate for a mediator, he belonged to the opposite moiety. He requested the two brothers to sit together in the centre of the village and ordered their wives to place platters of food before them. He made a short formal speech urging them to eat together and return to co-operation along the old lines. My Dap neighbours assured me that the fact that someone from the other moiety had intervened would make them too ashamed to abuse each other openly no matter what might lie in their thoughts.

For a short interval all seemed to go well, but Fandum soon took both his wives to the house of a cousin in Mwarok. Everybody knew the reason — try as he might, he could not obliterate the knowledge of what had occurred. The sight of Kaiaf made him want to punch and fight and accordingly it was better to avoid him, so he told me. In a month or two he might not feel so bitter.

Before the time was up the government vessel arrived with police on board to arrest a deserter who had failed to complete his labour contract (in those days the indenture system carried penal sanctions). Kaiaf, with the object of stirring Fandum to pity, announced that he would seek a passage in her to the plantation where he had worked as a youth. His wife and four children could stay for the present, but as soon as he was settled he would send for them. Despite urgings from Marigum and others, Fandum did not try to stop him, and, convinced that there was now no alternative, Kaiaf left in the ship. Four months later, as he had promised, he made a brief return visit to fetch his family.

STRIKING THE GONG

The first move of a husband determined to publish his anger is beating the slit-gong. His acknowledged aim, as we have seen, is to ensure a circle of listeners. People recognize, however, that the very act of banging away with a stout pole on the hollowed-out piece of tree-trunk, and raising a great deal of noise in the process, can in itself have a therapeutic effect. The just man may, indeed, be he who hides his spleen under a cloak of silence and equanimity, but what if in the face of extreme provocation, and the consequent strong emotion, this is beyond his power? An expression of feeling is then allowed, even admitted to be beneficial, though only provided violence is turned against inanimate objects. I draw attention once more to the proverb, 'When cross with your wife you should smash a pot; otherwise you'll be out of temper for a month.' The islanders repeatedly told of their satisfaction once somebody known to be concealing resentment at last advanced upon the gong and said out loud what was the matter with him. 'This is far as it will go,' they would reassure me. 'Now we know there'll be no taking down of spears and arrows.'

7 Cases of Adultery and Theft

ADULTERY WITH THE WIFE OF A HEADMAN

Fandum had passed through the nomination ceremony and thus was truly a headman, but in 1934 he was no more than thirty-five and so far had scarcely made an impression outside his own cluster. The events surrounding the liaison between his half-brother Kaiaf and Jongotaia hence gave little indication of the reaction when someone is discovered in an intrigue with the wife of his leader. Briefly, the lover is in extreme jeopardy. The affront to the husband's dignity is so great that, as he has the authority, he usually sees fit to override the obligations and responsibilities of kinship. His other followers, except perhaps those who belong to the adulterer's immediate family, are also sensitive to the slight and ready to give him their full backing. For an example we must return to Kajug, the younger half-brother of Janggara, the second Gol headman. It will be recalled that this man eloped with Kole, one of Kawang's wives. I have already discussed how in the final stages of the affair, in 1947, Marigum gave orders for the Wonevaro seniors to murder him (p. 63). Now I want to go back to the beginning.

It all started in March 1934, when one morning neither Kajug nor Kole could be found. Soon people realized that during the night they had made off together for the forest. Kawang at once sent his — and my — brother Sangani around the island to report their absence to the various headmen and request them to take steps to prevent anyone offering the pair sustenance or shelter. Sangani spent the night in Dap and was for a couple of hours with me. I learned that some of the older men from Gol had had to be physically restrained from pursuing Kajug then and there with spears and that even Janggara had declined to petition Kawang for mercy. 'They deserve to die, both of them,' he had pronounced. 'He's my brother, but I would seek no vengeance should he be killed.'

After a month, during which they ate wild roots or stole from the gardens, Kajug and Kole turned up one evening in Falala at the house of her sister's husband, who gave them a meal and allowed them to stay the night. But in the morning the headman Kaman sounded the slit-gong for some minutes and solemnly ordered Kajug to leave. Kole, he declared, was to remain, and he would return her to her lawful spouse. Kajug departed immediately, and later in the day some of Kaman's relatives led Kole to Gol. She crept into Kawang's house, but he took no notice. Then the next morning when she attempted to start out for the cultivations he told her to stop at home until he gave permission for her to leave. That evening she tried to help with the cooking, but he dashed the knife and dish from her hands.

The following day at about noon, when the rest of the villagers were all away at work, Kajug climbed down from the hills and begged her to come back to him. She must have been infatuated and needed little persuasion. They fled to the forest once more, and no one saw them for two or three weeks. This time they appealed to Kaiaf, who was married to Kajug's sister (Kaiaf's adultery with Jongotaia had not yet occurred – or was for the present unknown – and he was still living in Bariat). He helped Kajug to build a shelter in the foothills behind the village, and this the couple were occupying when I departed during the December. Kaiaf let them take taro from his gardens until their own, planted on land he made available, was ready. The two Bariat headmen, Fandum and Kauni, remained silent, presumably because, lacking in presence, they felt inadequate to deal with the situation (Fandum, as was mentioned, was no more than thirty-five, and Kauni might have been slightly his junior).

After some time Kajug began appearing in public once more, and I occasionally saw him in Bariat sitting with the men during the evening. They showed no discomfort in his presence but neither invited him to share in communal tasks nor gave him any assistance with his gardening. Once he showed up in Gol, though he took pains to keep out of Kawang's way. A food festival was in progress, and killing was therefore taboo, but the guests were amazed at his boldness and lack of shame. On the other hand, he never once set foot in Dap. This was just as well according to Marigum, who said he would have aimed a spear at him.

The rest of the story I heard in 1974–5 when I was trying to find out how Jaua had died. Kajug kept on in Bariat for only a week or two after I left the island. Early in January 1935 he went by canoe with Kole to Koil and from there took the first schooner to the mainland, where he joined Kaiaf on the plantation. All returned to Wogeo – the two men, their wives, and the children – in 1942. Five years later, as already recorded, Kajug, after wounding Jaua in self-defence, allegedly became the victim of sorcery administered at Marigum's instigation in punishment for the wrong done to Kawang, who by then was dead. Kaiaf survived for a decade or perhaps longer. My informants, a few of whom had been in their late teens at the time of the original adultery, were positive about the reasons for the precipitate voyage to Koil and the subsequent sojourn on the mainland. They admitted that Kajug had lost his main protector with the flight of Kaiaf, but much more significant, so they maintained, was my own departure. As long as I was there he felt reasonably safe, but with me gone Kawang, and Marigum also, would have no compunction about removing him either directly with some weapon or indirectly with *yabou*. After the lapse of years he imagined that he could count on forgiveness — but discovered to his cost that pardon is seldom if ever forthcoming for an offence against a headman.

Fandum was dying of tuberculosis when I went back in 1948, and not long afterwards Kauni perished after being gored by a wild boar. It was hardly a general opinion, but two or three men, none of them resident in Dap, were a quarter of a century later still convinced that sorcery was responsible, engineered by either Kawang's relatives or Marigum. The deaths were a judgement for not driving Kajug out of Bariat, they said. I pointed out that Fandum was the son of Marigum's half-sister, but they dismissed this as irrelevant.

Jaua also was guilty of adultery with a headman's wife, but as the offence was not discovered I shall for the present delay giving an account of what happened.

A husband whose wife is unfaithful with a man of high rank has no redress apart from giving her a beating. But a headman who too often takes advantage of his position suffers a loss of reputation and soon forfeits the respect of his followers, who become dilatory in carrying out his wishes. None of the leaders of today is notorious as a womanizer, although Marigum seduced Matiti, who became his third wife, while her spouse lay dying. The liaison caused much gossip at the time, but his prestige was not seriously affected. This was his only lapse since early manhood, so the people believed, and they were prepared to overlook it.

There has been no case in recent years of a headman committing adultery with the wife of someone of equal standing. If we were to accept the statements about past incidents we would say the penalty was death by sorcery if not by the thrust of a spear. As I have explained in an earlier chapter, however, such stories are not to be trusted (pp. 66, 67). When in due course the alleged offender dies, sometimes after years and years have gone by, the person injured, or his successor, always brags that the account is now settled; but as sorcery of the *yabou* type has no reality we can disregard what he says.

ADULTERY WITH A WOMAN FROM A NEIGHBOURING VILLAGE

The residents of the same district are all related, some of them just as closely as the householders of the one village, though in different ways. As was mentioned, the sons of two brothers are likely to be living in adjoining dwellings, but the sons of two sisters, or of a brother and a sister, more often than not belong to distant settlements. Adultery with a woman from a kilometre or so away is therefore considered to be almost as bad as with one from across the street. People say the wronged husband, on learning of what has been going on, should hold his peace, at all events for the time being. His chance to punish the wife's lover will come at the next food festival, when for a short period the rules governing the behaviour of kinsfolk are suspended, and every person is allowed to attack those against whom he holds a grudge, thereby ridding himself of his pent up indignation (p. 166). Weapons are barred, and in consequence severe wounds are unlikely, but I have seen stones flying; and black eyes, cuts, and bruises are a commonplace. Once when the fighting started earlier than expected I found myself hemmed in a corner near some of the combatants. On the signal for them to stop I was dripping with blood, not mine but theirs. Then there was the occasion when I saw a man pick up a dog by the loose skin of its back and hurl it in the face of his opponent. (The animal was killed in the fracas and its carcase added to the feast.)

I shall discuss the four cases that took place in the Wonevaro district during 1934 but in the reverse order to their occurrence. The repercussions were progressively less serious, and hence it will be convenient to begin with the last and work backwards to the one resulting in the worst upset. In the mildest example the young man Kamagun of Job, married for about a year, was the husband, and Sawang of Dap the lover.

How Kamagun came to doubt his wife I do not know, but when he taxed her she admitted an intimacy with Sawang lasting a couple of months. He struck her in the face and round the shoulders and then went outside to enlist the support of such of the men as were present in the village for a march on Dap, where he intended, so he said, to beat the slit-gong and announce to everyone what a scoundrel Sawang was. His contemporaries were prepared to accompany him, but the elders urged caution. It was unfitting for anybody so young to turn his back on custom and bring public shame on a relative even if the latter was in the wrong, they argued. Marigum would also be annoyed, and there was always the risk that, as Sawang was his nephew, he might upbraid the accusers for insolence. Kamagun must wait till the next ritual fight. Though initially unwilling to accept such counsel, he in the end agreed. For the next few weeks he and the men of his cluster indulged themselves by dwelling on the drubbing they intended to give Sawang later.

7 Cases of Adultery and Theft

By the evening the story had travelled to Dap, where it formed the main topic of conversation. The villages were critical of Sawang, though they showed little bitterness and avoided the subject if he was actually present. He continued to go about his work as usual and in the afternoons sat with the rest of us in the club or on the beach. People assured me that he felt uncomfortable, but if so he must have been an expert at concealment. Dal remarked with some satisfaction that he would inherit the same system of love magic but added piously that he would reserve it for winning over girls who were as yet unwed.

Shortly before this Tafalti was found to have committed adultery with the wife of Waj, a villager from Kinaba. The latter was in his late twenties or early thirties and already had a couple of children, but he was a retiring type and allowed his elder brother Tago[2] to act as his spokesman. Tago was content to beat the slit-gong but in his own settlement alone. He reviled Tafalti and ended up by saying that he was the worst wrongdoer in the whole of Wonevaro. Many marriages had been spoiled through him, and were it not for his being the son of so great a headman as Marigum those he had injured would have arranged for sorcery to be performed against him.

Later I asked Tago why he had confined his tirade to Kinaba and not repeated it in Dap. That would have been inappropriate, he explained. Waj, as a kinsman, ought not to confront Tafalti; and, besides, Tago himself was married to Marigum's sister and thus had to consider the additional affinal relationships.

Again the Dap folk passed strictures on the culprit, though they did not scorn his company. Like Sawang, he went about his business with apparent unconcern.

In the third case Sawang had the role not of lover but of husband. A party of pig hunters ran across his wife Bara in the company of Kajikmwa, a man from Job. They were deep in the forest, and an innocent explanation was out of the question. She did not try to excuse herself but made her way home as fast as she could. The hunters told Sawang of their discovery, and that evening he came and sat in the centre of the village. Marigum was away, but it was a fine night, and the other men gathered around him. He told them how angry he was and of his wish to accuse Kajikmwa openly. Before taking such a step, however, he wanted to know what the others thought. Should he swallow the insult and keep quiet, as he admitted might be correct, or would it be reasonable to march on Job? At first opinion was divided, with some arguing one way and some the other, but in the end the hot-heads carried the day, possibly because Marigum was not there to restrain them. They determined that the descent should be made the following morning soon after daylight. Waru was especially vehement. He paced up and down waving his arms and exclaiming, 'Do they think we are children? Who does Kajikmwa imagine he is? Are we his cooks?' (When a feast is taking place the most junior persons present have the arduous and unpleasant task of preparing the oven, and to call a man a cook is to imply that he is of little account.)

While the discussion was in progress two or three women paid a visit to Bara and scolded her for her looseness. She left during the night to take refuge with relatives in Mwarok, but these also found fault, and she soon came back to suffer the usual beating from her husband.

When the group broke up I walked back with Waru and entered his house for a further talk about the affair. His wife was serving dinner, and he began by recounting what had been decided. I soon gathered that he was not as distressed as his earlier statements had led me to believe. It appeared that a few days before he and Sawang had had a slight brush over some garden work and had parted with hard feelings. He agreed therefore that underneath his expressed rage was a measure of satisfaction at Sawang's dishonour. He had 'two insides' *(ilo rua)* and was simultaneously filled with pain and pleasure.[3] He told me that, naturally, when somebody humiliates your close kinsman you too are demeaned. The links between you and your relatives are strong, and an injury or insult to them is the same as an injury or insult to you. The reputation of the whole lot of you is lowered, and each must do his part to restore the good name. By such means mutual protection is achieved. Punishing an offender serves as a warning to others who might contemplate following his example. But where the kinsman suffering the wrong has himself previously provoked you, then deep down you may also rejoice. You always hide these sweet thoughts when abroad, reserving them for ventilation solely at the family fireside.

I wanted to know why, when previously he had insisted that with adulteries in which the parties were from the same district retaliation should be postponed till the next ritual fight, he now urged Sawang to take immediate action against Kajikmwa. Was this a case of still a third inside? Not at all, he replied. Normally, indeed, in circumstances of this kind the husband ought to bide his time; but here was the exceptional situation. Dap was the village concerned, and, as I well knew. it was a special place. Had I not chosen it myself? Marigum's living there made it the most

7 Cases of Adultery and Theft

important settlement on Wogeo, and the residents were entitled to expect deference from all, not hurt. Further, Sawang was not only Marigum's nephew, the son of his half-brother, but also an elder in his own right and far from a mere boy. He was to be commended for proceeding cautiously and seeking the support of his fellows before striking the Job slit-gong, and, of course, they all backed him up. But other people should not accept this as the pattern for what ought to go on always. The general rule for them was still to try and forget till a festival provided the chance for an answer.

Neutral observers, men with no immediate Dap connections, as, for instance, many from the Bagiau and Ga districts, dismissed Waru's arguments as specious. The Dap residents were not entitled to particular privileges — they were no different from other people — and the fact of Marigum's being one of them was not pertinent, they reiterated. Sawang should have put resentment at the back of his mind until a suitable occasion presented itself for a fight with Kajikmwa.

The expedition set out for Job in the morning headed by Sawang. Marigum was still absent and took no part (he may in any case have avoided doing so, for his wife Yam was originally from Job, and he would have had little desire to entangle himself in a dispute with his affines). Sawang beat the slit-gong while his supporters took up a menacing attitude behind. He swore at Kajikmwa in the vernacular and in pidgin English — which to the islanders sounds rather worse — and generally vilified him. Then, after about ten minutes, they all retreated. The Job villagers remained within their houses and did not attempt to reply.

For some weeks Kajikmwa kept to himself and avoided the neighbours. He left for the gardens soon after daybreak and returned just before nightfall, making straight for his dwelling (he was a married man). At no time did he enter the club, and he made no visits to Dap or any of the other settlements till about a month had passed. The Job elders agreed that he ought to pay Sawang three or four dollars as compensation, but as he had little cash of his own one of them undertook to take up a collection. This man subsequently handed the money over to Sawang. He also warned Kajikmwa to mend his ways. People might sympathize with him this once, but he must beware of trying their patience too often.

In the final incident to be recorded here the erring wife was our old acquaintance Sanum, the ill-used daughter of Marigum, married to the bullying Kakameri of Mwarok. Veu of Job was the lover, a handsome young man not long returned from completing his contract as a plantation labourer on the mainland. Kakameri, quick tempered as always, did not even seek guidance about what he should do. During the early evening he struck the Mwarok slit-gong, told the villagers of Sanum's disgrace, and announced that he was off to Job to revile Veu. A few minutes later he strode out, followed by most of the men. Arrived at his destination, he beat the gong loudly and then ran among the houses gesticulating wildly and shouting that had the government not prohibited killing he would have speared Veu on the spot. As it was, he would report the matter when next the District Officer made a patrol and see that the offender spent a long term in gaol (at that period the maximum sentence for adultery was six months). Those who were accompanying him did not speak — this was unnecessary — but stood in the centre displaying all the signs of rage. Finally Kakameri sounded the gong again, spat loudly in the direction of the house where Veu was living with his parents, and made a dignified exit. The supporters walked away behind him.

Veu, like Kajikmwa, kept out of the way for some weeks. During this period he gave two dollars, part of the wages he had brought back, to a senior kinsman with a request that this man should offer the money to Kakameri. The latter made no further claim, but Sanum for several days bore the marks of the firestick with which he had beaten her.

The Dap folk found fault with Kakameri for his over-reaction, which they described as unpardonable. Some of them even said it was without precedent, possibly because at that stage I was a relative newcomer and might not have known any better (as I pointed out, this was the first adultery to be discovered during my stay, and the cuckolding of Sawang, with the resulting tirade against Kajikmwa, was still in the future). They wasted no pity on Veu but were sympathetic to Sanum, who before her marriage had been one of themselves. Their excuse for her was that, with such a cruel husband, it was not surprising that she should take a lover. The Mwarok villagers justified Kakameri on the ground that she had so repeatedly been unfaithful. What else was to be expected of him than an instant foray against Veu?

At a later stage I wanted to know why Veu and Kajikmwa had so plainly been abashed at their unmasking and kept out of sight, whereas Tafalti and Sawang seemed not to be affected and went about their ordinary avocations. People said this was partly a question of age and experience, partly the public censure or lack of it. The first two were younger and had also been in their own villages in the presence of kinsmen, who were obliged to take a share in the shame. Tafalti and Sawang, on the other hand, both older, could pretend that they still possessed an unsullied reputation. But this was not the whole story, Jaua and Waru reminded me. Temperaments differ, and while some men are naturally sensitive and shrink at criticism, others are less susceptible or, as we would say, are thick-skinned and obtuse. Tafalti, declared Waru, vituperative against him as usual, was well known as a person blind and deaf to disgrace.

INTER-DISTRICT ADULTERY

Adultery across district borders is rare because most of the villages are too far apart. The sight of a man from Bariat in Ga, for example, unless he is clearly there on legitimate business, inevitably gives rise to mistrust. The householders tell one another he is up to no good — it could be for purposes of adultery or sorcery, nothing else — and keep a watch on his movements till he leaves.

Opportunities mostly arise when the women have planned to collect coral or shellfish in a body or to weed a large garden. Such tasks are carried out by females exclusively, and their menfolk are never on hand. My informants, males every one, said that the invitation always comes from the women. 'It's mainly the newly married wives who are anxious to even things up with their spouses,' Kalabai told me. 'They send word to any young men they've met in other places, and couples go off into the bush together.' Invariably the secret comes out, and then the injured husbands send a challenge to the philanderers. In the past a fight with spears would have followed at a spot agreed upon near the boundary between the two districts. The headmen and elders stood nearby and as soon as anybody was wounded ran between the combatants yelling at them to stop. No tradition exists of a killing ever having occurred either by design or accident. Later an exchange was arranged, sometimes of food, sometimes of ornaments and other valuables. Today, with fighting forbidden, a football match takes place, or what passes as such (the vernacular expression is *kik kros*, adopted from pidgin English). No rules are accepted, nor is there any notion of selecting teams of matching strength with equal numbers. The struggle goes on till one side admits defeat and withdraws. Probably the hurts inflicted in the way of punches and kicks are worse than the discomforts resulting from the battles of former times.

THE PREVALANCE OF ADULTERY

Why when people inveigh so much against adultery are they prone to committing it? Probably every mature married man has at some time or other had an affair with at least one married woman from his own district, and if the names of those from different areas are absent from the catalogue, then it is simply on account of the impracticability of arranging a meeting.

The first point to be borne in mind is that the disapproval expressed is not backed up by any specific religious prohibition with supporting sanctions. The only occasion when supernatural forces are supposed to come into play is when the erring couple are close affines, as a man and his brother's wife. Then there is also no general invoking of the death penalty in the secular sphere. A headman may claim the right to kill his spouse's seducer, but an ordinary householder who acted in so high handed a manner would be judged a murderer. A further factor is the attitude to fornication. A youth, once he has passed through the final stage of his initiation and received instruction in how to rid himself of female pollution, is permitted to indulge himself as often as he pleases, but he and his partner take precautions to avoid discovery lest the villagers should tease them and perhaps the girl's parents show resentment. The householders have a rough idea of what is going on, but as long as a decent silence is preserved they pay no attention. This must tend to foster the view that in sexual matters much is permitted if not found out. Each person's continual eulogizing of his ancesters is also relevant. All too often the seniors when giving moral instruction to the young pause and then in the next breath relate how a forbear, or a forbear of a headman of the cluster, triumphed over his enemies when his conduct, from the point of view of probity, was on their own showing indefensible. They seem to be unaware of how they are contradicting themselves. I several times heard old men giving long accounts of how their grandfathers were successful in the most flagrant adulteries and then within the hour lament that the members of the rising generation, unlike themselves in youth, have no respect for the marriage tie. The story told by Gubale of Job is worth repeating. The audience, apart from myself, included four lads aged about 17. His grandfather Morus was such a mighty warrior, Gubale boasted, that he routed a group of men from Bagiau who were pursuing his nephew Nagambol with the object of despatching him with their arrows. Nagambol belonged to Wokibol, where he had conducted an intrigue with the headman's wife. Naturally the husband wanted revenge, but Nagambol ran to his uncle in Job. Morus came to the rescue, defeated the would-be avengers, and took Nagambol into his household. That was the end of the episode, and the young man remained there for the rest of his

7 Cases of Adultery and Theft

life. 'Yes, Morus always showed real concern for his kinsmen,' Gubale concluded.

Finally, adultery may be attractive just because it is forbidden. I once remarked to Jaua that, he being the man he was, I felt confident of the excellence of his love magic and supposed he had won great success with it. I had nothing definite in mind but thought he might yield to the flattery and perhaps confess to overriding the rule against moiety incest. To my amazement he replied that the spells were so powerful that they had enabled him to have intercourse over a long period with Yam in her younger days. This was trebly dreadful – she was married to a headman, her husband was Jaua's uncle, and she belonged to the same moiety. Without further prodding he gave me the history of the affair with the minutest details, over each one of which he paused to luxuriate (of course, the story may have been a pure invention, but I do not think so). On one occasion he was saved from discovery only because he also owned magic to render himself invisible. I wanted to know was he not embarrassed when in Marigum's company. Far from it, came the answer. He often took meals with him to disarm suspicion. He gave up only when Yam became pregnant, and afterwards, with the weaning of the infant, she was no longer so attractive. (The offspring, Dal, resembled his mother's husband too closely to have been illegitimate.) Apart from me he had told no one except Waru – it would be the height of folly to broadcast the tale.

I used the same gambit with some of my other associates, but two only made surprising admissions. One claimed to have conducted an intrigue with the wife of a near relative from within the housing cluster, and the other told me with relish that he had forestalled a cousin on the latter's wedding day and found the bride still a virgin. Such boasting, whether or not based on fact, is in itself sufficient to indicate the appeal of adultery.

THEFT

Pig stealing causes most of the trouble, but a word may be said first about petty thieving, as of garden produce. This is infrequent, for the offender by his very pilfering admits that he is idle and improvident. To be without food is disgraceful, and only those indifferent to their reputation or too ill to work would steal from hunger. The man robbed may abuse the thief roundly, but no one else pays much attention except perhaps to express contempt. If the offender continues in his evil ways and becomes branded as a *rabis man*, a term taken over from pidgin English ('rubbish man'), he loses caste completely. Persons whose goods have been stolen do not as a rule then bother to retaliate unless something of great value has gone. They can only upbraid him, and, as they point out, what is the use when he has already proved himself shameless?

One family in Dap was the object of wonder and universal disparagement — wonder that the members could go on living as they did, disparagement that they had sunk to such a level. I doubt, however, whether they were really to blame. The husband, Sabwa, from Bagasal's cluster, had all the appearances of a consumptive and I suspect lacked the energy for gardening. He spent much of his time lying down, though occasionally he was able to go fishing. The wife, with no land cleared for her, could not provide cultivated foods, and her contributions to the larder were confined to shellfish and wild greens. They had one daughter aged about eight. The other villagers usually took pity on them, mainly because they realised that failure to do so would result in the plundering of their gardens. If no one had sent a meal and the little girl began crying the woman would take her to the most likely of the neighbours and ask for food. A weeping child always commands sympathy, and the householder quickly handed something over.

Waru first called my attention to this sad couple when Sabwa stole a fine bunch of his bananas reserved for presentation to relatives in another village. He was most vexed and told me what he thought, though he said nothing in front of the offender. Shortly afterwards a second bunch went. I was in Gol at the time, but Jaua intimated that Waru was beside himself on learning of the loss and went direct from the orchard to the settlement, where he picked up a handful of gravel and flung it at the house where Sabwa lived with another family. Then, shaking with rage, he insulted and swore at the pair. It would be better if they left and took to the abode of the wild pigs, he concluded.

Mention must also be made of the ceremonial theft of garden produce during the initiation rites. The elders in charge of the boys send them to plunder the cultivations in a district other than their own. Success is held to be a mark of their virility and skill.

PIGS

The animals are valued mainly for economic reasons, though an owner becomes attached to those he has fattened and then kept for a long time in readiness for a projected festival. He gives each one of them a name, to which it answers, and treats it as a pet. When he sits in the village during the evenings two or three may crowd round him to have their back and ears scratched. His wife feeds them in the morning and at dusk, but in the daytime they

7 Cases of Adultery and Theft

wander about in the bush, sometimes to a distance of two or three kilometres. Every pig bears the earmark of the household to which it belongs, but even at a distance people recognize those from their own village or district.

Pigs are killed only for feasts, never for daily meals, and it is an inflexible rule that no one, nor any member of his family, may eat the flesh of an animal for whose nourishment he was responsible. When the celebration takes place the host reserves nothing from himself: his turn comes afterwards when the guests in turn entertain him.

Theft is facilitated by the conventions about what ought to be done when a beast breaks into gardens and destroys the crop. The cultivator has the obligation of keeping his fences in good repair, but the unseasoned softwoods from which they are constructed soon decay and must constantly be replaced. Often in the meantime a pig from the village forces its way in. If it consumes a quantity of vegetables the gardener is free to spear it, though he has no right to the carcase. He must report his action to the owner, who can then use the meat to repay one of his debts. But often the killer hopes to escape detection, and he then carves the beast up and builds an earth oven in the bush nearby. There is always too much for one family, and he distributes the joints among his closer relatives, warning them to partake as discreetly as possible. The householder who has thus been robbed may simply conclude that his pig has joined the wild herds or been bitten by a snake, but the greater likelihood is that he will institute a search. Should he locate the culprit he claims an animal of equivalent size to cover his loss.

Theft of this kind when the two men concerned are neighbours or close kin living some distance apart probably never occurs. Apart from the consanguineal or affinal ties, which we know carry great weight, little advantage would be gained. In the ordinary course of events when someone slaughters his pig or gives it away and receives another in exchange he always shares with his relatives. If he has been robbed beforehand, obviously he will have nothing left to present and therefore cannot hope to attract a counter gift. Not only is he the loser, but so also are the others. A further consideration is the near impossibility of avoiding discovery. The bulk of the gardening areas belonging to the members of the same cluster are located within sight of one another.

Thieving from householders of the other cluster within the village must also be rare. The worst offender in the early 1930s was Bagasal's son Gireno.[4] In 1934 he was away in employment, but it seemed that he had made a habit of seizing pigs for the sheer pleasure of courting risks. Often he was successful, and if in after months the secret leaked out the owner's anger had subsided. He gave joints to his father and uncle but ate the rest in the forest with young companions. Perhaps his best joke was to kill one of Waru's pigs and send him a leg with the message that the day's hunting had been satisfactory. Even Waru saw the humour of this and was the first to tell me about it.

Probably the most common form of stealing is across village boundaries within the district. The first case in Wonevaro during 1934 was in Kinaba. Karem missed one of his herd during their evening feed, and as the animal also failed to turn up in the morning he concluded that it had been taken, though there was no clue as to whom the thief might be. That night, however, one of his wives returning from a visit to Mwarok reported noticing a strong smell of roast pork while she sat on Kakameri's verandah. Karem collected the men of his cluster and a few others and set out spear in hand to accuse Kakameri and demand a replacement. The latter denied the charge and told him to look elsewhere. But within a day or two a cousin of Karem's resident in Mwarok disclosed that Kakameri had lied and had killed the animal when he found it in his garden eating the taro. Karem said nothing then but six weeks later speared a pig belonging to Kakameri, trussed it up, and with the assistance of some Kinaba youths carried it home, where he cooked it openly and distributed the meat. Kakameri forthwith sounded the Mwarok gong and reproached Karem as a robber. Then he walked to Kinaba, flung his spear into the thatch of Karem's dwelling, and, standing in the centre of the village, several times asked for monetary compensation. His words drew no response, and eventually he returned home. He repeated the performance the next morning but with no better result. The incident was then closed except that Kakameri later admitted to me that he had carried out magic to blast Karem's harvest.

In a subsequent case Kaunara of Kinaba and some younger companions when out hunting killed an animal belonging to Kumun of Job. They had set up their nets with the intention of taking a wild pig, but this domesticated beast had run into the snare, and they had speared it. That evening every Kinaba household had a pork dinner. The story rapidly drifted through to Kumun, who the next day arrived, backed up by a few relatives, with a bunch of dry coconuts. Standing before Kaunara's house he threw the nuts on the ground and shouted, 'This is pig food. Call up your herd to eat it, and I'll pick one of them to take as a return for that which you people stole.' Kaunara descended

7 Cases of Adultery and Theft

instantly and replied proudly, 'I can give you one pig, two pigs, three pigs, four pigs. Here, take that fellow. It has been my pillow since its birth.' He pointed to a beast he was feeding up for some celebration, one much bigger than that of Kumun. The latter, crushed by the offer of more than the equivalent of his loss, walked away, indicating that he too could be generous. Kaunara did not accept the withdrawal and told some of the youths to capture the pig and take it to Job. This action served to enhance his reputation. He avoided blame for the offence and derived extra prestige. Kumun made no further complaint.

Marigum was less liberal when he found himself similarly placed after spearing a pig belonging to his brother-in-law Tago of Kinaba. It managed to escape with the barb fast in its hide, but though it afterwards died, the carcase was already rotten when discovered. A good deal of taro had been destroyed, and Marigum decided to remain silent. Tago was in two minds about what to do. He was angry at the loss and wished for redress, but, on the other hand, he could hardly cast reproaches on a close affine who was also so prominent. As a way out he proceeded to Dap and there charged not Marigum but Wiawia, a matrilateral cousin, using only the mildest language and offering no insults. Fortunately Wiawia understood the difficulty and had the delicacy to keep quiet. Tago told me he wanted Marigum to realize that he was not a man to be trifled with. Again there was no further reaction.

The last case is worth quoting on account of its ramifications. A few preliminary explanations are necessary. Sakum and Kalal did not belong to Dap by birth but had married two of Marigum's nieces, sisters of Jaua, Wurun and Mwal respectively, and had taken up more or less permanent residence there. Sakum, moreover, had given Waru an infant daughter for adoption. By rights the adopting father ought not to have minded the real parents continuing to show the child affection, but in fact he disliked their doing so, though he concealed his irritation. Matters came to a head when Sakum killed another pig belonging to this same Tago, who was one of Waru's closest relatives. Before Tago himself could complain or make a demand Waru strode over to Sakum's house and delivered a loud denunciation, imputing all sorts of additional offences to him. Sakum's only reply was to yell, 'Give me back my baby!' Tafalti was standing nearby and joined in on Waru's side with further abuse. As the argument continued he picked up a stone and threw it at Sakum, hitting him in the back. The latter had given a joint of the pig to Kalal, who was thus in honour bound to offer support. He stepped down from his verandah and called to Sakum to take the child from Waru's wife. Then he aimed a stone at Waru, though a bystander, a woman, caught his arm and spoiled the shot. Waru closed with Kalal, while Tafalti hurled another stone at Sakum, who stood screaming with rage and pain.

Jaua and the other men now rushed across and separated the combatants. Were they not all ashamed of themselves, men from the same cluster (he used the word *dan*) shedding one another's blood, he chided. As Waru retired into his house Kalal followed with imprecations. In a final thurst he scattered a handful of gravel in the doorway. After this all returned to normal. Sakum without any further urging presented Tago with a large pig.

Except for Mwarok of Wonevaro and Falala of Bagiau, and Gol of Bukdi and Maluk of Takul, the villages of the different districts are too far apart for the pigs to do much trespassing. At the same time, one found on the wrong side of the border has little chance of escaping alive no matter whether it has or has not done any damage. Once Waru requested a loan of my gun, which I used for shooting pigeons, to dispose of a wandering animal from Bagiau. This was early in my stay, and I complied, accepting his protestations that it had already ruined several gardens, a statement I soon found to be untrue. 'Well, the Bagiau folk would shoot our pigs on sight if they had a gun,' was his excuse when I remonstrated with him.

As with adultery, so with theft, the contradiction between ideals and practices can be traced back to early training. Like parents in other societies, those of Wogeo strive to inculcate in their offspring a respect for other people's property. The stock admonition when a child begins to meddle is, 'That belongs to So-and-so; if you break it he'll be cross and perhaps slap you; you'd better put it down.' In other words, teaching would seem to be founded on the adage that honesty is the best policy.[5] Among the To'ambaita of north Malaita in the Solomons the reproof is worded differently. There the parents warn, 'That isn't yours; it belongs to So-and-so; you'd better not touch it.' The aim is thus to cultivate self discipline. It is surely no accident that the missionaries in Malaita found a word by which they could translate our expression 'conscience', a concept notably lacking in the Wogeo language. Perhaps it is significant that while among the To'ambaita I used no locks and never had anything stolen, whereas in 1934, though not in 1974, although I had locks on every box, the Wogeo helped themselves to as much as they could lay their hands on.

8 Marigum and Tafalti

I want now to consider a prolonged quarrel between these two, the father and the son. Crisis followed crisis over a period of months, and although when I left they were again on speaking terms, everybody said this might be no more than a temporary truce. The affair is not only of intrinsic interest but also sheds light on what the headman means to the community at large. In one sense therefore my account belongs to the earlier part of the book; but the ramifications are better understood against the background of our present knowledge of the character of the various participants, those who played minor roles as well as the principals.

Theft of a sum of money sparked off the trouble. The incident erupted into bitter wrangling, and it became apparent that the recriminations were linked with disagreement over the choice of husband for a daughter of the family, Magar. Marigum wanted to send her to Kabub, a man belonging to the neighbouring village of Job; whereas Tafalti, who was her full brother, determined that she should be espoused to his brother-in-law Kalaua, the son of Kaman, a headman from Falala in Bagiau. Neither candidate was a perfect physical specimen. Kabub, on the brink of middle age, had lost the sight of one eye, and Kalaua, although much younger, suffered from a contagious form of ringworm covering his entire body.

Then beneath the second struggle I discovered a still deeper layer of tension, though this was never referred to in the open arena of civic life. Fundamental to the conflict was the flexibility in the rules of succession permitting a headman to decide which of his several sons should be the heir. People whispered in private that Tafalti resented his father's preference for Dal and wanted the nomination for himself but hesitated to make the grievance explicit lest the old man might punish the effrontery by employing a sorcerer to encompass his death.

It would appear on the surface that here was a contest over

the exercise of power, in the future if not at once; and Epstein, in an analysis of the dispute based on an earlier article of mine, insisted that it ought to be looked at as part of the political process.[1] But Tafalti must have been aware of Marigum's overwhelming influence and realized that out-manoeuvring him, except perhaps briefly, was not remotely feasible. Dal was within a year or so of maturity and once officially inducted into the office would be unassailable, totally immune to the artifice and plots of any competing half-brother. Only if he died during the short remaining months of his minority could Tafalti hope to win the coveted prize; and in that event wiles and stratagems would be uncalled for.[2] No one else was eligible, and his father, hate him as he might, would have to pick him.

The verdict of the Dap villagers was that Tafalti's conduct was an instance of sheer bloody-mindedness, and with this I concur. His intention, they argued, was to provoke exasperation by every available means short of direct confrontation. It must be stressed, however, that throughout his cantankerousness was directed against Marigum alone. Never once did he find fault with Dal or reveal the slightest animosity towards him.

I should also mention that Tafalti's championship of Kalaua could not have been in any sense an endeavour to enlist extra allies. His own marriage to the daughter of Kaman, who, apart from thus acquiring the extra status of a father-in-law, was already a cognate in his own right, a first cousin once removed, had created the closest affinal ties with the residents of this cluster in Falala (Kaman's mother, Damalina, was the full sister of Marigum's father, Jaran). Equally, Marigum, when about twenty years before he took as a wife Yam, daughter of the Job headman Kaneg, became entitled to the maximum support from that quarter. Further links through Kabub would merely duplicate existing obligations.

In the beginning, as I said, a thief stole some cash that Tafalti had left for safe keeping in his father's house. Furious with temper, he blamed Yam, accusing her of being so busy persuading his father to force Magar into marrying her kinsman that she had neglected the proper care of the dwelling (Yam and Kabub were parallel cousins in the classificatory sense and referred to one another as 'brother' and 'sister'). Marigum, much as he resented the implication of being under his wife's thumb, also wished to avoid an irreparable breach. He showed his displeasure not by arguing but by clearing out of the village. Early the following day he left for a distant garden hut on the beach beyond Bariat, where he remained for a fortnight.

Soon afterwards some villagers stumbled by accident on the girl in the embraces of a Takul youth who was spending some weeks in Dap. Kabub, anticipating his rights as a husband, clamoured for vengeance. Tafalti was indignant and announced that in the event of a wedding taking place he must receive compensation. Marigum again took umbrage and departed for the hut. During this second absence Kabub tried to bring matters to a conclusion by attempting rape, an action that inspired Tafalti to further denunciation. Several weeks later Marigum came back and this time complained about such unfilial behaviour. A pause followed, and gradually things seemed to settle down.

The next year, some months after my departure, Magar and Kalaua were married, but unfortunately I do not have any knowledge of the surrounding circumstances or whether Marigum gave a reluctant consent. They were alive in 1975 and twice entertained me. She was then fifty-eight and still active, but he, some six or seven years her senior, suffered from cataracts and could barely see.

In the initial stages the people were terrified lest Marigum might lash out indiscriminately, and as long as this fear persisted they all condemned Tafalti despite the reasonable assumption that he was acting at Magar's behest and in her interest. Later on, when they came to realize that they would be unlikely to suffer physical harm, several began offering excuses for him.

The discovery of the encounter with the visitor from Takul came as a great surprise, and people now concluded that the girl probably had no special liking for Kalaua. Tafalti, they surmised, was pushing him forward on his own initiative. This served to confirm the minority in their opposition to him, but others stayed vaguely approving on the ground that, although Marigum had full authority for favouring Dal, it was natural for an older brother to feel mortified when he saw his junior given precedence.

To start with, the attitude to Marigum was one of sympathy. Many of the seniors backed him up almost to the end, but he alienated the goodwill of the younger folk by his continued insistence that Magar must become the bride of Kabub, whom so clearly she hated. If Tafalti was wrong in advocating Kalaua as the prospective husband out of malice, they said, Marigum's support of Kabub to spite his son, or perhaps to please his wife, was just as reprehensible. Finally the entire village became so fed up by his prolonged absence that the universal blame originally reserved for Tafalti was now transferred to him.

At one point in the proceedings, and arising directly from them,

Kalaua accused Kabub and Dal of performing misfortune sorcery against his father Kaman. No regular method exists for dealing with a dispute between residents of different districts, but people recognize that a meeting between the parties, preferably under the chairmanship of a neutral, provides the most likely means of achieving a peaceful settlement. Marigum decided to follow precedent and requested Wakalu, a headman from Mwarok, to act. This man invited plaintiff, defendants, and witnesses to attend in his village, directed the discussion — though not without difficulty — and after the sifting of the evidence pronounced a verdict of innocence. Ordinarily the person found to be in the wrong hands over some form of compensation, but in this instance relations were so strained that probably an offer would have been refused.

THE FIRST CLASH

Tafalti's opening outburst occurred during the preliminary stages of Magar's coming-of-age at the time of her first menstruation.[3] On such occasions the girl and a few young companions work during the morning for a period of about ten days at a little light weeding in the gardens of the leading men, and the women reward her labour with gifts of food. Each afternoon they carry across bowls of stew or pudding to her mother's house, where they all spend the rest of the day eating, playing games, and singing songs in her honour. The festivities close with a distribution of pork supplied by her father and a picnic on the mountain top. The men, who hitherto have taken no part, now intervene to drive the women home with sticks and stones, telling them they have been neglecting their household tasks for too long.[4]

Magar menstruated on 31 March 1934, and the entertainments began at once. Late in the afternoon Tafalti, when searching for something else in his basket, which hung from a hook among the rafters of Marigum's house, discovered that some silver coins worth about a dollar in all had been stolen. Standing in the midst of the assembled women, he abused them roundly. They ought to be at home instead of gadding about, he roared. I give his words as one of those present later reported them. 'You women think you're the same as men, arranging this and that instead of leaving them for your husbands to settle. You should be at the fire cooking for the children, every one of you: that's your place, not sitting there talking about things that concern us men.' At this point he turned on his cousin Mareia, who was standing alongside, and knocked her down with a blow from his closed fist. 'Get out of here,' he went on. 'You're thieves, the lot of you. You've taken my money. Women! They run this place. My father listens to their babbling: that's why he talks of betrothing my sister to Kabub. Left to himself he wouldn't interfere with what she wants; he'd let her wed Kalaua. She doesn't wish to live with that old scoundrel Kabub. Who's the headman of this place, is it a man or his wives?'

Those present were too astonished to move, but Marigum, sitting outside, had heard the commotion, probably also the words spoken, and now appeared in the doorway. Tafalti, though still angry, was apparently in sufficient possession of his faculties to feel abashed and pushed his way outside. Pausing only to exclaim, 'My sister shall not marry Kabub: I'll stop it,' he left the village.

The women filed out quickly. Those from other places returned home, and the rest gathered up their children and retreated indoors.

PEOPLE'S FEARS

Several men had been standing about, and these now hurried down the few yards to the beach, where they seated themselves on my verandah, already a favourite spot for gossiping away an idle hour although I had been on the island for but three months. Their main desire was to be out of Marigum's sight. Not within living memory had the son of a headman spoken in such a manner to his father, and they expressed alarm at the possible consequences. Some of them sat with their eyes glued to the pathway leading to the settlement, and when a youth, approaching unobserved from the opposite direction, suddenly spoke, those close at hand leapt to their feet in preparation for flight. I noted also that, although all were heavy smokers, not one had the patience to roll himself a cigarette.[5]

Jaua summarized the discussion for my benefit. 'The wrath of a headman is terrible to see,' he explained. 'We are all much afraid of Marigum in his rages. Once when angry he burned his house down, and often he's aimed spears at every person within sight. Here in Wogeo nobody, not a single one, quarrels with a headman. When we hear his voice raised we run away, just as you see we're now doing. But you needn't be afraid — he'd never harm you — that's why we came here for protection. He wouldn't touch us while we're in your house. Yet I tell you truly this is a serious matter, and we're frightened, frightened lest he should make us suffer. Tafalti's to blame — he was wrong to have spoken in that way and so put the old man in a temper.'

As yet nobody mentioned the theft or referred to the possibility of Marigum's causing a famine, but talk continued till nightfall of the dread lest he might become violent and perhaps wound or even kill anyone wandering around the village. There were many reproaches also against Tafalti. When at last hunger drove those assembled to seek dinner — no woman emerged with a bowl of food, as would have been usual — they left quickly and stayed behind closed doors.

At daybreak next morning, when the various households were just beginning to stir, Marigum seated himself on his verandah and delivered one of the monologues to which he was much addicted when wishing to rebuke his followers. He spoke apparently to himself but so loudly that his voice penetrated from one end of the settlement to the other. 'My son alleges that the women direct our affairs here,' he pronounced. 'Does he wish to take over? Very well, he's the headman now! See, he's a truly important personage — look how extensive his gardens are, stretching far and wide. My son is great indeed, like the headman of olden times.' He then departed, with Yam and another of his wives bringing up the rear.

The men came outside and, following their regular custom, stood around small fires warming themselves while the women heated up last night's leftovers as breakfast for the children. This new development was the sole topic of conversation, and some expressed relief as in their opinion the affair might now blow over. They probably thought that Marigum's speech, succeeded by a brief absence, would make Tafalti mend his manners. If so, they faced disappointment.

Before many minutes had passed Tafalti, emerging from his house, called Magar to fetch a knife and help him and his wife gather material for rebuilding his father-in-law's dwelling, which was falling in ruins. Girls are not prohibited absolutely from performing other tasks during their first-menstruation rites, but people do not expect them to undertake more than the token amount of weeding. Tafalti's order, on the most favourable interpretation, was therefore unconventional, and in the light of recent events the only conclusion was that he was determined to antagonize Marigum still further. The villagers were aghast, but he took no notice of them and stalked after the women on the road to Falala.

Everyone spoke at once. What would happen now? Nothing could prevent Marigum from having one of his worst rages. Had not past headmen when in a state of fury speared their most willing supporters? True, the government today punished murder with hanging, but a man in a passion has no thought of penalties. Who ever heard of a son guilty of such defiance? Tafalti was thoroughly evil, careless both of the respect due to a parent and of the binding obligations owed to his kinsmen.

Talk continued in this fashion for several hours, with men and women in separate groups. The older children, aware that something unusual was afoot, were at first subdued, but after a time they began to argue with one another, and before long a fight broke out. Ordinarily the parents would have separated the contenders and sent them off in different directions, but on this occasion one of the mildest of the householders, who normally was incapable of scolding even his own offspring, boxed their ears soundly and told them to shut up.

At last someone remarked, 'Come, the gardens must still be attended to,' and one by one people sorted themselves out, took up their baskets and tools, and departed.

In accordance with an arrangement made some days previously, Waru arrived at my house during the early afternoon for a formal interview. Although before we began I enquired would he like to delay the talk, he expressed his willingness to proceed. Yet no matter what subject I brought forward he always returned after a few minutes to his anxiety about Marigum or his jeremiads against Tafalti. This was the first time I had heard about the headman's weather magic, and he repeated over and over that we might expect too much rain and consequent damage in the gardens. 'We may all be scourged just because one of us has done wrong,' he lamented. Finally he admitted his uselessness as an informant and suggested postponement till he was in a better mood. 'Fear so turns my belly that I can't listen to what you say. You can hear, my speech is from my mouth alone. I beg you not to think I'm lying – I'm not putting you off because I've work to do in the garden. If that were so I'd tell you and know you'd understand. Today everybody's like this – you heard us this morning – we're scared out of our wits.'

That evening the men again crowded on my verandah. Some of them brought word that Yam, passing a relative along the road, had confided that Marigum would not be back until Tafalti had completed the last of the celebrations for Magar. The rest agreed that the news might have been worse, but they still continued to cherish misgivings, especially now at the prospect of perhaps not having enough to eat. Some said they would feel easier if only they could take positive action. Jaua expanded on this point for my benefit. When in difficulties the group looks to its headman for guidance, he said; but here they were in the worst trouble known, and the leader was missing. The solution was a reconciliation, and who among them could attempt to hasten that? When two ordinary persons quarrel the headman can speak to them and compel them to settle their differences — that is his job — but when the headman himself is caught up in the affair there is nobody to interfere. One householder put forward the notion of inviting Kawang to act as an intermediary. Several discussed the suggestion seriously but ultimately rejected it, partly because they felt that he would have offered already had he thought he might help, partly because of Marigum's probable wrath at such an initiative. A further problem was finding a negotiator, an office none was willing to accept.

By the morning the gloom had to some extent lifted. People were still censuring Tafalti, but otherwise they talked more of hopes than fears. Sawang went so far as to say that their misgivings might have been exaggerated, but with this the others did not agree. During the course of the day numbers of persons assured me, however, that the worst was now over and that as Marigum had so far not been violent they were safe. 'Yesterday we trembled, for in the heat of temper a headman may do anything, even murder. But as nothing has happened, all will be well. We know Marigum, and his rage is already cooling. A man may be angry with distant kin for a month, two months, or for longer, but the son is his father's semen, and their disagreements don't last. In a few days you'll see Marigum back.'

The assertion that the villagers were trembling with anxiety was amply supported by their own statements: in the space of thirty-six hours each one had confessed to being thoroughly frightened. Such words were confirmed by their conduct. Never previously had they come to my house without some at least bringing work — perhaps an axe handle to be fitted, a food bowl to be carved, or cord to be twisted — never before had they refrained from rolling cigarettes, and never before were they so jumpy.

THE THEFT

Sawang's optimism went on growing, and during the evening of the same day I overheard him trying to convince the neighbours that really their alarm was without justification. 'A headman has to demonstrate he's cross when a follower defies him, but how do we know Marigum wasn't pretending?' he went on. 'He was aware Tafalti had just had his money taken and must have known he'd be stirred up by such a loss. Then we've often remarked among ourselves how casual Marigum is about feasts and such like — that when another man would take four days to prepare a celebration he might take eight. As for myself, I don't think he was seriously vexed. Of course, he'll soon be back again.'

At that moment Tafalti walked over and joined the group. The subject was quickly changed, but he silenced the speaker with a glare and then expressed regret for having charged the women with stealing. He had no evidence against any of them but was put out by the shock and said more than he ought to have done.

All listened quietly, and then one of the elders, Wiawia, gave as his opinion that each should contribute ten cents to make up the sum missing. Relatives are under the obligation to offer mutual assistance, particularly in times of misfortune, he reminded them. They would have helped Tafalti in punishing an evil magician who aimed at destroying his gardens, and in the present distress had they not a similar responsibility?

Several murmured agreement, but the party soon broke up, and as we walked away Jaua muttered to himself, 'I've no cash to spare: they'd do better to search for the thief.' Asked why then he had not opposed the scheme, he replied that tacit support was a way of showing sympathy. Perhaps, too, other people might donate something.

The majority of the villagers, with their previous criticisms apparently forgotten, were soon telling one another how sorry for Tafalti they felt, and if I had listened only to conversations when several persons were present I might have concluded that they were in full agreement with Wiawia. I noted down many such statements as these: 'This is the same thing as a heavy piece of work; I'd put my efforts at Tafalti's disposal for that and intend to help him now' and 'Tomorrow I must ask my brother-in-law to give me back the fifty cents I lent him for his tax; yes, I'll do it tomorrow and give Tafalti twenty cents.' Enquiries as to when the money would be handed over met with such replies as 'Soon' or 'The day after tomorrow.'

As it turned out, public protestations and private intentions were at variance. When I spoke to individual householders I found that each one, regardless of his neighbours, was fully determined not to give anything at all. Had they failed to turn up a culprit I doubt whether a single cent would have changed hands. Most of them were reluctant through sheer lack of cash. 'If it was a question of garden work or building a new house I'd be there,' Sawang maintained, 'but as for money, I haven't any. If I give away a coin now, how shall I pay my tax?'

Others justified their unwillingness with less plausible excuses. Wiawia, for example, argued that the closest relatives ought to come up with something first: his motive in speaking earlier was to draw the attention of men like Waru, who was Tafalti's uncle, to their liabilities. The older men persisted in the view that Tafalti had forfeited all sympathy by his attack on Marigum. His tactics were disgusting — how could they help a man so oblivious of his duty as to oppose his father; a man, further, who had brought them into danger?

By April seven people had abandoned their pretence. I have a reference in my diary that during the morning I heard five men talking together among themselves agree that nothing should be done. 'I can't afford a gift, and you others, I know, are the same,' said Jaua. 'I'd help if I had more than my tax money,' Sawang affirmed. 'I'm sorry at the loss and agree that relatives ought to be able to call on one another: but if a thief stole my money who'd give me anything? Well, you four would, I daresay, but not Tafalti,' Waru added. 'Why should we rescue someone who's made our headman angry?' Kalal concluded.

In the meantime Tafalti, though replying cheerfully if spoken to, was keeping to himself. Most days he left the village soon after sunrise and at dusk returned to his own fireside. Magar he ignored, and although her ceremonies were now suspended, he refrained after the first day from ordering her about. The neighbours did not seek his company but, trained as they are to be polite and show consideration to relatives, had no hesitation in passing the time of day when meeting him along the road.

The morning of 8 April brought a momentous announcement. Wakalu, the headman from Mwarok, came over to tell us that while on a visit to relatives in Ga he had heard that early in the afternoon of the day the theft was discovered two of them had caught sight of Sabuk's young son Karing descending from the verandah of Marigum's house. Their presence in Dap had been fortuitous in that they were just passing through after calling on a sick kinsman in Bariat. They had not given the matter a thought until Wakalu began bringing them up to date on local events but now agreed that the evidence might be relevant as the boy had had no business to be there.

Jaua, Waru, and Sawang at once went to pass the news on to Sabuk and suggest that he question the boy. The interrogation revealed that Karing had indeed been alone in the village for a short time and entered Marigum's house, though he denied touching anything there. Sabuk did not wait to scold him but took two twenty-cent pieces from his bag and presented them forthwith to Tafalti, who by now had heard the tale from Wakalu. 'This is all I have,' Sabuk apologized. 'I'm ashamed, but if my son did steal your money he gave none of it to me. Take this now and let me go away.' In spite of Tafalti's protestations that so small a child could barely have reached the basket, much less stolen anything of value, he returned to his dwelling, took an axe, and quickly disappeared. Tafalti kept the gift, an action I thought strange until Jaua and Waru explained that to have refused it would have been ill-mannered.

In discussing the incident people stressed Sabuk's giving the money rather than the boy's conduct. That positive evidence of guilt did not exist, they agreed, but entry into a house during the owner's absence was inexcusable, and the father was right to accept full responsibility. 'Had he not offered cash straight away we'd have said he was taking advantage of his son's being a thief,' Jaua argued. 'Yes, you're right when you point out that we don't know for certain whether the boy's to blame. The money could have been taken a day or two before. But that's unimportant, and men would still have gossiped. Now they'll keep quiet. Sabuk has saved his good name.'

Opinion regarding Karing's culpability was divided. Those who disliked Sabuk maintained that he was just the sort of shiftless person who might have instructed his son to rifle the basket and bring out the contents, but others were convinced that one so young could not have kept the secret.

Later in the day a messenger arrived from Yam bringing a further fifty cents. She let it be known that she owned nothing herself but had borrowed from a kinsman. Her motives were unclear, and persons I questioned did not seem to be interested. 'Perhaps she's ashamed because Tafalti referred to her influence over Marigum,' said Waru. 'Or perhaps she realizes she ought to have taken better care of the house and not left it unguarded. Who can tell? But now Tafalti has most of his money back. That's the main thing.'

Once the theft had been cleared up to the general satisfaction — obviously any solution was welcome however disappointing it appeared to me — the village returned to normal routine. Marigum stayed away for some days yet, but everyone was confident that he would be back soon. The majority of the older men held to the view that Tafalti had behaved badly, but members of the younger generation were inclined to shrug the offence off. He was distressed at his loss and ought not to be held wholly at fault.

TAFALTI AND MAGAR

Marigum on his return resumed the sponsorship for Magar's festivities, and the concluding feast took place on 29 April, four weeks after she had first menstruated. The quantity of food provided, though adequate, disappointed many of the women.

In ordinary circumstances a betrothed girl goes to her husband immediately after she has come of age. Magar was not formally affianced, but as her father had spoken so frequently of her marrying Kabub, the villagers were surprised when the days passed and still he did not fix a date for the wedding. They admitted he had the right to dispose of her as he saw fit, but several of them, concluding from Tafalti's earlier remarks that she had a liking for Kalaua — wrongly as we were soon to realize — maintained that it would be foolish to coerce her into a union for which she felt small inclination. 'You can't make a woman live with a man she doesn't want, and it's silly to try,' Waru remarked. 'She'll keep on running away until the man grows tired of fetching her back. You'd think with the lesson of Sanum before him Marigum would have learned sense.'

During the third week in May a favourable opportunity presented itself for me to ask his intentions. Yes, he was determined that Magar should go to Kabub but not at once as his wives still needed her help in the gardens, he said. Had I not heard yet that a father always likes to have one daughter marry into the village whence her mother had come? No? Well, there it was. By this means he made a fitting return for his own wife, repaying her kinsmen for the loss suffered when he took her away. Yam came from Job: was it not proper then that Magar should go there to live? Yes, yes, I was quite right — Magar was born of his first wife Maijabra, not Yam. But Maijabra had died long ago, and Yam, taking over her duties, had brought the girl up, thereby allowing herself to claim motherhood. Whose hands had been soiled by excrement when Magar was a baby? — Yam's: whose dress stained with urine? — Yam's; and who acted the part of grandfather, curing the child's ailments with his magic? — not Maijabra's father but Yam's.

But this was not all. I knew that a sister always nurses her brother in illness? So I had seen examples. Should Tafalti become ill his elder sister Sanum was ready in Mwarok to look after him. But what of his younger brother Gabis (at that time a wage labourer on a plantation)? And of Yam's son Dal? (Dal had a full sister, Jauon, but in mid 1934 she was less than two years old.) If Magar went to live in Job she would be close by in the hour of need to tend Gabis or Dal.

There were excellent reasons for the proposed match, I agreed. But what of Magar's wishes? (Like everyone else at this stage, I supposed she was eager to marry Kalaua.) She would do as he bade her, came the irritated reply. A child must obey his parents. The father and mother feed and care for him, and he therefore acts in accordance with their wishes. Magar would be a good and dutiful daughter and wed the man chosen for her.

A couple of days later I sought out Tafalti to see whether he could make out as good a case. It was nonsense for Marigum to assert that Magar was Yam's daughter, he told me. The girl had been born of the same woman as himself, Maijabra. The correct proceedure accordingly was to seek a husband in Maijabra's village, Falala, to which Kalaua belonged. Marigum had a further obligation to the folk there in that they had supplied Tafalti with a wife — they had thus given two women and so far received none back. Then why should Magar be compelled to do something repugnant to her? For that there could be no justification. She would either remain with Kabub and be miserable or else keep running away from him. Finally, he was too old for her.

I put these two points of view before Waru and Jaua. They agreed that Marigum's argument was more orthodox but insisted on Tafalti's being perfectly reasonable. Even an obedient daughter likes to have a say in her marriage, for she and not the father will have to spend the rest of her life with the man. Marigum was unfair to go on browbeating Magar. Probably, as Tafalti had hinted, Yam was behind his intransigence. The aim no doubt was advancement of her kin, of which Kabub was a member, by a further alliance with Marigum's family. It was a fact that fathers like to give one of their daughters in marriage to her mother's relatives, but, although Yam had reared Magar, the primary obligation was still to the residents of Falala, the village of Maijabra's birth.

Then early in June two lads when roaming in the bush during the evening came across Magar in the ardent embrace of the young man Kanakula from Bwanag in the Takul district. When in employment he had been fully trained as a cook, and I had recently persuaded him to join my establishment in Dap for a few weeks to give lessons to Gris, the youth who was looking after the kitchen, hitherto with but moderate success. The boys of the vicinity were delighted at the excuse to rag and laugh at Kabub for allowing himself to be forestalled. He was very angry and threatened to spear Kanakula but eventually was persuaded instead to challenge him to a football match after the manner of the *kik kros* already referred to (p. 115). Everyone thought that Kanakula would be able to assemble a team of reasonable size as a few days before a schooner had landed a batch of returning labourers, several of them from Takul, who were waiting in Dap for kinsmen to come and help them carry their baggage home. These men not only refused their support, however, but even toyed with the idea of backing Kabub. They argued that, as during their absence Kanakula had been debauching their sweethearts, here was a welcome opportunity for seeing him punished. He was a well set up young fellow and I concluded they were envious of his success with the opposite sex. In the end Kabub took the field with a side of fifteen to Kanakula's three, himself and his two workmates. Dal, because of his relationship with Kabub, whom he referred to as a mother's brother, was reluctant to play any part until he saw how uneven the conflict would be. His loyalty to Kanakula then carried the day. It is needless to relate the results of the match.

When it was all over Kanakula retired to the kitchen and gave himself up to a fit of violent weeping. This was not a ritual lament, and there is little doubt that his tears and sobs were a genuine expression of grief and self-pity. His kinsmen had derided him and let him down, and he felt isolated and alone.

Kabub's assumption that he was justified in regarding Kanakula's behaviour as a personal affront sent Tafalti into another of his rages, and he went around the village complaining, 'This man must think he's married to Magar already.' On the day of the football he went further and told Kalal, Marigum's closest companion (although they were only distantly related) in the hearing of some of the most senior men of the place, 'Magar is my own sister, daughter of my mother Maijabra, and she ought to marry someone from Falala. If my father wishes to think of her as Yam's daughter, then he cuts me off from her. Is it not just that I should receive something to recompense me for the loss? I want money to even things up, and Kabub must pay me two dollars.'

Claims of this type are an innovation, for in Wogeo, as we saw, the transfer of wealth forms no part of the traditional wedding ceremony. Nowadays men who while abroad have become familiar with the custom of bride-price sometimes insist on a small payment if a sister or daughter elopes with a man from a settlement located at some distance, but a demand for cash when the girl was to marry the man of her father's choice was without precedent and, according to Kalal, indefensible. Marigum, to whom he reported the speech, apparently was of the same opinion, and in the morning he once more retired to the garden hut.

People were less upset than on the earlier occasion and expressed no concern for their personal safety. The more responsible men were becoming worried, nevertheless, about what the ultimate outcome might be. Clearly it was not a simple case of marrying a girl off against her will, as they had all thought. 'We know Magar hates Kabub: she's often said so,' Jaua remarked one evening over dinner. 'But if she likes Kalaua, why this affair with Kanakula? You know I've come to the conclusion that the Kalaua business is her brother's doing alone.' He explained his earlier mistake as based on the natural inference that she had confided in Tafalti and asked him to intercede on her behalf. 'This is what sisters are always doing; but I doubt now whether Magar ever spoke to him at all.'

Kanakula confirmed Jaua's suspicions. He told us that, far from his seeking her out, she had approached him; moreover, she had begged him to carry her away to the mainland, protesting that she was tired of her father and brother using her for their own ends.

Normally firm bonds unite brother and sister, and everyone with whom I raised the topic deplored this attempt of Tafalti's to exploit Magar. I was puzzled about his motive until Jaua, speaking behind closed doors, disclosed the rift over the succession, a subject about which till now I had heard not so much as a murmur. 'Dal, as you must be aware, is Marigum's favourite, and he wishes to have the boy in due course take over from him,' Jaua continued. 'This angers Tafalti, who, as the elder, thinks he has the right. Since the Kanakula episode we've decided that Tafalti's been helping Kalaua not for Magar's sake but to defy their father. The quarrel is a serious matter, serious for us in Dap — indeed, for all here in Wogeo. I can't tell where it will end. If Tafalti goes on opposing him, the chances are that Marigum will boil over and use his magic to bring endless rain or scorching sun till not a taro shoot is left growing in the gardens.' Other men agreed, warning me to keep to myself what they had said. Tafalti chafed at Marigum's greater love for Dal, they affirmed. The old man was holding fast to every shred of authority, determined to hand it on intact. They also were alarmed lest the bitterness and frustration should cause him to spread famine throughout the land.

SUCCESSION TO OFFICE

Armed with this information, I proceeded to investigate this subject in earnest, something I had so far neglected (a field anthropologist cannot study every aspect of a society simultaneously). If I thought about it at all, I suppose I imagined that honours went automatically to the eldest son, just as in ordinary families he it is who receives the biggest share of the real estate and movables. Simple primogeniture would have appeared to be the most fitting as the father's firstborn is normally only about twenty-five years his junior and hence sufficiently mature to assume full responsibility. I now learned of the frequent partiality for the offspring of the second or third wife. At the same time, his extreme youth rendered the desire to give him the advantage difficult of attainment — he might be as much as two decades younger again. Despite the delay in the formal appointment of the heir, many a headman had been compelled by an attack of mortal disease to cast aside his dream and name the oldest of the half-brothers. From the start this one had thus a fair hope of enjoying the title even when he was not the best loved. I investigated forty recent cases — though few of the headmen were as outstanding as Marigum or Kawang — and found that in no less than twenty-four the distinction went, either by desire or default, to the son of the first wife. In ten it passed to a brother or nephew of the dead man and in only six to the son of a later spouse.

The reason advanced for the headman's greater affection for the child of the woman who arrived on the scene last is the influence she herself can exert. Still sexually attractive when her co-consorts are already showing signs of age, she is in the position to push the special claims of her progeny. Some of the seniors also gave it as their opinion that the father might be jealous of his older offspring's sexual conquests. They suggested that Marigum could well have resented Tafalti's pursuit of young girls whom he himself desired. Dal's escapades, on the other hand, would be unlikely to cause him distress, for as with the passing years the boy's interest in the opposite sex developed, so his would decline. Another possibility is that the real firstborn is a constant reminder of approaching old age and the enforced surrender of temporal power. Waru's statement quoted below, p. 146, is relevant here.

Kalal and Wiawia once stated that a son descended from headmen through both parents had better qualifications than those of one whose mother was not an aristocrat. Rank was bound up with boar's tusks, which may only be worn by a headman and his children, daughters as well as sons, they explained. Any man, no matter what his position on the social scale, was forced to give more of his possessions to his own firstborn son than to those who come afterwards, but headmen were permitted to retain some of their boar's tusks for younger sons and also to hand over a few to the eldest daughter. Thus where a headman's second or third wife alone was of high rank, her son's double inheritance, from his father and from her, might give the boy a certain superiority. Maijabra's parents were commoners, and Tafalti in consequence would receive only one set of tusks. But Dal, whose mother was the eldest daughter of the Job headman Kaneg, would inherit two sets. These, outnumbering those of Tafalti, would entitle him to precedence.

Other people dismissed this rigmarole as special pleading for Dal, the result of Kalal and Wiawia's regard for Marigum. A headman must have tusks, they allowed, but the quantity was not of much significance, and Tafalti's mother's humble status would have been relevant only if Marigum were unable on other grounds to make up his mind which of his sons to pick as his successor.

In polygynous families of low rank, where a similar preference is sometimes noticeable, trouble is prevented by the fact that the father, however much he may desire to do so, is not permitted to leave the bulk of the property to his darling. In these households the eldest, with nothing to lose — except perhaps some magical knowledge — has little excuse for openly displaying jealousy. Further, he will not have had the same early encouragement for aggressiveness as the children of headmen and in consequence is inhibited from challenging his parents.

In my view this complacency about the unruly behaviour in headman's families goes a long way towards accounting for such an anomalous system.[6] Leaders, accustomed from infancy to having their own way, have probably overridden the conventions for so long that the right to pass over their firstborn is now fully acknowledged.

Favouritism is not as such condemned, and whatever the situation may have been once, all now admit that a headman can choose whom he likes from among those eligible — provided, of course, the one selected is fitted by age, knowledge, experience, and character. The residents of other villages were agreed that, although Marigum's handling of Tafalti might have been unwise, he was doing him no injustice; and the Dap folk assured me that they would be perfectly prepared to accept Dal as their master — as eventually they did. Again, nobody ever blames prominent men from previous generations for passing over their eldest sons. I often heard how Marigum's father Jaran picked him instead of his older half-brother Gerobo, and not even Sawang, Gerobo's son, complained that this might have been wrong.

Many people were at pains to tell me, nevertheless, that a headman who has a leaning towards a younger son is asking for trouble: the eldest, they said, is almost certain to stir up strife. When the far past was under consideration, or cases in which the speaker was but distantly related to the individuals concerned, although he stigmatized the behaviour of the culprit as reprehensible, he still showed some understanding of the man's state of mind. 'It's bad for relatives to quarrel, and a son must defer to his father, even one who has become querulous and tiresome,' said Jaua when telling me of Gerobo's resentment against Jaran. 'To offend when the father has custom behind him is still worse. But we always expect such conduct from a son who's been passed over. It's wrong of him to act so, but how can he help it? He becomes inflamed at seeing a young stripling so pampered. What else would you expect? He grows increasingly sour and starts reviling his father, though not to the old chap's face. He'd be in danger of death if he did that.'

Judgements about a disgruntled eldest son who is also a fellow villager are not always so benevolent. As we saw in the earlier part of this chapter, when Tafalti's implied insults led to his father's first departure from Dap neighbours were almost hysterical in their condemnation. Yet this reaction did not arise solely from outraged moral susceptibilities; it was brought about just as much by fears of personal consequences. Although the senior men were firm in their disapproval, the evidence indicates that after an interval the younger members of the community felt a good deal of sympathy. This conclusion is further supported by Jaua's comments on a statement by Marigum when I called on him at the garden hut just after he went there for the second time.

'Tafalti's an idle fellow and for years now hasn't helped me in any of my work,' Marigum had said. 'I clear the ground for new gardens alone, and I go fishing alone. He never gives me any assistance, no never. And he's also disobedient. Who ever heard of anyone's disputing orders about a daughter's marriage or asking for money? He's a ruffian, a trouble-maker, and strife follows wherever he goes. It's sad to have a son like this, a son who calls me father but doesn't treat me as a parent. Truly, I am his *tama*, not his *maia*.'

A literal translation of the last sentence is impossible, but the inference was that Tafalti regarded Marigum as a distant relative. (Sons and daughters address the father as *mam*, the vocative form of *maia*, which might perhaps be rendered as dad: they refer to him, his brothers, and the patrilateral kinsmen of his generation as *tama*, though these others they call by their names.)

On my enquiring the reason for Tafalti's attitude, Marigum replied that his own father Jaran was the villain of the piece. The grandfather had been too fond of the boy and petted and spoiled him. Whenever he, Marigum, had attempted discipline, Jaran had taken the lad's part, with the result that he had grown up ill-mannered, inconsiderate, and unmanageable. Jaran was already dead before Dal was born, and was it any wonder that he therefore was the better son?

On my repeating the conversation to Jaua he insisted that, in the first place, Tafalti was not lazy. 'Yes, it's true that when earlier you commented on his being absent from his father's gardens I gave indolence as the reason,' he continued. 'But in those days you were a stranger, and I was ashamed to tell you about our quarrels. Now, dear uncle, I confess everything. No, Tafalti isn't lazy. Have you ever seen him gardening with other people or hollowing a canoe dugout? He works as hard as anyone else. It's resentment that makes him avoid his father and withhold assistance. He's like Gerobo used to be or any other son who's been passed over. Yes, yes, he ought to help his father more, but you know how it is with such men – we've talked about it before. And as for Jaran's interference in his childhood, that's also nonsense. Jaran paid the same attention to Tafalti as he did to me, for we were both grandsons. Old folk are always fond of children and try to prevent their being beaten. Marigum was only in the right when he called Tafalti a trouble-maker. Arguing accompanies him everywhere. As you well know, he's always stealing other men's wives.'

An incident that took place later on, in the August, also revealed an understanding of Tafalti's feelings, and half a dozen men remarked afterwards that his pique was hardly surprising. Marigum was preparing a new garden and, with the object of teaching Dal and his nephews Jaua and Sawang the appropriate spells for a good harvest, summoned them to assist him in the rites. He instructed them about which leaves to gather and told them to hold these in a bundle close to his mouth while he recited the hallowed formulae, which they had to repeat after him. Subsequently they buried the magical objects among the plants. Why, I asked on the way home, had he not called in Tafalti? Did he not wish to instruct his eldest son? 'If Tafalti were a good son he'd be here already,' came the answer. 'I invited Jaua and Sawang because they're only nephews, and I don't expect them to be always on hand. It's the same with Dal. Even if he weren't working for you he's still young and so busy with childish things. But a father shouldn't have to send for his grown-up son — Tafalti ought to have been present without my asking. If he doesn't choose to come to the garden, how can he expect to learn my magic?' Then when we had gone a few yards further he added, 'I gave Tafalti his clothing: that's enough: my spells he shall not have.'

ATTEMPTED RAPE

One evening during the third week in June, just a month after the two boys had found Kanakula and Magar together, a crowd of us were on the beach seeking relief from the heat when suddenly loud wails echoed from the village. We hurried up the path and found Magar in a fit of hysterics, alternately crying and shrieking out an account of how Kabub had sprung from a clump of bushes along the road and tried to rape her. One of the women persuaded her to come indoors, and immediately afterwards Tafalti began an harangue in the style of Marigum. He did not beat the slit-gong but sat on the verandah talking so loudly that all could hear what he was saying. 'I have spoken, and everyone knows that Kalaua is to be Magar's husband. She is not to marry Kabub: I forbid it, and our father's words are of no consequence. My elder sister Sanum married to please him, and one daughter's experience is disaster enough. Magar shall have the man she's chosen, Kalaua. For the future I place a taboo on her going beyond the northern boundary of Dap.' (Job, Kabub's village, is located on that side.)

  The men slunk away to the beach in dismay. Marigum would be furious, and who could blame him? The trouble was that he would take vengeance not on Tafalti alone but on everybody. He might attack them, or he might destroy their property. The best they could count on was having the present crops spoiled by black magic bringing too much rain or too much sun. How unfortunate it was that Tafalti was their kinsman! He was the cause of this pile-up of misfortunes! If he did not soon put a curb on his tongue, said Waru, they might just as well abandon Dap to the jungle and distribute themselves among relatives in other places. 'Tafalti's insane,' Jaua added. 'Of course, he was enraged with Kabub; that was to be expected. But why did he drag in Kalaua's name again? Magar doesn't want to marry the man. It must have been sheer malice, spite against his father. He doesn't defy Marigum right out when they're together — that would be inviting death — but really he ought to think of the rest of us, for we'll have to answer for him. Then, he never was one to consider others. I'm miserable and fear the worst.'

Kalal and a few others were apprehensive about the ban on Magar's going northwards — the thought of her disregarding the order seemed not to occur to anybody. It prevented her both from visiting Job, reasonable enough in the light of Kabub's barbarity, and also from going to Marigum's garden hut. 'Such truculence!' was Wiawia's comment. 'Even Gerobo never behaved so badly.' (This was probably untrue.)

The inquietude was apparent for two or three days, but the regular routine was not seriously interrupted, and as far as I could tell work went on as usual. Then the emphasis began to change, and men like Jaua, Waru, and Sawang, though still hostile to Tafalti, began murmuring that Marigum must bear a share of the blame. Why, why, must he persist with the stupid plan of foisting Kabub on poor Magar?

MARIGUM'S PROLONGED ABSENCE

After about a week I saw evidence of a new fear — perhaps he had decided never to return. The neighbours began lamenting that to be without a leader would be worse than having to submit to one who was angry. Who would help them to settle their disputes, protect them from sorcerers, supervize their garden work, organize feasts and ceremonies, and direct the overseas trading expeditions? At the end of June Kalal made a journey to the hut with the object of persuading Marigum to come back.

The following evening I heard the sound of the Dap slit-gong and on approaching the clubhouse to discover what was going on found Kalal striding up and down as he delivered an oration. 'Marigum, four days ago you agreed to return, and yesterday when I asked you, you replied you'd be here today,' he declaimed. 'Why haven't you come? Aren't you our headman? Then you must stay with us. If you want to garden in some distant spot you should tell us, and we'll clear the land: if you fancy fish from some distant reef you should also tell us, and we'll set out with nets and spears. You are wrong to go by yourself. The sorcerers will attack you when you're alone, and what'll become of us then? What are your wives doing to allow you to be absent for so long? You are the headman of Dap, not of the remote forest. We need you here to stop us quarrelling, protect us, make us do our work properly, and give us feasts. And is not Ian Hogbin here from Sydney especially to learn from you? For a long time now you have not given him food. Is that the way to treat your brother? Come back to us! Come back! Tomorrow you, Waru, his other brother, and you, Jaua, his nephew, must go and fetch him.'

As Kalal subsided Jaua stepped forward. 'Waru and I will be with Ian Hogbin tomorrow,' he said. 'We two don't belong to Dap any more: we're men of Ambuala [the name of the area where my house was located]. Marigum should be brought back, but others must fetch him.' He later confessed that he was determined to avoid so unpleasant a duty, which would be certain to result in Marigum's abusing him, and this was the first excuse that came into his head. But he still wanted something done. 'A village without a headman is like a canoe without a steersman. Every man's hand is raised against his fellows, no task is properly performed, and soon the houses are in ruins and the fires cold — the people have all died, killed by sorcerers.'

After Kalal retired Wiawia and various of the seniors went over to his house to express agreement with him and to say they also were anxious to have Marigum back. Waru and Sawang remained aloof, and I presently strolled across to hear what they were saying. The whole exhibition was just the sort of thing one might have expected from Kalal — all talk to no purpose, they maintained. Everyone disliked being without a headman, but what effect could an utterance to the empty air have? Kalal was always opening his mouth wide: his continual babbling was as deafening as the sound of the heavy surf on the exposed side of the island. Then, having finished with Kalal, they went on to abuse Marigum still further for shrugging off his responsibilities. 'He knows Magar will never agree to marry Kabub and continues to support him only because Tafalti's putting forward someone else,' said Waru. 'All this fuss has arisen from his anger at not getting his own way for once. What's the matter with him? Can't he think of us for a change?' Then, rising wearily to his feet, he had an afterthought. 'And when he does come back we'll have to put up with his complaints. He'll moan and groan and say we've neglected things in his absence. For days on end we'll have to listen to his reproaches.'

By the next day even Wiawia had turned against Marigum. 'We're tired of it,' he wailed. 'We can't understand what all the bother's about. Kabub wants Magar, but she won't have him: Marigum insists on her marrying Kabub: Tafalti wants her for Kalaua: apparently she doesn't like Kalaua either. How silly it all sounds! Certainly Tafalti is a bad son, but Marigum is a bad father and a bad headman, carrying on like a small child in a tantrum.'

THE RETURN

The wanderer at last made his reappearance on 3 July. I noted his sullen expression, and several people commented on how ungracious he was when replying to their questions. What chiefly surprised them, however, for they had never previously seen him so self-conscious, was his studious avoidance of Tafalti: they had expected him to rant and rave or else to pretend that nothing had happened. Three days later he delivered one of his stage-managed soliloquies. 'I am alone, a poor unfortunate to whom nobody shows respect. My son disobeys me and bars the road to prevent my daughter coming to see me. How desolate I am! My relatives think of me only to laugh at my troubles and urge my son on to further iniquity. A dull lot they are, too, showing no care for my affairs during my absence. Even my brother Waru neglects me and complains about Yam beating one of the young girls in my household. I have returned to Dap now only that I may talk once more to Ian Hogbin and share food with him. After he leaves I shall seal up my house here and go away also. I'll live on the mainland where I won't be able to see these relatives of mine who are so unkind.'

Tafalti, who was sitting in a house across the street, now descended and suggested that the two of them should thrash the matter out then and there. They advanced to the centre of the village while the rest of us took our places at a respectful distance. Tafalti, to everyone's surprise, put his case remarkably well. Speaking clearly and without heat, he described Kabub's attempt to rape Magar and how pitiful were her tears. Acting as any brother would have done, he endeavoured to protect her from the risk of meeting such a brutal attack in the future. Emphatically he had no thought of setting himself up as a headman in competition with his father. If Marigum was determined to marry her off to Kabub let the wedding be arranged; he was certain she would refuse to go. He admitted the demand for compensation from Kabub, but the government had given its approval for payment. (This was incorrect, but others shared the illusion, and I am sure he honestly believed that the law was on his side.) Finally, he accused the women of carrying tales (why he should have absolved the men I did not understand). If his father had only heard with his own ears all that had been said he would not have taken offence. The accusation that Waru had blamed Yam for beating somebody was a case in point: this was nothing but the invention of a malicious housewife.

At that stage Yam joined them with a further denunciation of Waru. She knew for a fact, she insisted, that he had spoken against her for striking Sirai, an orphan betrothed to Tafalti's younger brother Gabis, at that time absent in employment.

This was another example of rebuking an affine by indirection (in an earlier instance, p. 121, Tago, instead of accusing his brother-in-law Marigum of pig stealing, chose rather to blame Wiawia). Marigum's widowed sister Makwa, another Dap villager, had made the charge, but for Yam to have scolded a sister-in-law would have been a grave breach of etiquette, and she therefore chose an oblique method of showing her resentment. She must have asked Marigum to name Waru as the offender, the latter explained to me afterwards, thereby giving additional proof of her undue influence. He was not prepared to accept the rebuke and, unlike Wiawia, denied loudly that he was in any way concerned.

Marigum put an end to the discussion by turning on his heel and stalking away, remarking as he did so, 'None of you has any esteem for me — no, not one of you. I'm alone, and soon I'll be leaving you to yourselves.'

In the ensuing buzz of conversation many people expressed their amazement at Tafalti's guts; he had stood up against Marigum resolutely and answered him point by point. Father and son were equally stubborn, it was agreed, and as neither was likely to give in, the prospects for reconciliation were not bright. Condemnation of Yam as a mischief-maker was unanimous, and probably the majority continued to feel indignant at Marigum's obstinacy. Waru was particularly acid in his comments, as might have been expected from the unjust charge levelled against him. Tafalti was now a married man of some experience, he reiterated. He was like the seed which, having fallen to the ground, was already putting forth shoots and showing indications of a good harvest, whereas the yield of the parent tree was diminishing. Marigum, instead of resenting his son's maturity, ought to recognize his worth and listen to his advice. As the seasons pass, so the reputation of the father, reluctant though he is to admit it, begins to grow cold, while that of the son becomes warmer (the word used was *fila*, literally 'speech'). Marigum must be aware of all this and perhaps for that very reason was jealous, but surely his dignity did not demand cruelty to Magar. Tafalti's conduct might have been exceptionable, but it was not without some justification. As for Dal, he need not at present come into the picture. The date of his induction as heir still lay in the future.

8 Marigum and Tafalti

BLACK MAGIC

A month passed quietly, and then on 3 August Kalaua publicly accused Kabub of taking Dal and casting evil spells over his father Kaman's gardens, causing the taro plants to wither and die.

An unimportant ceremony was taking place in Mwarok, but for a number of reasons I decided not to attend — I had seen it performed several times already, no one from Dap was going, and a storm seemed to be brewing. At the conclusion of the rites, when those present were standing about chatting, Kalaua, who was part of a contingent of guests from Falala, approached Kabub, one of the Job party, and charged him, in loud and angry tones, with blasting the gardens. 'Kakameri from Mwarok saw you and Dal there in the middle of the cultivations chanting the incantations and burying the evil medicines in the plots, and already the leaves are beginning to curl up,' Kalaua shouted. Kabub enquired when this was supposed to have happened. 'You know well; during the afternoon of the day before yesterday,' came the reply. 'Wait,' called Kabub, 'I'll fetch Dal, and we'll see what all this is about.' He ran back to Dap and told the story. Marigum was there but only three other men, one of them Jaua. They each grabbed a spear and, without pausing to consider, hurried in a body along the road to Mwarok. Fortunately, someone warned Kalaua of their approach, and he retreated quickly to his home village.

The party returned to Dap, according to Jaua growing angrier with each step. Marigum beat the slit-gong to recall everyone from work, and the enquiry began. Tafalti alone took no part and remained silent in his house. He owed allegiance to both the accuser and one of the accused, his brother-in-law Kalaua and his half-brother Dal, and so had no alternative but to remain aloof. At first all brandished their spears, twanged their bowstrings, and shouted at the tops of their voices that Kalaua must die. One or two became incoherent and literally foamed at the mouth.

Not till a long period had elapsed did anyone think of questioning Kabub and Dal as to their whereabouts at the time of the alleged offence. The former denied that he had been near Falala and was able to call on various companions as witnesses, and I soon realized that I could provide Dal with an alibi — he was with me developing photographic film.

Now that the innocence of the pair was established, the fury of the villagers seemed to increase, till Marigum was forced to remind them that a killing could well lead to official intervention and that they had better put away their weapons. Then he called to Jaua, handed him a spear decorated with cassowary feathers, thereby appointing him as his special representative, and bade him proceed to Mwarok and approach the headman Wakalu with a request that he arrange a meeting of the residents of Dap and Falala in his village for the next day. Kalaua must be there and also Kakameri, who asserted that he had seen Kabub and Dal performing the magic (Kakameri, as we know, was Marigum's son-in-law).

In the morning Tafalti left early for his garden to be out of the way, and at about nine o'clock the rest of us set off together for Mwarok. Notwithstanding Marigum's warning, all were fully armed, himself included. On arrival we seated ourselves under the trees on one side. Soon Kalaua and Kakameri approached from the opposite direction, each backed up by a crowd of relatives. Kaman was there but remained in the background and did not speak. Wakalu sat on the steps of his house in the centre and opened the proceedings with a short announcement that Marigum wished to see Kalaua and Kakameri about their accusations. Marigum then pranced up to the two of them and shook his spear at their chests. How dare they try to brand his son-in-law and son as sorcerers, he exclaimed. To say such a thing was also casting a slur on him! He and his relatives were not the sort of people to avail themselves of black magic in secret — if they had a complaint they would come right out with it in a public denunciation. Was it feasible to imagine that he and his son would resort to anything underhand? That was for little people: he was a headman well known for never doing a shabby or mean act. In any case the indictment was absurd. Kabub did not go near Kaman's gardens, and on the day named Dal was doing a job with Ian Hogbin and had not left his side. Kalal and Jaua followed and for the most part repeated Marigum's sentiments. At that point I joined in, imitating them as best I could. Shaking a stick as though it were a spear, I protested that to speak ill of Dal, who was part of my establishment, was the same as picking on me. How could he have been in two places simultaneously — processing films at home and in Kaman's gardens?

A general clamour then broke out, and for some minutes I feared lest someone might be wounded, even killed. Wakalu was also anxious. He jumped from his place and ran up and down between the two groups begging them to withdraw to the sides and listen to the argument. 'Come, Kakameri,' he called, 'tell us what you saw.' The latter then admitted he was a long way off when he sighted two people standing near Kaman's garden. At the time he felt sure they were Kabub and Dal, but he could have been mistaken. The older was wearing a dark-coloured loincloth, the

8 *Marigum and Tafalti* 149

younger a red one. Here was further evidence of wrong identification — all Dal's loincloths, supplied by me, were khaki. Wakalu then drew the meeting to a close with an announcement that Kabub and Dal could not have been guilty, and the sooner the incident was forgotten the better.

As we walked back to Dap it was agreed that the Falala villagers — Kalaua's kinsfolk — were 'now our cooks'; that is, 'we have proved them wrong and made them eat humble pie.'

The final outcome was that, at my suggestion, Marigum taught Dal, and me, the magic to blast growing taro. The lad then took an afternoon off to visit relatives in Falala and on the way made a detour to pass Kaman's gardens, where he cast the spells so recently learned. Here was underhand behaviour after all.

THE LAST DAYS

Nothing further having a direct bearing on the relations of Marigum and Tafalti occurred during the remainder of my stay on the island, and when I left they were treating one another in the same way as at the time of my arrival — politely but without cordiality. People were convinced, nevertheless, that, given provocation, Tafalti would again champion Kalaua and the daily routine in consequence might once more be upset.

After a sufficient interval had elapsed to allow Jaua to see the different events in perspective I asked him for his considered opinion of the affair. It was to be regarded as a tragedy of temperament, a clash of two men with iron wills neither of whom would give way, he said. The only solution would be for someone to elope with Magar. Marigum might fly into a rage and possibly threaten the young fellow with death, but if the two were prepared to stand up to him he would come round in the end, especially after an offer of compensation. Yet such an outcome could never be hoped for. Nobody would dare to place himself in such jeopardy. Moreover, after the girl's marriage was settled Tafalti would be sure to find other excuses for opposition. Father and son were alike indifferent to public opinion and determined at all costs to have their own way — characteristics also of Dal, young as he was, Jaua reminded me. Such qualities are desirable in a headman but out of place in a follower, and between them the wreck of Dap seemed inevitable. Fortunately Dal was growing up fast, and Marigum would soon be able to appoint him as successor. Once this was done, though Tafalti would be cross, he must give up. In the meantime there was always the risk he might resort to violence. If he did so Marigum might order his death, or he would have to run away to the mainland or one of the other islands of the Schouten group.

I much regret my lack of information about what went on when in 1935 Kalaua and Magar were married. If there were fireworks, as I have no doubt, Marigum must with the lapse of time have come to forgive the past. Thirteen years later, in 1948, though the couple lived in Falala, they often made the journey to Dap bearing gifts for the old man, who received them most graciously.

As for Tafalti, he became resigned to his subordinate position once Dal had been nominated, as Jaua forecast he would. Yet the suspicion about his encompassing Marigum's death indicates that people were convinced of his lingering hatred.

9 Food and Politics

This concluding chapter will be devoted to an account of the major social occasions punctuating the monotony of the daily round. They are of two types, the *walage*, which concern the residents of a single district, and the *warabwa*, when a headman and his followers and partners make a presentation to persons of comparable rank from a different district. Any islander asked in 1934 why Marigum and Kawang enjoyed such great renown would without hesitation have given the answer that they sponsored so many of these festivities.

The *walage* are but simplified versions of the *warabwa*, and I can therefore pass them over in a few introductory paragraphs. Briefly, they serve to enhance the reputation of the organizer, sort out his followers, confirm the closer ties of kinship, and attest the individuality and internal cohesion of the smaller local groups and build them up into a broader ensemble. How these ends are achieved will become clearer in the later discussion.

Headmen arrange *walage* to mark events of family rather than community importance, such as a younger son's accomplishing some act for the first time – perhaps planting his own garden – a daughter's coming-of-age, or the lifting of a taboo on visiting the dwelling of a favourite relative after the death of his wife. I shall describe the proceedings in Dap when Marigum's son Sabwakai, who was sent out for adoption in infancy to the woman Nyem, began wearing a rattan waistbelt.

In mid April, about a month before the main harvest of the Pacific chestnuts *(Inocarpus edulis)*, Marigum took a bullroarer beyond the confines of the village and swung it for some minutes, making a deep whirring noise. On his return he hung plaited streamers of white coconut leaflets on the front of his house and warned all and sundry that forest spirits had arrived to prevent any collection of the chestnuts, which must be left lying on the ground where they fell. The young men carved other bullroarers and swung them daily in the early mornings and late afternoons.

At the end of three weeks Marigum declared that the instruments were to be heard no more. The men and women had now to pick up the nuts while the youths gathered a stock of dry coconuts. About 300 would be enough, he said. Each household for the time being kept its own supply and busily removed the husks.

Meantime Marigum invited the headmen and elders of the other Wonevaro villages to attend on a certain date (3 May) and receive a gift of chestnuts. None of these had issued a corresponding ban, but the people immediately set out heaping up a quantity, as they explained, 'to help Dap.'

During the afternoon of the day appointed the Dap folk carried their chestnuts across to the clear space in front of Marigum's house. He watched from the verandah but asked Jaua to take charge. All the nuts went into three huge baskets, which they filled to overflowing. Alongside each Jaua placed fifty coconuts. The surplus 150 remained in a heap at the back.

One by one the different sets of villagers entered, first Job, then Mwarok, then Kinaba. Their chestnuts filled three more baskets, which Jaua ordered to be lined up with the rest. The Job people alone brought a supplement of coconuts, fifty of them, and he therefore split the pile at the back into two, one each for the Mwarok and Kinaba containers.

By now it was clear that there would be no appearance of anyone from Bariat. A dispute had occurred there a few days previously, and one of the headmen had left temporarily in disgust for Bagiau. The householders were so upset and disorganized as a result that they decided to stay at home.

Towards sunset Marigum gave the word for Jaua to go ahead with the distribution. He presented the Job basket and coconuts to Mwarok, the Mwarok basket and coconuts to Job, and one of the Dap baskets to Kinaba. The women from each place advanced and, assisted by the Dap housewives, filled their carrying bags with the chestnuts. Simultaneously the men took up the coconuts, and the various parties left for home with the older boys in the lead waving torches to light up the path. The elders in each case subsequently made an equal division among the component households.

The chestnuts and coconuts left over Jaua halved. He told the youths to carry one lot to my house, where it could stay till the morning, when they were to take it to the Bariat elders for sharing out. The rest he separated into three equal portions, the first for the villagers at the southern end of Dap, the second for those at the northern end, and the third for Marigum, who lived in the middle and had the greatest number of dependants.

That night each woman boiled a dish of chestnuts, which she served with almonds as an accompaniment, making a rich repast.

There was no passing to and fro of the chestnuts, as we shall see takes place with the pork at a *warabwa*, though a few men sent small parcels to relatives in Gol, where they are in short supply. The trees grow best on the verge of swamps, of which in hilly Bukdi there are but few.

WARABWA PROCEEDINGS SUMMARIZED

These festivals, by contrast, commemorate really significant happenings — the headman's appointing an heir, the construction of a grand new dwelling for himself or a clubhouse for his fellow villagers, or the settlement of a serious dispute. The gifts of food are not handed over in bulk but go from one man to another, called his *lasa*, who may be anyone from the corresponding cluster of the second village. Thus the organizing headman treats solely with a leader of similar rank, and each of his followers who takes part as a principal makes his offering directly to an individual householder on the other side. The purported aim, apart from personal aggrandisement, is to express honour and goodwill; but deep down the donors hope to inflict humiliation by an overwhelming extravagance of generosity. Often a man temporarily beggars himself and until fresh gardens come into bearing — never longer than a few weeks — has to rely on the hospitality of distant kinsfolk or partners *(bag)* not immediately concerned in the transaction. To even things up the recipients must later, after a not too protracted interval, deliver goods of equivalent worth. On this occasion, however, display and ceremonial are considered inappropriate. The headman selected as the object of the original presentation, if he now wishes to reverse the balance, can at last plan a festival on his own account.

Obviously the gifts arouse mixed feelings. The extra food may be welcome, enabling the family not only to enjoy the luxury of a meal of pork — as we know, pigs are never killed just for an ordinary household dinner — but also to discharge obligations incurred over the previous months by accepting shares from others; but nobody likes to be shamed or put out of countenance. When people suspect that a headman may be contemplating a festival the seniors from other places therefore avoid him lest they may become the focus of his attentions. Generally he has to trick one of them into paying him a visit, as, for instance, by shamming illness. When he has the victim safely inside the house he announces his intention by hastily performing a rite, the principal feature of which is bowling an orange-coloured coconut along the floor to where the man is sitting. Concealed witnesses come forward beating hand-drums, and refusal to accept is impossible. The word for this variety of coconut is *warupo*, the term also applied to the rite.

During the next few months much work has to be done. The pigs, if not already in prime condition, must be fattened, the almond harvest stored away to smoke in great crates over the fireplace, and extensive areas of land cleared for new cultivations. At last, when all the food is available, the actual presentation is preceded by further ceremonies. First the donors, accompanied by their wives and daughters and some of their kinsmen and partners from other places, visit the village or villages they are about to honour — or humble, according to the point of view — and identify who the various recipients are to be. This they do with the same variety of orange coconuts, now each representing a pig — one, two, or three as the case may be — which they hang over the entrance to the dwellings of the men chosen. Givers and receivers then dance together, though the latter soon retire to cook a light repast, of which everyone partakes. Then comes a brief period of four or five days for the final preparations — constructing the display platform, harvesting the taro, collecting coconuts, catching the pigs, and so forth. On the afternoon after the various tasks have been completed the women from the households where the supplies are to go, together with numbers of kinsfolk, make their way to the organizing settlement for a dance. Again the locals take part, except that this is an affair solely for female performers. The husbands in the host community therefore stand looking on until it is time to cook a meal for the women. The visitors eat and depart just before sunset. A couple of hours later their menfolk have a turn. First a small group enters the village and ritually cleanses and fumigates it by marching around, with much stamping of feet, flourishing of spears, and waving of torches. This time the donors stand to one side till the party has left, when they shoot arrows and fling stones and billets of wood after the supposedly frightened evil spirits. The rest of the receivers then enter, and another dance takes place. Early the following morning the hosts decorate the platform with the pigs and baskets of almonds and vegetables, adding also bananas, coconuts, areca nuts, and betel pepper. The guests arrive at about ten o'clock, but a ceremonial fight takes place at the gateway to the village before they actually enter and for ten minutes or so the normal rules of conduct do not operate. A final dance goes on till well into the afternoon, but eventually the gifts are distributed, and the crowd disappears.

I have no information for the period before about 1925 but gathered that from then on two or sometimes three festivals had been held each year. In 1934 there were two, one originating in Gol, the other in Ga. In the former the identification of the recipients took place on 23 July, the men's parade after the woman's dance on 27 July, and the final presentation on 28 July. The corresponding dates for Ga were 9, 13, and 14 August. The July-August-September quarter is usual, after the second almond crop in June and while the prevailing winds are still from the southeast. The northwest-monsoon season is ruled out owing to the risk of bad weather.

Now let us deal with the ceremonies in turn.

THE WARUPO

I cannot describe the rolling of the coconut at first hand — during 1934 it never took place — but am able to give from hearsay some account of the tricks headmen play to secure a dupe.

Probably early in 1932, about two years before my reaching the island, Marigum completed a new house, the sort of event that inevitably calls for a celebration. The headmen of Bagiau and Takul on either side of Wonevaro were therefore wary of visiting Dap, the more so in that a couple of them had already received presentations from him and had not yet been able to repay their debts. Accordingly he picked on Ga. The sole village in that district had the customary two leaders, and the problem was how to lure the senior of them, Wakera, into such a position that the symbolic coconut might be passed across.

Marigum's first step was to confide in his highest ranking father-in-law — as a polygynist he had more than one to choose from — Kaneg by name, a headman from neighbouring Job. This man readily agreed to a conspiracy and took to his bed with a pretended illness. He complained of severe pains in the chest and would accept only broth to eat, and even the householders from next door were taken in. At the end of a fortnight he summoned two young kinsmen and instructed them to announce to Wakera the probability of his dying (by bad luck he succumbed to a real disease, represented as sorcery, before the year was out). 'Tell him I feel death approaching and long to see his face before I depart,' said

Kaneg. As proof of the genuineness of the message he gave them his spear to take, thereby conferring upon them the formal role of envoys. Within forty-eight hours Wakera and some companions were on their way laden with delicacies to tempt the appetite of the invalid. As they passed through each settlement the villagers struck the slit-gong to announce to the sorrowing residents of Job that the party was approaching.

The visitors stayed for a few hours to comfort the now almost speechless Kaneg and then departed on the return journey. As they entered Dap some minutes later the householders there bade them pause to partake of food, which was cooked ready, and have a smoke. Marigum, naturally, accepted the responsibility for entertaining any headman, and he beckoned Wakera into the new house, where a platter of vegetables could be seen resting on a mat. All unthinking Wakera mounted the steps and sat down – to decline the invitation would in any case have been discourteous. Without a second's hesitation Marigum bowled the coconut at him, and the men in the corner immediately played a roll on the handdrums. Wakera showed concern and attempted to leave, but Marigum calmed him down, or perhaps reminded him of his manners, by pointing out that this was a shot not with a spear but with a nut and soon there would be plenty of pork. By the evening Kaneg was up and about laughing heartily at the joke. I assume from other stories I heard about him that he was something of a natural comedian, unusual for a headman, though Janggara of Gol would have kept him company.

In the following year Marigum turned his attention to Kaman, the leading headman of Falala in Bagiau. Once more some time had to elapse before a favourable opportunity presented itself for giving him proper notification.

Gale-force winds had been blowing for several days, and some of the houses in Wonevaro were damaged. Such misfortunes are often attributed to the black magic of the residents of other districts, and accordingly a band of young hotheads descended on Bagiau. They accused no one in particular but made a nuisance of themselves by behaving offensively and uttering threats of vengeance once they had discovered the culprit. A scuffle took place in Urawo, a village close to Falala, and a couple of people suffered a few bruises. On the young men's return, despite the fact that several came from other places, Marigum scolded them for taking matters into their own hands. It was his task to punish wrongdoing, he said. Then he called one of them over and told him to go immediately to Kaman with a demand for a pig as compensation for the storm havoc. Kaman, though no doubt angered by the implied charge of performing sorcery, did not even bother to plead innocence: he ignored the order.

After a few days Marigum sent a second messenger inviting Kaman and the other Bagiau residents to a public meeting at Dap to discuss the trouble. They accepted, and after some talk it was agreed that the episode should be forgotten. The Dap villagers then produced food, and all sat down to eat. At the conclusion of the meal Marigum suggested to Kaman that they might withdraw to his house for a quiet smoke. Within a few minutes those outside heard the sound of drums, and Kaman's followers realized that he also had been caught. The presentation that eventuated I was to see paid back in April 1934. I shall describe it presently.

An earlier case had still more unusual features. The originator was Janggara, who wished to make a festival for this same Kaman. As fellow conspirator he selected Mangora, a headman of Takul to whom he was bound by strong kinship ties. This man tore his clothing and smeared his face with pig's blood and, acting with consummate skill, then ran to Kaman's house begging for help to avenge a raid on Bwanag village by a party from Kwablik in Bukdi. Kaman quickly assembled the men who were at the time in Falala, and, armed with spears, they set out for the offending settlement. As they marched through Gol Janggara seized Kaman by the wrist and dragged him away on the pretence of arguing him out of his intention to attack. The coconut was in readiness, and the poor man did not realize till too late how gullible he had been.

These examples could be multiplied, but I shall conclude with one in which ambition was frustrated. It concerns Banggai, Wakera's fellow headman in Ga. Instead of keeping his own counsel he allowed his plan of offering Kaman a presentation to become public property (ostensibly it was to be a reward for taking the main part in the mortuary ritual for Banggai's aged father). On hearing the news Kaman organized his followers into a working bee shelling almonds. 'Yes, we've decided to start early,' he told enquirers. 'You see, Banggai is arranging a festival, and I want to help him.' The result was that the enterprise had to be scaled down to a minor enterprise, a *walage*.

The incident proves the wisdom of secrecy and discretion. At the same time, the leader does well to have guarded discussions with seniors he can trust. To be sure of success he must have the full backing of the men of his own cluster and promises of support from a number of the headmen from the villages round about. If some of these have heavy commitments hitherto undisclosed and are likely to be embarrassed by an additional demand on their resources, postponement may be called for.

A week or two after the *warupo* ceremony the headman places a ban on his followers slaughtering pigs until the completion of the cycle. This he does by exercising his right to summon from the other world the spirit monsters called *nibek,* whose voices are represented by bamboo flutes.[1] Killing an animal while these are present would amount to sacrilege.

IDENTIFYING THE RECIPIENTS

This ceremony is described as opening, or clearing the way, for the festival. The name is *wag jale: wag* is the term for a ballet with an underlying theme or plot, but *jale* apparently has no other meaning, though some people suggested that it might be a corruption of *jala,* road or pathway.

During the morning each man who is presenting a pig — usually there are from fifteen to twenty — brings an orange coconut to the clubhouse, where a member of the headman's household fastens them to a two-fathom length of rope decorated with ginger stalks, red and yellow ornamental but inedible fruit, and multicoloured Croton leaves. This he hangs for the time being from the rafters over the doorway.

From about ten o'clock onwards groups of kin and partners from outside arrive. At the Gol *wag jale* the party from Wonevaro, me included, reached there at midday. We consisted of over eighty men and women, youths and girls. Some said their main motive was to give adequate support to Marigum: he would be joining in with Kawang, whom therefore they would also be helping on Marigum's behalf. The others were interested rather in backing up their Gol connections more directly. The majority of the residents of the other two Bukdi villages, Bajor and Kwablik, were already present, as well as a number from Ga and Bagiau and, at the time to my surprise, a couple from Takul, men whom I expected to be lined up with the recipients. On the other hand, at least one of the Gol elders was missing, a close relative of Janggara. Thinking he might have been ill, I enquired as to his whereabouts and learned that he had joined the other side. The total in the village must have exceeded 400.

We spent an hour or so chatting, bathing, and chewing betelnut or smoking, and the men then began painting their faces with patches of red and yellow ochre, charcoal, and pipeclay. Once finished, they and the women donned their best clothing, and we

9 Food and Politics

were ready for the departure to Takul. We moved off at 3 p.m. and were soon gathered on the outskirts of Maluk, the nearer village, where we put on our ornaments. There were necklaces of shell discs or dog's teeth, straps sewn over with small cowry shells to be worn crosswise over the chest, dog's teeth waistbands, mother-of-pearl pendants and breastplates, anklets of dried seed-pods or dog's teeth, and dog's teeth armlets and leggings gay with sweet-smelling herbs, flowers, and coloured leaves. Many of the men wore head-dresses of feathers also — cockatoo, bird of paradise, or goura pigeon — but the women favoured triangular caps of twisted palm spathe.

Now came the ceremonial entry. The wives, or in some cases the daughters, of the pig donors, bearing aloft the rope of orange coconuts, led the way. Their gait was rhythmical, following the singing of the rest and the beat of an orchestra of hand-drums played by a dozen of the men, but, as is usual with their sex, there was no abandonment to the music, and they seemed to be shuffling along with bent legs and flat feet. Behind came the men in twos, some holding spears, with the drummers half way down the line. These were much more agile and, keeping strictly in time, lifted their feet high, leapt in the air, and twisted and turned. On either side were the remaining women, grouped into sets of threes and fours with arms linked round one another's backs.

On reaching the centre of the village the women at the front tore the rope apart and hung the coconuts on the thatch of the houses of the men who were to receive the pigs. Five were left over and lay for the present near the club. These were to go to Bwanag, the other Takul settlement, when later in the afternoon the proceedings were repeated there. The rest of the party crowded in behind and formed a tight circle round the drummers, with the women in the outer ring. Maluk is built on uneven ground, and space in consequence is restricted. Some of them for lack of room had therefore to take up a position on outcrops of rock, where they stood waving branches of coloured leaves. One by one the local residents and those who were assisting joined in, and for nearly an hour a great wheel of gesticulating and gyrating figures slowly revolved in front of the club.

The extras from outside who had aligned themselves with the recipients included several from Bagiau and a sprinkling from Wonevaro, Ga, and Bukdi, as well as the elder missing from Gol. I estimated that they and the Takul together made a total of over 250. Three quarters of the entire population were thus concentrated that afternoon in Maluk. Another hundred or so waited in Bwanag.

Suddenly the rhythm of the dance changed, and the women withdrew to the sides, allowing the men to form a long double column. Clenching pendants between their teeth and waving spears, they made a great procession around the houses, first advancing, then retreating a few paces, only to go forward once more. At last the drums ceased, and they paused and stood erect. Kawang, the sponsor, accompanied by his one adopted son, who was still a child, now strode up and down between the two rows. As he went along he slowly recited in a low voice the spell to cause his renown to spread till all the places in the known world – that is to say the Schouten and neighbouring islands and the adjoining New Guinea mainland – were speaking with awe of his reputation as the holder of food festivals. On completing the magic he and the boy withdrew so that he could rinse his mouth with salt water to rid himself of the taboo incurred by contact with such powerful supernatural forces.

The next phase was upon us before we could draw breath. The men who had received the coconuts rushed from their houses bearing presents in both hands for the male visitors – fishlines, bundles of hooks, lures, gaily painted canoe paddles, bunches of areca nuts, and rolls of home-cured tobacco. Hard on their heels came the wives and daughters with gifts for the women – bags, baskets, clay pots, wooden platters, and coconut water-bottles. There was wild confusion and for a few minutes much boisterous hilarity.

At this point some of the story ballets should have begun, but as the hour was late and we still had to go on to Bwanag the idea was abandoned. (Nothing in Wogeo starts punctually, and we had delayed our first arrival for too long.) The party hastily gathered itself together, and soon the entry, dances, and spells were being repeated in the second village. Some members stayed on and ate there, and others went back to Maluk, where by then a variety of dishes was set out. Most of the visitors to Gol preferred to spend the rest of the night there, where till past midnight more dancing took place, but a few returned to their own homes by torchlight.

The Ga *wag jale*, held in the Bagiau village of Urawo, was in all respects similar, and almost as many people were present. Here also a late start resulted in the omission of the ballets. I shall therefore postpone my description till we come to the end, when in both places several hours were devoted to them.

FINAL PREPARATIONS AND THE WOMEN'S DANCE

The main job in the next few days is building the platform for the display of the food. The Gol villagers with a few helpers from other parts of Bukdi, and also the Ga villagers in their turn, erected it in the front of the clubhouse but slightly to one side, leaving plenty of room for the dances. The supporting piles were a metre high and the frame over thirty metres long and four metres broad. On this they constructed a canoe — a dugout with outrigger, booms, and decking — of green timber and black-palm wood. The sides they filled in with white unbroken coconut leaflets, and along the gunwales they hung swags of coloured leaves interspersed with bright vermillion fruit, regrettably inedible.

Once the platform is fixed the food can be collected. The youths gather hundreds and hundreds of green drinking coconuts, bunches of areca nuts, and stocks of betel pepper; and they also catch the pigs and tether them alongside the owners' houses. Meantime the men cut down whole banana trees, and the women dig up the taro and other root crops. Then with a mighty effort they combine to bring almost everything to the village. At this stage the banana trees alone go on the platform, where the men stand them upright and tie them to the rear of the canoe hull so that the bunches rest on the decking. Each householder leaves behind in his garden a few small baskets of taro and a hand or two of bananas. These he stands in a conspicuous spot near the fence with covers of leaves and old mats as protection from the weather.

While the host villagers are carrying out the various tasks their supporters from elsewhere are also busy preparing contributions. For the Gol festival Marigum wished to present Kawang with two pigs, but as he had only one of his own to spare he demanded the second from Waru, much to the latter's annoyance. ('The gains from being a headman's brother don't make up for the disadvantages,' he announced to me in private.) The rest of the Dap residents and some of Marigum's closer relatives from elsewhere brought their supplies to his house to be piled up as part of the gift. The remaining Wonevaro folk attending, from Mwarok, Kinaba, Job, and Bariat, retained theirs to give as personal donations to Gol kinsmen or partners. When the time came for our departure we fastened each pig by its legs to a pole, which relays of young men transported. The rest of us followed, men and women all laden with baskets of goods that grew heavier during the seven-kilometre journey. On arrival we took the animals with Marigum's offering to Kawang's house. The other food, naturally, went to the particular persons already chosen.

For reasons explained earlier, my information from Ga is less satisfactory than that from Gol, but it is certain that no pigs went from Wonevaro, although several people, including Marigum, took almonds and vegetables. Two headmen from Takul gave Wakera one each, and a headman from Bukdi contributed a third.

    The recipients, warned beforehand, are ready on the penultimate afternoon for the women's dance, a literal translation of the vernacular term *veine gela*. At the Gol festival the Takul females and those accompanying them made their entry around two o'clock. The settlement was at that period located on a ridge, and they formed a column of six abreast in the valley below. Then to the steady beat of the drums, played on this occasion by some of the older housewives, they ascended the zig-zag pathway to the gate. Each had borrowed the finery of her husband or brothers, and their appearance was stunning. The Gol women and supporters stood on either side to give them a welcome and afterwards closed in at the rear. As before, a great wheel began turning, and a throng of perhaps 200 went round and round in front of the club. Most of the small children watched from nearby, but a few women danced with a baby on their back. The men took no active part and generally continued with ordinary work, pausing from time to time to clap with cupped hands, strike a note or two on the slit-gong, or call out loudly as encouragement, '*Wa, wa, wa!*'

    This continued for half an hour, when after a short pause a series of figure dances began, with various leaders, who always had to be persuaded and pushed to the front. In what was perhaps the most picturesque a troupe of about fifty made a line one behind the other with hands on hips and a shell pendant between the teeth. They shuffled forwards till each reached a certain point, then she turned, the first to the right, the next to the left, the third again to the right, and so on, seized a spear proffered by a bystander, and retreated in the opposite direction, interweaving with those who were still advancing. On coming to the end of the line they faced about and went through all over again. Several of the figures called for sets of small circles, others for different rows facing the same way, and a particular one for a hollow square in which the two sets of opposite sides alternately mingled and separated. There were also games using a coconut or taro corm as a ball. In one of these a woman hit a girl betrothed to a son of Marigum harder than had been intended on the back of the head. Her future step-mother-in-law, Yam, immediately rose to her feet — she was too old for dancing — and with immense dignity ordered the offender to take better care.

    Periodically the Gol hostesses made for their dwellings and

emerged with presents for the guests, such goods as clay pots, food bowls, baskets, bags, armbands, and skirts. At about four o'clock most of them retired to cook the meal that the rules of hospitality demanded. This they served sufficiently early to permit the party to be on the road before dark.

DANCE FOR THE MEN

While the women are dancing the men from the receiving villages visit the donors' gardens and coconut groves to collect a pile of dried coconut leaves, which they bind together for use later as torches, and a stock of ripe coconuts. Any sweet-smelling herbs discovered in the forest or the cultivations they pluck and stick in their armbands and the holes in their ear-lobes. Such plants are a normal vehicle for beauty magic, called *ngarul*, and from this term the subsequent ceremony and dance derive their name. The men cook and eat the food left for them in the baskets, perhaps bathe, and then proceed to a rendezvous with their womenfolk, who are now on the way homeward. While waiting they paint their faces.

After the dance in Gol the Takul women reached the meeting place as night drew on. They exchanged a few desultory remarks with their husbands and brothers, handed back the borrowed finery, took most of the ripe coconuts, and continued on their way. On reaching home they were supposed to prepare oil to rub on themselves the next day, but while a few did so, the others said they were too tired or had to busy themselves looking after the children.

The men arrayed themselves and when satisfied strode on to the valley below Gol. By then it was quite dark. Twenty separated from the rest to perform the purifying rite whose object was to drive away any intruding ghost or other kind of evil. They formed up in pairs, the man on the left brandishing a spear on which he had impaled a coconut and the one on the right holding up a flaming torch. As they ascended the path the members of the orchestra, who for the time being stayed with the rest at the bottom, began beating their drums and blowing conch-shell trumpets. The sound gave the signal for an elder within the village to follow the steady throb on the slit-gong beneath the clubhouse. The others took up stations where they could see without being in the way. My relatives warned me to stop quietly in the place they had suggested, a high rock, and not descend into the street till the first part of the show was over. 'You know quite well nobody would want to harm you, but these people are in such a state of excitement that you might be pushed over if you hindered their progress,' it was explained.

Now the group was upon us. The men marched as one with an unbroken stamp, stamp, stamp of the feet till the ground itself seemed to be trembling under the impact of a minor earthquake. They had the mother-of-pearl breastplates clenched between their teeth and contorted their faces into a transport of rage. The seniors were all in traditional costume, but the two or three youths wore new white loincloths and had powdered their faces.

As in other purification rituals – for example, after a funeral or when the spirit monsters are despatched back to the world of the supernatural – the noxious influences have to be driven out by fire and weapons. The members of the party therefore went around each dwelling with one man waving his torch under the eaves and his partner poking at the thatch with his spear. Twice they did this and then with the same stamping descended the hill to their fellows. Never have I been present at a more dramatic performance. We waited in our places till they were out of range before shooting arrows and hurling blocks of wood and stones into the surrounding bush at the evil forces already on the run.

Now came the dancers. There were six sets, composed at random according to where people happened to be standing, following behind each other at short intervals. These remained separate as they stepped up and down the village street. The pair formation was repeated, again with one man carrying a lighted torch and the other a spear, though this time without an impaled coconut. A crowd of boys brought up the rear bearing the remainder of the coconut-leaf flares, which they held out later as replacements when one by one the others burned down. But before long the moon rose, and artificial illumination was not necessary.

Gradually the Gol residents and their helpers from Wonevaro and elsewhere filed in behind, and soon still another wheel of performers was encircling the central area. Various formal dances followed during the next two hours, when the women brought out platters of hot vegetable stew. The majority of the visitors slipped away as soon as they had eaten, but many of the locals started up again and continued dancing till dawn.

THE LAST DAY

The work of arranging the food on the platform begins early in the morning. The different households produce their baskets of almonds, taro, yams, fruit, and coconuts; and the youths and men tip them into huge receptacles, which they place on the decking of the canoe. Then out come the pigs, each with legs fastened round a pole, now decorated with mats, white coconut leaflets, Croton and Cordyline leaves, and strings of the vermillion fruit. Some of the youths line the animals along the street while others sound leaf whistles, allegedly the voices of other spirit monsters known as *wakaka*, a noise that forces the women to go indoors.[2] The originating headman can now perform magic to enhance the flavour of the meat, increase the quantity of fat, and reduce the appetite of the recipients so that they will marvel at how far the joints go. Ordinarily the men suspend the bespelled pigs around the front of the platform, but if the headman is using the festival as a means of naming an heir the animals must be slung one below the other from two uprights representing the masts, thereby giving the structure the appearance of a vessel under sail.

At the Gol festival there were seventeen pigs, over six tonnes of taro, four tonnes of husked, dried almonds, and 200 ropes of bananas (over half a tonne of fruit), 5000 green drinking coconuts, and hundreds of bunches of areca nuts and betel pepper. How much of this Kawang and the members of his housing cluster supplied I do not know exactly, but my estimate was nine of the pigs, a third of the taro and almonds, and the bulk of the bananas, coconuts, areca nuts, and betel pepper. At Ga during that festival there were sixteen pigs, rather less taro, the same quantity of almonds and coconuts, but fewer bananas. Nine of the pigs had come from Wakera and his immediate supporters. On both occasions the hosts took immense care in creating the best aesthetic effect with their platform.

The ritual performed over the pigs at Gol was of particular interest. As soon as they were set in line and the leaf whistles had sounded, a close relative of Kawang, acting on his instructions, dabbed red paint on the head and rump of each. He then ceremonially cleansed them by emptying several bamboos full of bespelled coconut liquid over their flanks. These vessels, as sacred objects, he later threw behind the club. Kawang now advanced with a bundle of Cordyline leaves in one hand and in the other a half-coconut shell filled with oil, red paint, and grated coconut meat. He dipped the leaves in the container and thumped the neck of each animal, reciting his magical formula as he did so (this blow with the leaves gives the rite its name, *wun*, to hit). 'These pigs will now be pork for many,' he told me.

The workers may take a hurried bathe, but they refrain from using face paint and wear only a few simple ornaments. This is the day for the guests, they explain. They also take little part in the dancing, though they watch intently and applaud any special brilliance with the usual cries of *'Wa, wa, wa!'*

The proceedings open with the hosts blocking the entry to the village against the guests, who are thus obliged to force their way in. Instantly the women climb up to the house verandahs out of reach, and for about ten minutes, after which the headmen intervene, all is disorder. As has been mentioned, the rules of kinship behaviour are suspended, and persons who are ordinarily expected to treat one another with respect, such as affines and the members of opposite moieties, are allowed to indulge in abuse and to exchange blows. Weapons are forbidden, and tongues, hands, and feet must suffice; but black eyes, minor cuts, and bruises are a commonplace. What happens is not a brawl with two sides that remain distinct but a series of separate skirmishes between pairs of men or small groups. Some hosts fight other hosts, some hosts fight guests, some guests fight other guests. As I explained in Chapter 7, the purpose of the affair is to provide an opportunity for expressing grievances normally concealed, as of a husband against his wife's lover. For a brief period each man is permitted to bring into the open the irritations that hitherto he has been obliged to suppress.

At Ga the blocking of the road took place, and the ensuing fights went on for twelve minutes, then Wakera and Marigum and a couple of other headmen, clutching spears, demanded that everyone desist and allow the festival to continue; but at Gol Kawang did his best to prevent the mêlée. He requested two men to impersonate still another type of monster, the *lewa* or *tangbwal*,[3] and stand guard at the village gateway. They duly dressed up in the appropriate garments — a body covering of dyed sago fibres, a wooden mask, and a tall wicker head-dress topped with human hair — and as the guests approached ran between them and the hosts waving Cordyline leaves and ginger sprays as a sign of peace. The effort was of no avail, and within moments the fighting groups were buffetting them to right and left. Kawang, Marigum, and Janggara had eventually to rush in and threaten all sorts of dire penalties.

Once the fighting has stopped and people have recovered their normal poise the dancing begins. It goes on till well into the afternoon, and performances are restricted to ballets *(wag)* based on a theme or a story. The men alone take part, with the women serving as audience. Sometimes the music is drowned by wailing. Persons recently bereaved are confined to the house, and the gaiety and merriment in which they can play no part are a vivid reminder of their loss. Accordingly they give themselves over to lamentations.

There are dozens of ballets, with new ones frequently invented. The tunes are traditional, but several men have a gift for making up lyrics and working out fresh choreography. Inspiration comes in dreams, so people said. I often attended rehearsals on moonlight nights.

Among the more popular ballets are the snake and the pig, the fisherman, the hawk and her young, the pig hunt, and spearing the octopus. For the first some 20 or 30 men, all holding a rope with one hand, form a line with the other hand grasping the shoulder of the man in front. They dance around for some time curving to left and right in imitation of a snake, and at length the pig comes on the scene represented by a man hunched forward with his arms hanging down like a pair of forelegs. He pretends to root the ground and wallow in mud but is soon disturbed by the snake. He tries to run away and is then attacked and bitten. A good actor can die with great effect. In the fisherman ballet six troupes of eight men take the stage. They represent shoals of fish, and each dancer is on all fours with his buttocks in the air. Their skill in holding the rhythm as they crawl about with their behinds bobbing up and down always gives rise to applause and laughter. The fishermen enter holding barbed spears at the ready as they shade their eyes and peer into the distance. They catch some of the fish, which expire with great gasps, and others escape. For the hawk ballet the performers have women's fibre skirts attached to their arms to give the impression of wings. The mother bird protects her gaping young in the nest and dives for fish, which she regurgitates to feed them. The octopus requires a circular formation with eight projecting tentacles of four men each.

The most spectacular of the ballets is that of the almond collectors, which I saw in Ga. A group of men entered carrying poles with a crook at the end such as are used for pulling down bunches of nuts. They went through the motions of stripping several trees and then moved into the wings. Next the wives appeared – men dressed as women. They picked the almonds from the ground and dropped them into baskets, but while they were so occupied their lovers emerged stealthily as though from hiding and began urging them in mime to come into the bush. After much show of anxiety lest the husbands should find out they eventually agreed. Soon the men returned, and there was a fight with the lovers, who were driven from the stage.

I stress that I have been describing not games but dances. The performers' steps and gestures are always strictly in time with the drummers, who stand at the side beating out the rhythm and singing the different songs. There is no mistaking what is being portrayed despite the hightly stylized movements.

By early afternoon everyone is exhausted, and the organizing headman brings things to a close by publicly carrying out the magic to preserve the peace of the village and give it protection from attack. The rite is referred to as *kinaba,* the word 'to nod'. At Gol, Kawang as an act of courtesy invited the former headman of the other cluster to take over on his behalf. The man's name was Natuia, and he had long since retired in favour of his son Janggara. I judged him to be over eighty: he was blind, and a grandson led him by the hand.

Later on Kawang taught me the magical spell and how to perform the rite. First I must take ginger root and the leaves from two lianas, the *waluo* and the *dabara,* and chew them all together. Then I should stand firmly with my feet apart 'like an immovable rock' and chant the following words over the people present:

> The tree standing tall,
> Fastened securely, covered entirely,
> With *waluo* and *dabara* vines.
> My beloved village,
> Fastened securely, covered entirely,
> With *waluo* and *dabara* vines.
> Old baskets are black,
> Black over the hearth,
> Blackened by the smoke.
> Food to eat, much food,
> Fastened, secure, held tightly.

At the end of each line I must spit some of the contents of my mouth over the crowd to my left, then over that on my right, simultaneously giving a polite nod, *kinaba.*

He showed me how the *waluo* and *dabara* lianas envelop a tree so completely that the branches are locked together and do not rub against each other. It thus resists the force of the strongest winds and remains firm. Further, the thorny tangle is so thick that nobody can approach to take the fruit or wield an axe. The smoke-blackened baskets are a sign of continuing peace — they have remained undisturbed for so long. The magic gives the settlement stability. The different households do not dispute with one another, and sorcerers fear to carry out their wicked designs.

Immediately after the completion of the *kinaba* ritual the recipients come forward and without further ceremony strip the platform. The donors and their families offer no assistance, though each indicates the pig he has provided and who is to take it. The almonds, taro, coconuts, and other products are divided into roughly equal quantities for every pig. Those who are to bear the burdens, men and women, take up the loads, and within the hour the hosts are alone, often with only the barest scraps to eat. They subsequently dismantle the platform and throw the timber and rubbish out of sight behind the club. Before they do so, however, the headman has to despatch the *nibek* monsters back to the world of the spirits, thus permitting the new owners to kill the gift pigs.[4]

The initial cooking of the Gol pork and other food took place in Maluk and Bwanag, and I did not attend. As a resident of Dap I was identified with the donors, and it would have been thought rude had I intruded. I also missed the corresponding activities in Urawo after the Ga festival. But I had already been able to record much of what went on when the Dap villagers received the return for their offerings to Kaman and his followers in the festival of 1933. I shall give the details in the next section, and for the moment all I need say is that those first singled out divide the pork and other things among their relatives and partners, that these in turn make a division among their relatives and partners, and so on almost *ad infinitum*.

THE COUNTER OFFERING

People tell stories of headmen of the past who were so wealthy that they were able within a day or two to pay off the debts incurred by accepting a festival, sometimes before the sharing out of the food was completed. Such tales are unlikely to be accurate, for in the 1930s a year or more had to elapse before the pigs and other supplies were available in adequate quantity. Kaman waited fifteen months before he and his followers could settle their account with Marigum.

The repayment has no special name except that until the gifts are returned the original donors speak of their pigs as 'alive': an animal 'dies' only with the receipt of its equivalent. The aim is to make things even, 'to come from underneath' in the local phrase, and any fuss or flourish is felt to be out of place. The earlier accepters, now the secondary donors, abstain from decorating themselves or the animals and from arranging any dances or performing any magic. In certain circumstances, indeed, some men may act by themselves ahead of the rest. Thus Kaman's son Jaj, who owed a pig to Wiawia, gave him one before anybody else was ready. The beast in question had broken through the fence around a garden and destroyed a considerable area of growing taro. The owner of the crop speared it in the leg, as he was entitled to do, and told Jaj to remove it. The latter, fearing that it might die as a result of the wound, went straight to Wiawia with a request that he accept it at once. Wiawia agreed and set off in his canoe to fetch it. Jaj added a large basket of taro and three ropes of bananas.

A month after this Kaman sent a message to say that Marigum and his followers could collect the fifteen remaining pigs – together with the almonds, taro, coconuts, and fruit – in three days' time. That evening Marigum had a village elder sound the slit-gong to call the people together for the announcement. He sent no word to any supporters outside the district, and the working party therefore consisted solely of residents of Wonevaro. We reached Falala, where Kaman lived, at three o'clock and found the pigs ready trussed and pushed beneath the houses. There they were protected from the blazing sun, but clearly the motive was to avoid display, not to provide comfort for the animals. Similarly, coverings of leaves hid the goods in the baskets. We chatted with our hosts, who remained sitting on the verandah, and for a short time chewed betelnut and smoked. Then we loaded the canoes, which had come for the heavier cargo, and shouldered our burdens for the return journey.

Nothing was done that evening, and the pigs remained fastened to the carrying poles. They were already gasping, and during the night some of them died. Six came to Dap, three to Marigum and one each to three other householders.

After dinner most of the Wonevaro men adjourned to the Dap clubhouse, which was the largest and most comfortable in the district. The one topic of conversation was the, in general, miserable size of the pigs. Some householders, certainly, were satisfied and made no complaints, but the majority talked endlessly of how shabbily we had been treated. They spoke enviously of a legendary figure from the past, Mwog of Bajor, who they said was so angry at the inadequate return offered by his *lasa* that he refused to accept it. The man, admitting the fault, made amends with a bigger animal. I then joined in the discussion. Why, I wanted to know, had everyone left his grumbles till now? Surely the time to have spoken up was during the afternoon, when instead they had all been so amiable. And if it was agreed that the action of Mwog had been justified, why did nobody follow his example? Quite impossible, the assembly assured me; and as the pigs had been hidden, how could anyone see what he would receive? It is reasonable to speak of a person's faults when he is not there listening, but those with a proper upbringing never dream of shaming him to his face. If I had ever heard people counting over their wrongs regardless of who was within earshot I could depend upon it that they had been tried in the extreme. No, the Falala villagers and the rest of the residents of Bagiau were hopeless, without any sense of what is correct; they had always been mean and no doubt always would be. As for Mwog, he must have been really important, the sort of leader who could afford to ignore the rules.

I gathered that this was a normal reaction. After the counter gifts have arrived few of the original donors feel they have made a good bargain, and more often than not the *lasa* has to bear the criticism.

Next morning everyone in Dap was early on the move. The day was fine, and the villagers carried the pigs to the beach. Each owner and the senior members of his immediate household worked as a unit on their own animal, but the young people pooled their efforts and moved about from place to place according to the task of the moment. The first thing was to gather fuel and light a couple of fires over which the pigs could be held to singe off their bristles. This is the regular way also of killing those that survive the night, and the squeals are horrifying. I had to keep out of range till the last one had been dealt with (an anthropologist must remain an observer and, no matter what the provocation, avoid interfering).

Almost everyone is capable of cutting up a carcase, but in each place two or three men are recognized as especially skilled. Accordingly, the experts now took over and carved the pigs in turn. They slit open the belly to remove the entrails, a great delicacy that the youths immediately roasted. These lads then divided the pieces, and people chewed as they worked. The butchers next hacked off the legs, leaving the back and ribs intact. They cut the meat into long strips, which they tied tightly with the vines in order, so they said, to preserve the maximum amount of fat.

Meantime the women, helped by a few men, had been heating stones for a series of ovens. I said earlier that the islanders import clay pots from the mainland but use them mainly for boiling or steaming vegetables: pork they always bake. There was an oven for each pig, but the pieces were set in a row for public inspection both before and after cooking. During the intervening period most of the men whiled away the time by fishing, and the women collected shellfish off the reef.

But it would be a mistake to imagine that the opening of the ovens meant that the feasting could begin at once. The main concern was ensuring that obligations to relatives and exchange partners in other districts were met. So Marigum, for instance, set aside a third of his cuts, one whole pig, for Kawang; and Bagasal, the other Dap headman, who had received but one animal, picked out four pieces weighing a total of 30 kilograms for Janggara, another lot weighing 10 kilograms for a headman of Kwablik, and a third lot weighing 7 kilograms for a headman of Bajor. Some of the young men packed the joints into baskets, adding smaller amounts, carefully separated by pads of leaves, from other householders for their respective kinsmen or partners in the same villages. The men rehearsed their instructions to make certain there would be no mistakes, took up the loads, and attended to the delivery. Several women accompanied them with packages of almonds, taro, and bananas. The party stayed the night and was back again by early morning. The members of the families left behind took the rest of the pork to the houses and hung it on hooks out of reach of the rats in the roof and the dogs on the floor.

In the tropics meat soon goes bad, and after breakfast the next day the women, assisted by the youths, had to re-cook everything. On this occasion Marigum allocated some of the pieces from his second pig to Wakera of Ga and the headmen of Mwarok and Bariat in Wonevaro. Other people presented various cuts to relatives in Wonevaro and Takul — their maternal uncles, cousins, brothers-in-law, and so forth. Again what remained went back to the houses, only to come out once more in the morning for still another baking.

The Dap residents were not alone in wanting to fulfil obligations: their kinsmen and affines felt the urge no less keenly. So now, on the third day, quantities of pork and almonds began to come back into the village. This went on for the rest of the week, interspersed by the constant return to the oven of the pieces, which were becoming smaller and smaller as the householders cut portions off.

The same kind of thing was taking place in the other districts to which the earlier gifts had gone. Kawang divided and shared his pig, redivided it and reshared it, received other pieces back, and gave some of these away.

I went to the trouble of tracing the exact perigrinations of frag-

9 Food and Politics

ments of several joints. Each one, weighing at the start approximately 7 to 10 kilograms, ended up as six slices which had passed through from five to seven hands and in the process been cooked eight times. By then, depending on the part of the pig's anatomy, some were like disintegrating balls of string, and others resembled the sole of an old boot.

Equally confusing was what went on in the individual dwellings. Thus the three adult occupants of one, first received a piece weighing 6 kilograms, divided it into five parts, three of slightly more than 1500 grams and two of 500 grams, and gave all but the last 500 grams away; then over an interval of five days five different persons presented them with a total of 5 kilograms, two of which passed along to others. These housholders accordingly finished up with 3.5 kilograms for themselves and two children.

I found that a share of the meat, possibly as much as 50 kilograms, actually went back to Falala, apart from other Bagiau villages, some of it comparatively direct from Wonevaro and some by roundabout means through Ga and Takul. In this case, however, the givers took the greatest care, no mean feat, to find out who had reared the particular pig, for it would have been unpardonable to offer anyone part of his own animal. At the same time, Kaman, as the secondary originating headman, received nothing at all. Marigum had only a little, thereby confirming the saying that leaders think first of their followers and hence confine their own feastings to sucking the bones.[5]

By 1934 a few breeding boars and sows from Australia had been introduced, but the majority of the island pigs were still long-legged, narrow-shouldered, and scraggy, even though the owner did his best to fatten them. My spring balance was capable of weighing only the joints, and I had no means of measuring the dressed carcases. My estimate was 100 kilograms apiece.[6] The fifteen provided therefore made up some 1500 kilograms of meat. If from the population of 929 we exclude, say, 129 as infants and another 100 who had to go without, it appears that each of the remaining 700 must have finished up with little more than 2 kilograms. Considering that they would have to wait several months for the next slaughter, it would seem that the amount of animal protein in the Wogeo diet is scarcely worth mentioning.

FLEXIBILITY OF THE SYSTEM

The Wogeo islanders all have hundreds of kinsfolk and affines, as we know; moreover, such relationships imply mutal loyalty. A headman holding a festival, and the one selected for the receiving end, should therefore be able to count on almost unlimited assistance. The latter, as the immediate beneficiary, may not be in such dire need of support to begin with, though even at that stage he is obliged to provide hospitality for the crowds of visiting dancers. The full onus of responsibility comes to him later, when he makes his repayment.

The population is so small, however, that inevitably any two individuals share certain of their relatives, men who are cousins of both perhaps or cognates of the one and affines of the other. The more prominent the pair, the wider the circles of recognized consanguines and in-laws are likely to be and in consequence the bigger the area of overlap. Ordinarily, being in the middle does not give rise to competition in demands for help. With everyday tasks such as gardening and house construction, for instance, a man connected with headmen from his own and another cluster makes his services available to the first today and to the second tomorrow. But if they are respectively the giver and the recipient in a festival, he may find their simultaneous claims upon his time awkward. Unable to be in two places, he must decide on where he can secure the greater favour or incur the lesser displeasure. The most significant consideration turns out to be based on a combination of locality and genealogy. He tends to side with the headman of his own cluster, village, or district — the very one with whom he is likely to have the closer ties. But the rule is not by any means inflexible, and, as has been indicated, I sometimes missed householders from gatherings to which I had assumed they belonged and found them where initially they might have seemed out of place. Thus at Kawang's festival a man from Gol elected instead to join Mangora in Takul, and at Wakera's someone from Ga preferred for the occasion to transfer to Urawo. In the one case resentment at a real or fancied slight was the cause, in the other unwonted kindnesses and possibly the expectation of more to follow. Correspondingly, a couple of the Takul villagers went over to Gol and a couple from Urawo to Ga.

A resident of a district other than those of either of the headmen directly implicated has more freedom of choice. The example of Waru during the Gol festival is instructive. It will be remembered that Marigum demanded a pig to eke out his own contribution to Kawang. Refusal was impossible — Waru would not have dared to brush Marigum's request aside, and in addition the two were next-door neighbours and considered themselves to be the same as brothers. Yet in Takul, Waru also had a cousin to whom he was devoted, and when at nearly the last moment this man invited him to link up with the recipients he was tempted to accept. After long cogitation he reached a compromise. He remained with Marigum and hence Kawang, as was practically inevitable since they would have the pig, but despatched his wife, well stocked up with almonds and taro, to the cousin's. I noted two more Wonevaro householders who gave their spouses similar orders and an additional four, out of a total of about sixty, who went over themselves to Takul. I never saw the full cycle of the one festival but would hazard a guess that occasionally the odd villager might change sides half way through. Why not, if he can protect his reputation and has relatives in both settlements?

The stress on locality raises the question of whether the headmen from the more densely settled southern half of the island, comprising Wonevaro and Bagiau, have for this reason an advantage. The answer is that they probably start off a step or two ahead. Yet, in the long run, early superiority means almost nothing. Drive is what counts, and a leader obviously on his way up is never at a loss for want of followers. Kawang from sparsely populated Bukdi was no less famous than Marigum, but their contemporary Kaman from well stocked Bagiau was some way behind.

Marigum and Kawang overtopped the rest on account of the quantity not the quality of their festivals. The amount of food, give or take two or three pigs, seems always to be about the same. There was little difference between the heaps of supplies mounted at Gol and at Ga, and each time six to seven hundred were in attendance. But whereas Wakera, along with Mangora, Kaman, and Sami, held celebrations only at rare intervals — they had to return them more often — Marigum and Kawang did so frequently. They squandered their resources at a great rate, but as debts have always to be honoured, those of a dead man by his heirs, the equivalent comes back after only a slight delay. They depended upon their followers working with them to replenish the herds of pigs and enlarge the area of gardens, but all received a fair share of the ample rewards. In other words, the common people satisfy an appetite for pork and other things by attaching themselves to acknowledged leaders who, dismissing their own bellies as scarcely worthy of a thought, concentrate on magnifying such intangibles as their status and prestige.

EFFECTS OF THE FESTIVALS

In the cold light of common sense festivals must appear absurd. As each day passes the people put much effort into carrying the food backwards and forwards, its nutritional value diminishes, and the risk of illness caused by contamination and the multiplication of harmful bacteria increases. The rational procedure would be for households to kill their pigs as soon as the animals reach maximum size.[7] But the Wogeo see things differently. They prefer to save up for a celebration.[8]

My relatives explained to me that a festival makes the whole place straight. Each person reaches agreement with his fellows, those from his own village and those from elsewhere, and quarrelling is outlawed. The dancing points to the ideal of tranquillity, first all together in the settlement of the recipients, then all together again in the settlement of the donors. The festival is a time of happiness and rejoicing (*kanikani*, derived from the word meaning 'to eat', *kani*). Was I not myself aware of all the laughter, how even those who normally were of serious demeanour now wore a gay face and cracked jokes? And when the heart is light (the lungs in local speech), so is the entire body — the breathing, the muscles, the limbs. Work is accomplished with ease, and nobody becomes exhausted or irritable. Men run instead of walking, jump instead of standing still. Why the change? The answer is simple. Who does not enjoy dressing up in all his shells, dog's teeth, and feathers and showing himself off before an admiring throng? Who does not love the sound of the drums? Who is not overwhelmed by the steady rhythm of the dance? And who can resist the feeling of well-being at the sight of so much food?

Such statements seemed to be an accurate summing up of the situation. There was a general quickening, and people went about their business with relish and zest. Apart from the ceremonial fight, and this was soon over, aggressiveness was never manifested overtly.

The emphasis on the outward expression of ill temper is to be noted: nothing was said about what the smiles and easy comradeship might conceal. Yet deep down people do become annoyed, even enraged. On various occasions jealous husbands and lovers came murmuring to me, the sympathetic and understanding outsider who had proved so trustworthy with secrets, about the suspected intrigues of a faithless spouse or a flirtatious sweetheart with some attractive seducer, a host if the accuser was a visitor, a guest if he was at home. Once or twice I quoted back the proverb about smashing a pot, but the invariable reply was that during a festival you are forced to be tolerant and smother your indignation, to stifle it so that others cannot guess of its existence. Besides, the slightest show of petulence, no matter what the provocation, would call forth blame for ruining the spectacle. Every headman present would demonstrate his disgust, and the culprit, publicly shamed, might be driven to committing suicide.

I found myself thinking of the large family parties at Christmas in Western societies, and I wondered whether the main value of the affair might not also lie in the anticipation of an ideal. We too become sentimental about our gatherings, expend an enormous amount of energy on the preparations, and talk about the good time ahead. The decorated tree with its lights, and the fancy wrapping paper for the parcels, all have a resemblance to the Wogeo platforms with their coconut leaves, festoons, and garlands. Then the presents keep our kinship and affinal sentiments alive and underline our mutual responsibilities, though, like the islanders, we are apt to be dissatisfied with what we take home — the hideous ashtray for the non-smoker, the excruciating tie impossible to wear, or the book by an author held in derision. But we too keep our frayed nerves under control from the conviction that to give way to them might bring ruin.

The two magical rites afford a clue to the political implications. One is to enhance the headman's reputation, the other to bring concord to his village and enable it to stand inviolate. Ordinary people can achieve the smaller triumphs associated with housebuilding, births, and funerals; but he alone has the resources at his command for the endless series of festivals. Accordingly, his followers as a matter of habit come to look up to him. The result is an accretion of authority. Not only is he in a position to demand extra labour from them for further festivities, but he can also intervene in their disputes and by reminding them of what he has done on their behalf so humiliate them that they willingly accept his solution. 'Have I not given you many festivals, have I not initiated your sons?', was a common prelude to strictures by Marigum when he wished to stop an argument or persuade quarrelsome neighbours to heal the breach between them.

Serious conflicts within the village are rare, as I have so repeatedly insisted; yet the variation between the amount of bickering in settlements with or without a strong headman was striking. In Dap and in Gol, apart from the disputed succession in the former and the seduction of Kawang's wife in the latter, there was almost no trouble; in Bariat, in Mwarok, and in Jug, where the leaders were young and as yet untried, misunderstandings from time to time emerged into the light of day.

A headman exercises his sway primarily within his own housing cluster or village and seldom interferes in the goings-on in other places. When he does so, then, provided he is a real personage, people listen with attention. I saw Marigum put on a show of losing control once in Mwarok and once in Job, and on both occasions the offenders refrained from justifying themselves or answering back — they simply slunk away. Later they sent a pig to appease his righteous anger. The bystanders went on with their work pretending not to notice. Had they been critical they would have assuredly come to me that evening and deprecated the intervention: instead they remained silent.

It follows that the inhabitants of a settlement with a strong headman are conscious of their solidarity. They live in amity and in many situations willingly act together. In consequence, as is universally agreed, they are likely to succeed in all their major enterprises. Other groups, fearing reprisals, take care not to be an annoyance. In the past they would have pondered deeply before engaging in a raid and probably in the end have given up the notion.

People are so aware of the advantages of living under an outstanding headman that they maintain his presence gives them protection against even *yabou* sorcerers. This was one reason for the alarm in Dap, as Jaua made clear (p. 144), when Marigum became enraged with Tafalti and left. Not till his final return did the villagers feel safe once more. 'The sorcerers won't come near us now,' two men remarked to me. 'They realize that if they do Marigum will be able to get the facts so that we can round them up and slay them.' As proof they cited their own present good health and that of their fellows. It is indeed true that during my stay nobody in Gol succumbed and only one old woman in Dap; but the low death rate in these two places over such a short space of time must have been fortuitous.

Of vital importance also is the fact that those whose festival debts remain undischarged are under a moral obligation to refrain from either raiding their creditors or giving assistance to anyone else contemplating such a move. Odd examples may be quoted, again possibly legendary, of unscrupulous persons violating the principle, but their actions are deplored and condemned. After the Gol festival of July 1934, Kawang and his followers, and Marigum and those of his followers who helped, would therefore have known that for a year at least, when the return might have been expected, they had little need to be apprehensive of the ambitions of the Takul residents. The headman of Maluk was singled out as especially unfortunate in that a second presentation had come to him before he could return an earlier offering. 'Poor fellow, he carries a heavy log on each shoulder,' one of my kinsmen exclaimed. 'He'll be a long time throwing them off, and till then

9 Food and Politics

he won't be able to stand upright or look people straight in the eye. He'll have to keep watch on his tongue and go on saying "yes" to everybody.'

The creditors are also unlikely to attack their debtors, though morals scarcely enter into the situation when the practical reasons for not molesting them are so apparent.

The final point concerns the welding together of the clusters, villages, and district groups into a total society. The typical tribe as described in anthropological literature consists of a large body of people divided into a number of some such assemblages as lineages and clans and surrounded by like units similarly structured. Feuding and warfare are more or less constant, with each one pitted against the rest. The members of the constituent segments are obliged to settle any minor differences between them in order to combine against the common enemy. Outside hostility thus enforces tribal integration. Wogeo, by contrast, is detached and solitary. Formerly the only foreigners the islanders saw, and this at rare intervals, were their trading partners when an overseas expedition took place. Yet they managed to live together in comparative harmony and were not dogged by obsessive fears of violence. Petty raiding occurred from time to time, but the massing of hosts of armed warriors and wholesale carnage were unknown. The chief aim of the festivals was to exalt a particular headman, and by extension his immediate kin and affines; however, vast throngs from other places came along to dance and share the food. The final effect was a strengthening of the spirit of broader fellowship and a deepening of the feeling for the total community as a unique consolidated and enduring role.

Probably a case should be made out for judging Wogeo society of the era of early European contact as in some respects close to the perfect type. The people lacked the benefits of scientific discovery, medical research, and international trade, and the women were only secondary citizens; but the system of hereditary leaders, who, in addition, were obliged to demonstrate their worth, gave assurance of a fair measure of wealth and civil liberty for all. The headmen acted as a regulatory force and saw to it that persons whose rights had been infringed punished the wrongdoer strictly according to the seriousness of his offence. Further, an escape clause in the religious dogma relating to sorcery as the cause of human mortality meant that life was more secure than in some parts of Papua New Guinea. After the lapse of time death could be attributed rather to carelessness or accident, and the survivors were thus absolved from the obligation to seek out someone for blame and thence proceeding to vengeance. The ordinary islander going about his daily avocations might have occasional fears of a *yabou* attack without warning, but his alarm had no foundation in practical affairs, and he never felt called upon to post sentries around his cultivations, as is recorded of many communities. The chances were overwhelmingly in favour of his survival till in the end he died in his bed. Five murders in a total population of about 900 between 1933 and 1949, or, statistically, one per 1000 every three years, can scarcely be described as a devastating figure.

Reference Notes

1 Introduction

[1] The word 'New Guinea' can cause confusion. First of all, it was, and still is, correctly applied to the entire island, including the western part administered by Indonesia under the title 'Irian Jaya' (formerly 'West Irian'). From 1921 till the late 1960s, however, the name was often used, as here, to refer to the Mandated, later Trust, Territory of New Guinea, that is to say the northeast section of the mainland, plus the neighbouring Bismarck Archipelago and the two most northerly of the Solomon Islands. Then in 1970 the whole eastern half of the mainland and all the islands eastwards, with these same Solomons, became officially 'Papua and New Guinea'. Later still the 'and' was dropped in favour of the simple 'Papua New Guinea'.

[2] The word 'New Guinean' sounds awkward but is sanctioned by official usage, though generally in the spelling Niuginian. Nothing would induce me to adopt two other official terms, 'expatriates' and 'indigenes', the latter always mispronounced so that it rhymes with 'Aborigines', serving to distinguish Europeans and Chinese on the one hand and New Guineans on the other.

[3] Actually decimal currency was not introduced till 1966, and prior to that date pounds, shillings, and pence were used. Fifty cents represents the equivalent of five shillings. (On 1 January 1976, dollars and cents were replaced by a new coinage of the same value, respectively kina and toea.)

[4] R. M. Wiltgen, 'The Death of Bishop Loeks and His Companions', *Verbum: Romae Apud Collegium Verbi Divini*, vol. 6 (1964), pp. 363–97; ibid., vol. 7 (1965), pp. 14–44.

The fact that so many of the missionaries were German reinforced the Japanese view that they must be spies. Had they not supported the Allied cause, it was argued, the Australian government would long before have interned them.

A United States military commission which met in Yokohama during September and October 1948, although able to establish that orders for the massacre were delivered to *Akikaze* by seaplane at 10.13 a.m. on 17 March, could not determine who had issued them. By 1948 Lieutenant-Commander Sabe, captain of the destroyer, was dead and the ship's log book lost. The most plausible hypothesis is that Rear-Admiral Kamata, at the time in charge of the Base Force at Wewak, was responsible; but this was impossible to prove as he had already been hanged in Java, whither the High Command in Tokyo had at some later period transferred him (he would have travelled by submarine), on being found guilty by an Allied Military Court of beheading without trial 150 Dutch civilians suspected of planning a revolt. Probably Kamata made a sudden decision after learning that one of the missionaries (Father Manion, an American) had sent medicine to injured airmen, also American, from a bomber shot down over

181

Wewak. The plane crashed in the sea, and the survivors drifted in a rubber dinghy to Wogeo. Some of the people befriended them, and Mot of Job, an admirable character whom I knew well, made a voyage of over eighty kilometres at night and alone to the mission hospital on Kairiru Island for the medicine. He was not aware when setting out that the Japanese had brought all the other missionaries here while deciding what to do with them. When the airmen recovered Mot sent them by canoe eastward to the New Guinea mainland, but they were captured near the mouth of the Sepik River at dawn or before on 17 March. The news must have been transmitted at once to Wewak, and presumably Kamata lost no time in sending instructions by radio to Staff Officer Ando, Director of Civil Affairs in New Guinea, who was stationed in Rabaul, where there was a seaplane base. *Akikaze*, with the missionaries on board, was then at sea bound for Rabaul. On arrival they were to have been interned or held prisoner. If the surmise is correct, then Ando must have requisitioned the plane to carry the message; but again we cannot be certain as by 1948 he too was dead.

Curiously, Mot escaped punishment by the Japanese. He would have received an American decoration had he not been drowned with the rest of the crew when, in 1947, his canoe foundered in a sudden storm while on an overseas trading expedition. At least one of the airmen was alive at the end of the war and expressed his gratitude to the rescuers, who refer to him simply as 'Master Jim', by sending them a case of presents.

[5] The Trust Territory was combined with the Australian colony of Papua to the south. Together they formed Papua New Guinea. In 1969 Indonesia had claimed the western section of the main island, formerly Netherlands New Guinea, and is still in full control there.

[6] The Seventh-Day Adventist Mission had arrived in the Sepik region after the end of World War II.

[7] The vessel is a half-decked whale boat seven metres long with an awning of three-ply aft. She is fitted with a diesel engine capable of about six knots, and the single journey takes from six to seven hours; but she carries no compass, no life-jackets, and no distress flares. On my return passage in January 1975 the pump was out of order, and one member of the crew of three bailed out at the rate of fifteen buckets hourly. There were seventeen passengers including me and a full cargo of live pigs and general produce.

[8] It is of interest that when later Bernard received a transfer to his old school on Kairiru, close to Wogeo, his letters were full of complaints that he found it impossible to bank any of his salary towards the fare for a holiday in Sydney. A constant stream of relatives visiting Wewak on business made a practice of calling in and staying for a few days, during which period he had to provide them with bed and board. Turning a kinsman from the doorstep would have been unthinkable.

[9] This paragraph, along with the rest of the chapter, was written immediately on my return to Sydney in January 1975. Rereading it just before the MS. was despatched to the publisher, I was shocked to find that I had been so sour. I decided not to make any changes and simply to offer disappointment as my excuse. Forty years earlier dances lasting all night never upset me — but then I was not yet thirty and frequently a performer.

[10] Of the dozens of examples that could be quoted I mention but one, M. W. Young, *Fighting with Food*, Cambridge, 1971.

2 Place and People

[1] I. Hogbin and P. Lawrence, *Studies in New Guinea Land Tenure*, Sydney, 1967, pp. 54-8.
[2] The approximate ages of those born after 1942 may be obtained from the Mission register of baptisms.
[3] Hogbin, *The Island of Menstruating Men*, pp. 82-99.
[4] Not *Xanthosoma* sp. as I said in *The Island of Menstruating Men*, p. 15. Bernard pointed out the mistake.
[5] The trees are deciduous and for a short period stand bare, apparently dead. It is thought that a man who ate the nuts might die suddenly.
[6] I. Hogbin, 'Trading Expeditions in Northern New Guinea', *Oceania*, vol. 5, 1934-5, pp. 375-407.

The party as soon as it put to sea substituted nautical terms for those used on shore. We follow the same kind of practice when we speak of 'port' and 'starboard' instead of 'left' and 'right', 'fore' and 'aft' instead of 'front' and 'back', and 'deck' and 'companionway' instead of 'floor' and 'stairs'. Our seamen also have their own units for measuring speed, depth, and distance – respectively knots, fathoms, and chains.

[7] Sometimes men also apply *tina* to the descendants of female agnates married into other districts (e.g. the father's father's sisters' children and grandchildren).
[8] I. Hogbin, 'Wogeo Kinship Terminology', *Oceania*, vol. 34, 1963-4, pp. 208-9.
[9] A person may also refer to his father's sisters as *tama veine*, female fathers.
[10] A man applies the son-daughter terms to the offspring of his male cross cousins and the sisters' children terms to the offspring of his female cross cousins.
[11] *The Island of Menstruating Men*, p. 113.
[12] J. D. Freeman, 'The Concept of the Kindred', *Journal of the Royal Anthropological Institute*, vol. 91, 1961, pp. 192-220.
[13] Persons who are already kin may, of course, as a result of a marriage, become affines as well; for example, they may be simultaneously cousins and brothers-in-law.
[14] A Busama, for example, enumerates as his close cognates his grandparents, their children and grandchildren, his parents' grandchildren, and his own grandchildren. These are 'one blood' with him *(da-tigeng)*: the rest are his 'one stem' *(hu-tigeng)*. See I. Hogbin, *Kinship and Marriage in a New Guinea Village*, London, 1963, p. 14.
[15] I. Hogbin and P. Lawrence, *Studies in New Guinea Land Tenure*, pp. 1-44.
[16] It should be remembered that in the mid 1930s the study of lineage theory had barely begun. M. Fortes and E. E. Evans-Pritchard's *African Political Systems* was not published by Oxford till 1940, Fortes's article on unilineal descent systems, referred to below, not till 1953.
[17] 'The Rules of Relationship Behaviour in One Variety of Primitive Warfare', *Man*, vol. 47, 1947, pp. 108-10.
[18] I am speaking specifically of societies with a cluster-like organization, but several writers have drawn attention to the inappropriateness of the African model for the Melanesian scene in general. See J. A. Barnes, 'African Models in the New Guinea Highlands', *Man*, vol. 62, 1962, pp. 5-9 (reprinted in I. Hogbin and L. R. Hiatt (eds.), *Readings in Australian and Pacific Anthropology*, Melbourne, 1966, pp. 117-29); and 'Agnation among the Enga', *Oceania*, vol. 38, 1967-8, pp. 33-43; L. L. Langness, 'Some Problems in the Conceptualization of Highlands Social Structures', *American Anthropologist*, vol. 66, 1964, special publication (reprinted in I. Hogbin and L. R. Hiatt (eds), *Readings in Australian and Pacific*

Anthropology, pp. 130-58); and 'Traditional Political Organization', in I. Hogbin (ed.), *Anthropology in Papua New Guinea*, Melbourne, 1973, pp. 142-73; and M. de Lepervanche, 'Social Structure', ibid., pp. 1-60.

Recently an African scholar lacking in personal experience of Melanesia protested that Barnes and de Lepervanche were mistaken: New Guinea groupings, she said, are identical with those described by Fortes, jural equality and all (J. La Fontaine, 'Descent in New Guinea: an Africanist View', in J. Goody (ed.), *Character of Kinship*, Cambridge, 1973, pp. 35-51). It is ironical that A. Strathern, in a contribution to this same collection of essays, although at the time of writing he cannot have known of her arguments, should have made an effective reply to them ('Kinship, Descent and Locality: Some New Guinea Examples', ibid., pp. 21-33).

[19] 'The Structure of Unilineal Descent Groups', *American Anthropologist*, vol. 55, 1953 (reprinted in M. Fortes, *Time and Social Structure and Other Essays*, London, 1970). The quotation is from p. 79 of the latter publication.

[20] Kaneg, the Job headman, had before his death in late 1932 or early 1933 fixed everything for his son Gwaramun to be hoisted, but at the last minute the young man funked the publicity and ran away. The villagers hoped that next time, with Marigum's support, he would not be so foolish. I found out in 1974-5 that he had disappointed them.

3 Headmen

[1] Hogbin, *The Island of Menstruating Men*, pp. 42-9.
[2] I. Hogbin, B. D. Gagin, and T. M. J. Fandim, 'Wogeo Notes', *Oceania*, vol. 42, 1971-2, pp. 28-31.
[3] *The Island of Menstruating Men*, pp. 49-51.
[4] M. de Lepervanche, 'Social Structure', in I. Hogbin (ed.), *Anthropology in Papua New Guinea*, pp. 21-9; and L. L. Langness, 'Traditional Political Organization', ibid., pp. 153-4.
[5] I. Hogbin, *Social Change*, Melbourne, 1971, p. 196.
[6] Earthquakes are common, but I never heard of any great damage. Their lack of severity may explain the absence of a link with the headman's magic.
[7] *The Island of Menstruating Men*, pp. 175-6. The attitude to warmth and cold are discussed on pp. 84-5. The island is within three degrees of the Equator, and a day that the people may find uncomfortably chilly, with a temperature perhaps no more than five or six degrees below the average, will still appear decidedly hot to someone accustomed to a temperate climate.
[8] The technique of magic, and the way in which it is supposed to work, are discussed in *The Island of Menstruating Men*, pp. 168-87.
[9] Ibid., pp. 87-91, 121.

4 Sorcery in Real Life

[1] Women, who are not thought to practise *yabou*, are in consequence never the object of vengeance. They have thus some compensation for impinging so little on public life.
[2] See, for example, I. Hogbin, *Transformation Scene*, London, 1951, pp. 145-9.
[3] Ontong Java, an atoll to the northeast of the Solomons, in many respects resembles Wogeo. The number of inhabitants is about the same, and although skirmishes have occurred, they were minor affairs resulting in three or four

Reference Notes

deaths at most. Here the people attribute death to the spirits of the ancestors, considered to be the guardians of the moral code. Anyone dying is thus held to be reaping a just if unfortunate punishment for his sins, and equally the question of vengeance does not arise. See I. Hogbin, *Law and Order in Polynesia*, London and New York, 1934, pp. 143-65.
4. H. C. Brookfield and P. Brown, *Struggle for Land*, Melbourne, 1963; M. Meggitt, *Blood is Their Argument*, Palo Alto, 1977. Meggitt discusses the present situation in Chapters 9 and 10.
5. Sale was the natural child of Kaneg and Waki of Job, Yam's parents, but they sent her to Bagasal of Dap for adoption.
6. His name was really Dal, but to avoid confusion I have taken the liberty of changing it.

5 Marriage

1. I have discussed pre-marital sexual relations in 'Puberty to Marriage: a Study of the Sexual Life of the People of Wogeo', *Oceania*, vol. 16, 1945-6, pp. 185-209.
2. In all societies sexual intercourse is forbidden between certain classes of kin, but where the ban is imposed differs from place to place; for instance, sexual intercourse between uncle and niece, or nephew and aunt, is punished in Scotland and New South Wales but not in England. Within the one society these incest prohibitions do not necessarily coincide with those of marriage, and often sexual relations are tolerated between persons who are not allowed to marry. For a criticism of the accepted notion of incest see R. Needham, *Remarks and Inventions: Skeptical Essays about Kinship*, London, 1974, pp. 61-8.
3. Not to be confused with Bagasal's father Kintabi, referred to above on pp. 66, 67, after whom he was named. As both men are mentioned only once I have left them as they are.
4. His real name was Gris, but I have taken the liberty of changing it to avoid confusion with Gris, my cook.
5. The presence of enduring units does not necessarily make for exchanges between them. Thus the Busama are divided into land-owning matrilineages, but marriage is arranged on the basis of give and take between individuals. The result is frequent arguments about who owes a woman to whom. See I. Hogbin, *Kinship and Marriage in a New Guinea Village*, pp. 107-8.
6. I. Hogbin and P. Lawrence, *Studies in New Guinea Land Tenure*, pp. 23-5.
7. 'I was so ashamed that I vomited' is a characteristic Wogeo expression. I cannot vouch for it, but, so firm is the expectation, probably people do vomit when in fear of disgrace. Husbands are expected to suffer from morning sickness during the early stages of a wife's pregnancy, and I knew several who became ill.
8. I never discovered why Marigum had not previously sought a partner for Sanum. His failure to do so was the more surprising in that she was his eldest daughter.
9. The custom, in abeyance for decades, was revived for Bernard's wedding in May 1975, though it was preceded, as always today, by a ceremony in church.

6 Husband and Wife

1. The anxiety is seldom justified. Girls are accustomed from their early teens to cooking meals without supervision during the mother's periods.
2. I am speaking here of disquiet expressed openly in discussions when men meet face to face. I must leave others to decide whether or not the more rigorous

taboos surrounding the Malaita wife serve to magnify, or are a symptom of, qualms of which her husband is at the conscious level unaware.
[3] The child concerned, Gwa, a boy born in 1930, was already dead by 1948; but two girls, born respectively in 1932 and 1934, were still alive in 1974–5 and unmistakably Wiawia's offspring.
[4] He was really called Kanakula, but as someone else, to be referred to at length later, has the same name I have sought to avoid confusion by changing it.
[5] See, for example, E. E. Evans-Pritchard, *Kinship and Marriage among the Nuer*, Oxford, 1951. pp. 90, 91.
[6] Yet, as we saw, marriage with two sisters is permitted.
[7] Both Dal's widows remarried, but this was in the early 1960s, when the old traditions were already breaking down.

7 Cases of Adultery and Theft

[1] Hogbin, *The Island of Menstruating Men*, pp. 42–8. Wonka and Mafofo, as blood-brothers, must have belonged to opposite moieties. The former, in committing adultery with the latter's wife, and subsequently marrying her, must therefore have been guilty of the additional faults of ignoring the rules against moiety incest and exogamy.
[2] Really Kanakula: I explained in a previous chapter why I changed his name.
[3] The lungs are regarded as the seat of understanding, but Waru was speaking figuratively. He did not mean that a person can have two dispositions because he possesses a pair of lungs. The phrase is comparable with our usage when we describe a hypocrite as 'two faced'.
[4] Another change of name to avoid confusion. He was really Gris, the same as my cook.
[5] I. Hogbin, 'A New Guinea Childhood: From Weaning to the Eighth Year in Wogeo', *Oceania*, vol. 16, 1945–6, pp. 275–96.

8 Marigum and Tafalti

[1] A. L. Epstein, 'Law', in I. Hogbin (ed.), *Anthropology in Papua New Guinea*, pp. 174–81.
[2] As we know, Dal survived for almost a quarter of a century.
[3] Nobody knew in which year she had been born, but, reckoning from events of which I was aware of the exact date, such as the introduction of head tax, I judged her to be at least sixteen and probably seventeen. Much later, when I was living in Busama, near Lae, a young man who had had some degree of medical training informed me that the average age at which New Guinea girls first menstruate is thirteen plus or minus one but that a delay of up to five years is common. The reason for this late maturity, when compared with Europeans, may well be inadequacy of the diet.
[4] Hogbin, *The Island of Menstruating Men*, pp. 125–36.
[5] Made from home-grown tobacco, with dried banana leaf instead of paper.
[6] Anomalous, that is, in the Pacific; but many African parallels might be cited.

9 Food and Politics

[1] Hogbin, *The Island of Menstruating Men*, pp. 72–81.
[2] Ibid., p. 58.
[3] Ibid., pp. 59–71.
[4] Ibid., pp. 79–81.
[5] My comparison of headmen and an old-time Army officer met with warm approval. The officer looked after his horses first and then his men: only when horses and men were fed did he think of himself. (The islanders had all seen horses on the coconut plantations of the mainland.)
[6] I discovered in 1974–5 that in an earlier publication, 'Food Festivals and Politics in Wogeo', *Oceania*, vol. 40, 1969–70, pp. 304–28, my estimated weight of the pigs was too low.
[7] See M. McArthur, 'Pigs for the Ancestors', *Oceania*, vol. 45, 1974–5, pp. 87–123.
[8] Cf. the Taude of southern Papua New Guinea, 'who prefer to consume pork in the "irrational" manner of periodic orgies of gluttony — a mode of consumption which minimizes the benefits of available protein. These feasts are held in order to give renown to the hosts.' (C. R. Hallpike, 'Functionalist Interpretations of Primitive Warfare', *Man* (n.s.), vol. 8, 1973, p. 466)

Bibliography

Other publications on Wogeo not referred to in the text.

B. D. Gagin (Bernard G. Dalle), 'Some Wogeo Songs and Spells', *Oceania*, vol. 42, 1971-2, pp. 198-204.

I. Hogbin, 'A New Guinea Infancy', *Oceania*, vol. 13, 1942-3, pp. 285-309. Reprinted in J. Middleton (ed.), *From Childhood to Adult*, New York, 1970; and, in revised form as 'A New Guinea Childhood', in L. L. Langness and J. C. Weschler (eds.), *Melanesia: Readings in a Culture Area*, Scranton, 1970.

P. G. Sack, 'Mythology and Land Rights in Wogeo', *Oceania*, vol. 46, 1975-6, pp. 40-52.

D. Tuzin, a critical review of *The Island of Menstruating Men*, *Journal of the Polynesian Society*, vol. 82, 1973, pp. 429-33.

Index

adoption, 4, 7, 29, 96, 100, 121, 151
adultery, 17, 18, 56, 63, 66, 67, 74, 75, 78, 87-91, 97, 138, 141, 176; cases, 101-17; degrees of disapproval, 101; within the village, 102-6; with wives of kin outside the village, 109-15; outside the district, 115; prevalence of, 115-17; with the wife of a headman, 66, 67, 107-9, 116, 117; portrayed in dances, 167; *see also* jealousy
affines, 20, 30, 31, 36, 37, 62, 79, 105, 107, 108, 111, 113, 121, 124, 134, 162, 172, 179, 183; and reciprocity, 17, 31, 34, 36, 56; terminology, 30, 31, 98, 99; compared with kin, 31; and adultery, 56, 91, 101, 102; and remarriage, 98, 99; disputes between, 111, 121, 145, 146
African lineage systems compared with New Guinea, 36, 37, 67, 183, 184
agnates, 34, 35, 183
America, *see* U.S.A.
anthropologist, status of, 4, 7, 29, 171
arson, *see* destroying property

ballet, *see* dancing
Barnes, J. A., 183
Bernard Dalle Gagin, 7-11, 31, 62, 69, 72, 182, 183, 184, 185
big-man, compared with headman, 42
blood-brotherhood, 29, 30, 79, 101, 186
bride price, 69, 76, 97, 99, 136, 145
Brookfield, H. C., 185
brother-sister relations, 79, 80, 81, 85, 86, 92, 95, 99, 123-50
Brown, P., 185
bullroarer, *see* religion and magic
Busama, 183, 184, 185, 186

calendar, 20
chastity, *see* adultery, fornication, sexual relations
chief, 45; *see also* headman

childbirth taboos, 12; *see also* pollution
Chinnery, E. W. P., 3
Christianity, *see* missions
clan, 35-7, 69, 179, 185; *see also* African lineage systems, cluster of houses
climate, 19, 20, 44-6
clothing, 9, 14, 15, 20, 84, 164
clubhouse, 10, 17, 21, 23, 64, 66, 72, 95, 111, 113, 143, 153, 158, 161, 170
cluster of houses, 10, 11, 21, 33-6, 37, 38, 41, 68, 78, 82, 99, 101-9, 116, 117, 119, 120, 122, 153, 157, 165, 177
cognates, *see* kinship
commercial undertakings, 5, 8, 10, 13, 15, 19
compensation for injury, 18, 65, 85, 89, 104, 105, 113, 114, 120, 125, 126, 136, 149, 156, 178
conception dogma, 31
conscience, 12, 48, 67, 122
cook, as an insulting term, 112, 149
culture heroes, 24, 37, 41, 90, 92, 101

Dal, 4, 7, 27, 44, 69, 71, 72, 100, 102, 117, 123, 124, 125, 136, 137, 138, 139, 141, 142, 147-9; and Marigum's death, 58-62; death, 62, 186
dancing, 154, 155, 159, 160-4, 166-8, 176, 179
daughter-father relations, *see* father-daughter relations
death, *see* menstrual taboos, pollution, sorcery
decoration, personal, 20, 25, 37, 39, 44, 158, 159, 162, 163
descent, 25, 30, 35, 70; *see also* African lineage systems, filiation
descent group, *see* cluster of houses
destroying property, in anger, 17, 86, 106, 127; if offended by a kinsman, 28, 103
diet, 13, 14, 24, 119
disease, *see* menstrual taboos, pollution, sorcery

191

Divine Word Mission, *see* missions
divorce, 76, 94, 97, 98, 105
dowry, 34, 70, 71, 84, 97
drug plants, 24

economic development, *see* commercial undertakings
Epstein, A. L., 124, 186
equality, *see* jural equality
Evans-Pritchard, E. E., 183, 186
exchange partners, 29, 30, 63, 67, 153, 161, 170, 179; criticism of, 170, 171; *see also* trade
exogamy, 25, 68, 186

famine, 16, 44–6, 63, 127, 137; *see also* weather magic
Fandim, Tom, 8, 184
Fandum, 42, 104, 105, 106, 108, 109
father-daughter relations, 70, 72, 73, 74, 75, 79, 80, 81, 85, 123–50
father-son relations, 58–62, 67, 74, 75, 79, 123–50, 160
feast, 13, 14, 21, 23, 40, 60, 73, 76, 77, 83, 95, 118, 126; in 1975, 12–15; *see also* festival
festival, 37, 40, 41, 44, 108, 110, 143; minor, 151–3, 157; proceedings summarized, 153–5; as humiliating device, 153; return offering, 153, 169–73; introductory rite, 154, 155–8; preparations, 154, 160, 161, 164, 165; identifying recipients, 154, 158–60; ritual purification, 160, 163, 164; presentation, 159, 169; frequency of, 155; magical rites during, 160, 163, 165, 168, 177; women's dance in, 160–3; amount of food, 165; suspension of kinship rules, 166; distribution of food, 171–3; economic and social effects, 175–80; irrationality of, 175, 176; compared with Christmas party, 177
feud, *see* raiding
fighting, ritual during festivals, 17, 110, 112, 113, 154, 155, 166, 176; *see also* adultery, raiding, warfare
filiation, 35; *see also* land tenure
Fontaine, J. La, 184
food, *see* diet, feast, festival
football, in settling grievances, 115, 136
fornication, 116; *see also* sexual relations
Fortes, M., 36, 183, 184
Fortune, R. F., 36, 183
Freeman, J. D., 183
friendship, *see* blood-brotherhood
fumigation, *see* purification

Gagin, B. D., *see* Bernard Dalle Gagin
generosity, *see* status
Germany, 4, 181, 182
Gerobo, 67, 140, 143
Goody, J., 184
government, pre-independence, 3, 4, 6, 7, 8, 55, 59, 61, 65, 66, 100, 106, 114, 129, 145, 181, 182
grandparent-grandchild relations, 141

Hallpike, C. R., 187
headman, 4, 11, 16, 17, 18, 21, 35, 37, 39–53, 72, 99, 123, 139, 143, 144, 152, 155, 165, 169, 177, 178, 179; qualifications, 16, 37, 38, 39, 40, 42, 43, 44–6, 149, 195; and famine, 16, 44–6, 63, 127, 137; and kin ties, 26, 174, 175; inauguration, 37, 39, 165, 184; formal respect for, 39, 176, 177; hospitality of, 40, 156; and work, 40, 41; and wealth, 40, 41; the ideal, 40, 41; family of, 43, 44, 95, 139, 151; and sorcery, 49–52, 56–67, 140, 142, 143, 149, 178; and marriage of his children, 69, 70, 74; intervening in disputes, 89, 101, 130, 143, 176; as a mediator, 105, 106, 126, 130, 143, 144, 148, 149, 176, 177; reaction of when wife is adulteress, 107–9, 116; supports equals, 107, 108; as an adulterer, 109; restrains followers, 112, 176, 177, 179; and warfare, 115; fear of, 125, 127–30, 140, 142, 143; rebukes followers, 128, 144, 145, 177; protects followers, 143, 147, 148, 168, 177, 178; and politics, 151–79; and festivals, 151–79; consults equals, 157, 158; like Army officer, 187; and group solidarity, 177–9; *see also* Kawang, Marigum, Wakera
Hiatt, L. R., 183
Hobgin, I., other publications cited, 11, 183, 184, 185, 186, 187
house, description of, 10, 11, 21–3
housing cluster, *see* cluster of houses
hunting, 24, 65, 111, 120
husband-wife relations, 83–100, 124, 126, 127, 135, 146; division of labour, 83, 84, 94, 118; authority in household, 84–6; property rights, 84, 85; quarrels, 85–7; sexual life, 87–90, 115; affection, 90–2; widowers and widows, 62, 74, 92, 98–100; *see also* adultery, jealousy, marriage, polygyny

illness, *see* menstrual taboos, pollution, sorcery
incest, 25, 68, 69, 117, 185, 186

Index

inheritance, 28, 33, 34, 35, 47, 70, 84, 99, 138, 139, 140
inquest, 12, 16, 52, 53, 54, 55, 60, 62
Irian Jaya, 8, 19, 181, 182

Japan, 6, 63, 181, 182
Jaua, 4, 5, 33, 34, 53, 59, 73, 85, 86, 87, 89, 90, 91, 94, 95, 102, 108, 109, 115, 117, 118, 121, 122, 127, 129, 130, 131, 132, 133, 135, 137, 140, 141, 142, 143, 144, 147, 148, 149, 150, 152, 178; death, 63, 64
jealousy, sexual, 68, 88–90; father-son, 125, 138, 144; *see also* adultery
jural equality, 36, 67, 158; *see also* African lineage systems, compensation, raiding

Kaiaf, 63, 89, 105, 106, 107, 108
Kajug, 63, 64, 107–9
Kakameri, 73, 75, 76, 85, 89, 98, 113, 114, 120, 174, 175
Kalabai, 12, 29, 115
Kalal, 121, 122, 132, 136, 138, 139, 143, 144, 148
Kalaua, 9, 123–50
Kaman, 42, 46, 76, 77, 107, 123, 124, 127, 148, 149, 156, 157, 169, 170, 173, 175
Kanakula, 135–7, 142
Kawang, 4, 26, 35, 40, 41, 46, 49, 60, 62–4, 99, 107–9, 130, 138, 177; death, 62–4; and festival, 158, 160, 161, 165, 166, 168, 172, 174, 175
kindred, 11, 30, 31, 38, 69
kinship, 4, 7, 10, 11, 12, 13, 20, 23, 26, 56, 61, 62, 66, 67, 68, 74, 112, 114, 119, 132, 140, 141, 158, 161, 182; and reciprocity, 16, 17, 23, 32, 33; and grievances, 16, 17, 102–15, 166; suspending rules of, 17, 107, 158, 186; maintaining with gifts, 17, 27, 171–3; and genealogy, 25, 26, 31, 32; terminology, 26, 27; and behaviour stereotypes, 28, 29; and mutual loyalty and help, 28, 29, 47, 48, 131, 132, 153, 173, 174; and jural equality, 36, 67, 158; conflicting claims of, 37, 147, 148, 174, 175; and ancestors, 116, 117; *see also* destroying property

land tenure, 33, 34, 57, 58, 70, 71; *see also* inheritance
Langness, L. L., 183, 184
language, 5, 8, 10, 24, 25; *see also* Pidgin English
Lawrence, P., 183
leader, *see* headman
Lepervanche, M. de, 184

lineage, 35–7, 69, 70, 185; *see also* African lineage systems, cluster of houses
Loeks, Bishop, 6, 181, 182

McArthur, M., 187
Magar, 9; as a pawn in the Marigum-Tafalti quarrel, 123–50
magic, *see* religion and magic, sorcery, weather magic
Malaita, *see* Solomon Islands
Marigum, 4, 7, 26, 33, 34, 37, 38, 39, 40, 41, 42, 43, 45, 46, 49, 53, 64, 66, 67, 70, 71, 72, 73, 74, 75, 76, 77, 92, 93, 99, 100, 102, 103, 106, 108, 109, 112, 113, 121, 178, 184; death, 58–62; and death of mother-in-law, 54–6; avenges Kawang's death, 62–4, 108; and marriage of followers, 73, 74, 75, 76, 77, 81; expresses disapproval of offender, 74, 85, 87, 127, 177; and wife's adultery, 193, 194; commits adultery, 20, 109; and pig stealing, 121; quarrel with son, 123–50; and festival, 151–3, 155–7, 158, 161, 166, 169, 170, 172, 173, 174, 175, 177
marriage, 68–82; regulations, 68–70; betrothal, 70–7, 127, 134; elopement, 69, 74, 75, 76, 77–81, 93, 137, 149; by exchange, 69, 70; preferences, 70, 80, 81, 137; trousseau, 73, 79, 80; ceremony, 80; church, 185; by capture, 81, 82; and Magar, 123–50; *see also* bride price, divorce, dowry, husband-wife relations
Meggitt, M., 185
menstrual taboos, 12, 27, 54, 56, 83, 85, 103, 185
menstruation, rites at first, 73, 75, 126, 128, 134
messenger, official, 147, 156
Meyer, Father, 8, 58–60
missions, 3, 5, 6, 7, 9, 10, 11, 15, 122, 181, 182, 185
moiety, *see* social structure
moral judgements, 88, 101, 116, 117, 140
mother-child relations, 97–100; *see also* divorce
mwaere, 43, 54, 56, 95
mythology, *see* culture heroes

Needham, R., 185

Ontong Java, *see* Solomon Islands

Papua New Guinea, 13, 15, 18, 32, 35, 44, 45, 57, 179, 181, 182

patrilineage, 35-7; *see also* African lineage systems, cluster of houses
Pidgin English, 5, 9, 10, 15, 113, 115, 117
politics, 18, 36, 123, 124, 178, 179; *see also* headman
pollution, ritual, 12, 54, 56, 116, 179; *see also* menstrual taboos, religion and magic
polygyny, 23, 37, 42, 43, 60, 62, 63, 69, 70, 71, 72, 91, 92-7, 98, 138, 139
population figures, 3, 6, 15, 20, 38

quarrels between kin, 16, 28, 43, 44, 47-9, 62, 68, 123-50, 176; disapproval of, 101-15, 128, 129, 140, 176; *see also* destroying property, sorcery

raiding, vengeance, 5, 18, 28, 36, 42, 53, 54, 55, 56-8, 59, 61, 62-4, 67, 107, 178-80; directed solely against offender, 67; *see also* compensation, jural equality, warfare
rape, 81, 125, 142, 143, 145
reciprocity, *see* kinship
religion and magic, pagan, 7, 9, 11, 12, 21, 23, 25, 27, 37, 38, 40, 41, 42, 43, 46-56, 93, 101, 102, 116, 117, 120, 139, 141, 142, 160, 163, 165, 168, 177, 179; spirit monsters of, 21, 40, 151, 158, 165, 166, 169; *see also* culture heroes, inquest, pollution, sanctions, sorcery, weather magic
residence after marriage, 11, 32, 34, 35
responsibility, *see* jural equality
revenge, *see* raiding
ritual sanctions, *see* sanctions

Sabuk, 35, 95, 96, 102, 103, 132, 133
sanctions, religious, 25, 56, 101, 179, 184, 185
Sangani, 4, 8, 107
Sanum, 73, 75, 76, 85, 89, 98, 113, 114, 134, 142, 185
Sawang, 75, 103, 110-15, 130, 132, 140, 141
Seventh Day Adventist Mission, *see* missions
sexual relations, before marriage, 25, 65, 74, 75, 77, 80, 81, 116, 125, 138; after marriage, *see* husband-wife relations
Schulz, Father, 9
slit-gong, psychological effect of striking when angry, 17, 106
social structure, 25-38; moieties, 25, 26, 28, 29, 49, 68, 70, 78, 105, 165, 186; and conception dogma, 31; *see also*

affines, agnates, cluster of houses, headman, kindred, kinship, land tenure, marriage
Solomon Islands, 6, 7, 9, 88, 89, 122, 181, 184, 185, 186
sorcery, 5, 12, 20, 93, 96, 109, 111, 115, 126, 131, 142, 143, 144, 156, 179, 180; fear of, 12, 51, 55, 60, 65; and headmen, 16, 44-6, 168; protecting property, 47, 49; illness and misadventure, 17, 46-9, 55, 66, 147-9; cures for, 49, 91; death, 49-67, 109; unpopular people charged with, 57, 62-5; women and, 184; stories of as self-glorification, 57, 66, 67; *see also* weather magic
status and generosity, 40, 46, 77, 121, 153, 179; in 1975, 13; *see also* feast, festival
Strathern, A., 184
succession, 16, 37, 42, 123, 125, 138-42, 165, 184
suicide, 87, 92, 177

Tafalti, 46, 67, 76, 102, 111, 114, 115, 121, 122, 178; and Marigum's death, 58-62; quarrel with Marigum, 123-50
tangbwal, see religion
theft, 117-22, 123, 124, 126, 127, 128, 130-4; petty stealing, 117, 118; of pigs, 118-22
trade, 20, 24, 25, 30, 41, 143, 183; *see also* commercial undertakings, exchange partners
Trobriand Islands, 39, 45
trousseau, *see* marriage

U.S.A. 181, 182

valuables, 20, 25, 37, 39, 44, 115, 138, 139, 159, 162, 163
vendetta, avoiding, 56, 57; comparison with other peoples of Papua New Guinea, 57; *see also* inquest
vengeance, *see* compensation, fighting, raiding, warfare
village, *see* cluster of houses
Vokeo, 19

wage labour, 3, 4, 5, 15, 73, 74, 89, 134, 135; as an escape from public disapproval, 63, 104, 106, 108
Wakera, 39, 42, 64, 65, 155, 156, 162, 165, 166, 172, 174, 175
warfare, 18, 57, 58, 102, 115, 178, 179; *see also* fighting, raiding
Waru, 4, 33, 34, 65, 77, 90, 91, 102, 112, 113, 115, 117, 118, 120, 121, 122, 129,

Index

131, 132, 133, 135, 138, 142, 143, 144, 145, 146, 174
weather magic, 16, 45, 46, 65, 93, 94, 128, 142, 156
Wewak, 3, 6, 7, 8, 10, 15, 59, 61, 63, 181, 182
Wiawia, 4, 33, 41, 66, 72, 90, 103, 121, 131, 132, 138, 139, 143, 144, 146, 170, 186
widows, see husband-wife relations
Wiltgen, R. M., 181

Wiwiak, see Wewak
women, status of, 56, 76, 84, 85, 86, 87, 88, 89, 90, 110, 112, 115, 124, 125, 126, 133, 134, 135, 173, 184; see also divorce, husband-wife relations, *mwaere*
World War II, 6, 181, 182

yam, 43, 44, 54, 56, 93, 94, 100, 117, 124, 128, 129, 134, 135, 136, 145, 146, 162
Young, W. M., 182